SOCIOLOGY OF EDUCATION SERIES

Gary Natriello, Series Editor

Advisory Board: Jomills Braddock, Sanford Dornbusch, Adam Gamoran,
Marlaine Lockheed, Hugh Mehan, Mary Metz, Aaron Pallas, Richard Rubinson

Tracking Inequality

Stratification and Mobility in American High Schools

Samuel Roundfield Lucas

Teachers College, Columbia University
New York and London

Published by Teachers College Press, 1234 Amsterdam Avenue, New York, NY 10027

Library of Congress Cataloging-in-Publication Data

Lucas, Samuel Roundfield.
    Tracking inequality : stratification and mobility in American
high schools / Samuel Roundfield Lucas.
        p.   cm. — (Sociology of education series)
    Includes bibliographical references (p.   ) and index.
    ISBN 0-8077-3799-2 (cloth: alk. paper)
    ISBN 0-8077-3798-4 (pbk. : alk. paper)
    1. Education, Secondary—Social aspects—United States.
2. Educational equalization—United States.   3. Social mobility—United
States.   4. Educational change—United States.   I. Title.   II. Series:
Sociology of education series (New York, N.Y.)
    LC191.4.L85   1999
    306.43′2—dc21   98-47094

ISBN 0-8077-3798-4 (paper)
ISBN 0-8077-3799-2 (cloth)

Printed on acid-free paper
Manufactured in the United States of America

06   05   04   03   02   01   00   99   8   7   6   5   4   3   2   1

Contents

v

Foreword

Americans take pride that, unlike our aristocratic European cousins, we base upward mobility on ability, determination, and hard work in school, rather than on wealth or family connections. Many teachers, believing in the power of education, commit their lives to providing better life chances to deserving disadvantaged children. Yet the rhetoric of equal opportunity and merit masks a harsh reality—schooling still favors children from privileged families. Undoubtedly ability and ambition matter for success in school and in life, but that is not all there is to it. Ambition and ability occur with no less frequency in low-income families and among Blacks, Latinos, and immigrants, but relatively few from these groups are able to parlay those qualities into economic success.

What has gotten in the way? Most obvious, of course, is the inferiority of the schools that most poor and non-white students attend—schools with fewer qualified teachers, fewer advanced classes, and less access to the influential social networks students need to negotiate the complicated process of social mobility. More subtle, but no less powerful, have been the stratifying effects of high school tracking. For most of this century, a 14-year-old's initial assignment to the high school's academic, general, or vocational track determined his or her entire course of study, eligibility for college, and occupational choices. As Samuel Lucas points out in this book, high school tracking has allocated quite different instruction to students in different tracks, socialized them to accept their position in the school's status hierarchy, and signaled their appropriate futures to the outside world. And, true to the intents of those who fashioned high school tracking early in the 20th century, American schools have quite consistently assigned children from privileged families (usually white) to academic tracks, and those who are poor and non-white to the others. Many argue today that this has changed. In fact, as Samuel Lucas recounts, not long after Sputnik, most high schools did replace their overarching academic, general, and vocational programs with structures that allowed students to participate in classes in different subjects at different levels. This more flexible approach, in theory, unlocked the tracking system that so constrained academic and social mobility. Today, many high schools report they do not "track." Rather, their students "chose" from a menu of courses with varying levels of academic challenge.

In this fine book, Lucas combines thoughtful and thorough statistical analyses with sociological theory to explore the meaning and consequences of this seemingly dramatic change. He examines whether and how the newer arrangements (reforms) in high schools provide students with opportunities and mobility that the older system did not. What we learn is as sobering as it is insightful—when considering what matters most, little has changed. The implications for school reform are profound. Lucas' careful analyses reveal that the culture of stratification through schooling is uncannily robust. We can change the structure of inequality, it seems, only to have it re-emerge in a new guise.

Lucas makes us ponder deeper questions about schooling and sociology: How does our culture create and recreate such robust patterns of inequality in school? How do our notions of competition and merit press us to reinvent stratification, even as we work to invent more egalitarian structures? How does the widely discredited construct "intelligence" recede from prominence in policy only to be replaced with its proxies: "ability," "giftedness," and SAT scores? Why do we persist in equating intelligence and its proxies with merit in ways that produce a distribution of school accomplishment, power, and privilege that bears a striking resemblance to race and social class sorting? Why do our social theories fall short of explaining why well-intentioned efforts by educators and advocates to change such patterns only seem to make matters worse?

As sobering as Lucas' findings and the questions they raise may be, schools remain our best hope for achieving a free and democratic society where all have decent lives and rich opportunities. But, for schools to work honestly toward those goals, we must look beyond structural reforms. Rather, we must also abandon the wishful thinking that the wealth and happiness of advantaged Americans rests on a moral platform of merit, and that their children's advantages make them more deserving of schooling opportunities and life chances. We must struggle against the ruinous consequences that come when those with dismal lives place the blame on their own lack of ability, effort, or their failure to take advantage of schooling. No structural changes—detracking included—can bear the weight of changing these powerful norms and the political arrangements that hold them in place. What we need most is honest and public discussion about whether Americans are ready to extricate schools from perpetuating inequality, and, if so, what social research and political strategies might help do that. Samuel Lucas' probing work should inform that important discussion.

Jeannie Oakes
UCLA

Acknowledgments

Thinking is a social process. My thinking on tracking is the result of many conversations and much correspondence. The opportunities afforded me to study the measurement and implications of tracking and track location are the result of a vast social network that delivered aid in a variety of forms, including technical assistance, library materials, supplementary data, and other essential resources. And, I have been favored with several willing conversation partners who helped me explore the issues embedded in my research in several ways.

Although I wish to do so, it would be impossible to thank by name all of those who have aided my efforts. That said, I can begin by expressing my appreciation to Professors Adam Gamoran, Robert Hauser, and Robert Mare for their assistance and counsel on matters substantive, statistical, logical, and methodological, as well as for their overall support. Professors Michael Olneck and Franklin Wilson also aided my efforts in a variety of ways, for which I am most grateful. In addition, Doug Anderson, Elsa Elliott, Jeffrey Hayes, Jyh-jer Ko, Ryan Smith, Raymond Wong, and Yu Xie provided helpful insights, hints, and criticisms concerning the assumptions behind the measurement strategy. Thomas Conroy and Wai Kit Choi shared the fruits of their research in very different fields; our conversations helped me maintain perspective about my own work that proved essential to its completion. And many thanks to Anne Cooper, for teaching me many matters without which I could never have even read the data from the tape, and to Mary Rasmussen, for her tireless technical assistance and spirited interest in the project.

In developing the measures of track location, upon which this book is based, I was supported by a National Science Foundation Minority Graduate Fellowship held at the University of Wisconsin-Madison. I also received support from the Committee on Research at the University of California-Berkeley for virtually every other phase of the project.

My colleagues at Berkeley, especially Neil Fligstein, Mike Hout, Martín Sánchez-Jankowski, Claude Fischer, Ann Swidler, and Kim Voss, have been constant sources of support to the work and its dissemination. Grace K. Kim, Phillip Noel Fucella, and Carrie S. Horsey have kept me always moving forward toward the next step in our inquiry. My collaborator, Mark Berends, has provided important insights over the long-run of the study.

This is my first sole-authored book, and given all that that means, special thanks go to Series Editor Gary Natriello, and Susan Liddicoat, Peter Sieger, and Myra Cleary of Teachers College Press. All would-be authors should be as fortunate to have such able, gracious, and professional guides to the world of publishing.

I thank Kathleen Dzubur for helping me through the ups and downs of the entire process, including the writing and re-writing of this book, and, more important, for helping to make the process a pleasure.

Lastly, thanks does not begin to convey the debt of gratitude I can never repay to Hazel F. Lucas and Allison Lucas Ogden; the positive effects of their devotion through my own educational odyssey cannot be overstated.

All thought *is* social. But, as is customary, I as author accept full responsibility for any errors, including those of fact, approach, or interpretation. But, because I am optimistic that even in error a lesson may be found, the responsibility is not paralyzing. In this manner the social nature of thought proves to be the fundamental foundation of whatever progress we are blessed to realize.

CHAPTER 1

Introduction

Analysts have long debated whether schools serve to reproduce political and economic inequality by allocating cognitive training, differentiating socialization, legitimating differential treatment, and, ultimately, undercutting collective social protest by individualizing failure. One mechanism that furthered the reproductive role of schools was tracking, the practice of dividing students into programs that rigidly proscribed their courses of study and that admitted little opportunity for mobility from program to program. However, between 1965 and 1975 many urban school systems dismantled the procedures for assigning students to such overarching programs. By 1981 a majority of high schools had no formal mechanism of program assignment and thus no formal means of tracking. It is this dramatic change in school practice that I term the "unremarked" revolution, unremarked in that its occurrence has been noted but its implications—for how students are grouped in school, how students experience school, and how students transition from school—have been incompletely recognized. But in the wake of this revolution it is essential to investigate whether and how students are now stratified, and what the implications of the new in-school stratification system are for the relationship between schools and the economy, the polity, and the wider society.

This change in school practice was purposive and aimed specifically to reduce the reproductive role of schools. However, once we investigate this new school structure we will see that the unremarked revolution had many apparently unintended effects. It seems that the unremarked revolution transformed and submerged, but did not uproot, a stubborn stratification system. Indeed, the character of the consequences we will survey is such that the inadvertent result of the unremarked revolution may have been to actually *reduce* students' and parents' ability to effectively seize the opportunities for individual upward mobility that schools provide. In fact, the change in school practice also may have increased the tendencies that individualize failure and thus heightened the difficulties of generating transformative collective action.

The remainder of this chapter outlines the ideological and political underpinnings of the old in-school stratification system, the process by which

1

it seems to have given way, and the research efforts that have documented and responded to this change. In order to understand how this unremarked revolution came about and how its impact actually could reinforce inequality, we need to begin by describing in-school stratification in America in historical and cross-national perspective.

IN-SCHOOL STRATIFICATION IN AMERICA IN CROSS-NATIONAL AND HISTORICAL PERSPECTIVE

The common Western model of curricular placement is that students select and are selected into one of a few explicit curricular locations immediately before or shortly after entering secondary school. For example, between the ages of 11 and 13 Swiss children are tracked into one of three different types of secondary school—*Realschule, Sekundarschule*, or *Gymnasium*. After 2 or 3 additional years of schooling, *Realschule* students have the option of pursuing apprenticeship training or obtaining a job; *Sekundarschule* students have the option of apprentice vocational training, pursuing a job, or transferring to the *Gymnasium* curriculum; *Gymnasium* students can continue with their academic training or enter an apprenticeship. In short, by age 16 students select among three well-marked paths through school—quit, apprenticeship training, or college preparatory (Sauthier, 1995).

Regardless of the categories, and regardless of the criteria (e.g., tests, teacher recommendations), a policy of *explicit* allocation to different curricula is followed in the majority of Western nations. At the age of 10, students in Germany select from among three different school types—either the *Hauptschule* (which leads to apprenticeships after 6 years), the *Realschule* (which leads to continued vocational education or apprenticeships after 6 years), or the *Gymnasium* (which leads to university entrance after 9 years) (Hirsch, 1994). At the age of 12, students in the Netherlands are admitted to one of four school types on the basis of test results and the advice of elementary school personnel—either *VWO* (for pre-university education), *HAVO* (for higher-general education), *MAVO* (for lower-general education), or *VBO* (for prevocational education) (Hirsch, 1994). Historically, students in Great Britain have taken the 11+ exam at age 11; students' scores on that exam determined their curricular location.

Unlike these countries, the United States currently lacks an explicit system of in-school stratification. It was not always so. An explicit system of in-school stratification arose in America in concert with late nineteenth- to early twentieth-century changes in the organization of work, the incidence of immigration, and the expansion of schools. Immigration presented a particularly problematic challenge, for it brought to America's shores foreign cultures, disruptive ideologies of class conflict, and potentially revolutionary energy. In this environment many reformers looked to the school as a way to Americanize immigrant youngsters (e.g., Kelley, 1903). In order for schools to do so, however, the young had to be forced into school. The adoption of compulsory schooling laws accomplished this aim, but posed yet another dilemma. Should schools remain unchanged, teaching a classical college preparatory curriculum of Latin and Greek to students "just off the boat"? Or should schools elaborate the curriculum to provide different types of training? In short, what strategy of school organization would both Americanize youngsters and maintain the legitimacy of schools to diverse constituencies?

Historians and sociologists of education have documented that a complex process involving actors with a diversity of perspectives came together in this environment and, despite themselves, made the differentiated curriculum (ensconced in a compulsory comprehensive school) the ubiquitous organizational form for secondary school in America (Kliebard, 1995; Spring, 1972; Wrigley, 1982). This form allowed students to be given distinctly different cognitive preparation as well as distinctly different socialization. Ostensibly, the differentiated curriculum allowed students to be educated in ways relevant to their future social, economic, and occupational roles. Because projected occupations often were based on parental status, by providing training targeted to students' projected occupational positions, the school buttressed the existing social order (Spring, 1972). Thus, the differentiated curriculum harbored a pro-status-quo bias (Kliebard, 1995). This bias was manifest in that the curriculum was constructed not only to differentially allocate exposure to cognitive training, but also to allow instructional strategies to vary by track level. This second aspect of the tracking system facilitated differential socialization.

Ample evidence exists as to the pro-status-quo position of many curriculum differentiation advocates. Ross Finney (1928), an influential early twentieth-century sociologist of education, made plain the motivation for differential socialization when he contended that:

> Plato's scheme for locating leadership of society in its wisest minds failed of theoretical and practical articulation with reality because it contained no provision for assuring the followership of the dull and ignorant masses. He assumed that the masses would follow as a matter of course. But that is a groundless assumption, for they never do! . . . To date, in western society, the mobilization of the masses has never been secured except by force—or superstition. . . . And now come forward the psychologists with scientific data for headlining what we all knew before, namely, that half the people have brains of just average quality or less, of whom a very considerable percentage have poor brains indeed. How can intelligent political participation be expected of these duller

intellects? Successful democracy demands the ascendancy of the wise and good. . . . But if leadership by the intelligent is ever to be achieved, follower-ship by the dull and ignorant must somehow be assured. (pp. 385–386)

Finney (1928) goes on to describe *how* followership will be secured, namely, by training and socialization in schools.

The safety of democracy is not to be sought, therefore, in the intellectual inde-pendence of the duller masses but in their intellectual dependence. Not in what they think, but in what they think they think. For the dice of their conclusions are mostly loaded in advance by the beliefs that run current in the social mind, so that everything depends upon how the dice are loaded. The safety of democ-racy depends, instead, upon securing, through systematic social suggestion, the prevalence in the public memory of sound beliefs, so that when the barber parrots opinions he will parrot sound ones. . . . To load the dice of popular beliefs with the enlightened beliefs of enlightened leaders is the only preven-tive. How shall we go about it? . . . Every culture system accumulates an enor-mous capital of catch-words, proverbs, epigrams, slogans, witticisms, rhymes, old sayings, catechisms, and the like. They are the capsules in which concen-trated philosophies are swallowed. They are the token money, the credit sym-bols, by which intellectual exchange is carried on; they are as indispensable to a complex social life as checks, coins, and paper money are to modern busi-ness. . . . And it is principally through the schools that this new coinage of the collective intellect should be paid into general circulation. It is not enough that we teach children to think, we must actually force-feed them with the concen-trated results of expert thinking. To this end there is immense occasion for memoriter training and sheer drill. Ours are the schools of a democracy, which *all* children attend. At least half of them never had an original idea of any general nature, and never will. But they must behave as if they had *sound* ideas. (pp. 389–395; emphasis in original)

Finney makes clear, however, that only some of the students will be trained in this way; thus, the training and socialization will be allocated differen-tially.

What the duller half of the population needs, therefore, is to have their reflexes conditioned into behavior that is socially suitable. . . . The reader is reminded that superior intellects are not the subject of this chapter. Teach them to think, by all means. But for the duller half of the school population, teaching them to think is a well-nigh hopeless enterprise. (p. 395)

Overarching tracks were constructed on a foundational commitment to the idea of a unitary intelligence that determines capacity for learning in all domains. In this view, teaching advanced matters to students who cannot

learn them is a waste of resources. Moreover, to some it was also a danger-
ous endeavor, because it would ruin the chance that the dull would ever be
good followers. And, as Finney argued, good followers were essential to
social stability in a democracy. Making good followers and good leaders
required schools to divide students and socialize them differently.

Evidence suggests that schools were constructed with overarching
tracks whose existence was consistent with Finney's aims. In *Elmtown's
Youth* Hollingshead (1949) describes a high school with four explicit overarching tracks—college preparatory, general, general-commercial, and sec-
retarial-commercial. In a poignant passage Hollingshead details how three
girls enroll in specific tracks upon entering the high school. Although the
parents had supplied their daughters with specific enrollment instructions,
based in part on the parents' ability to pay for college and existing hardships
owing to marriage dissolution, on the way to school the three girls agreed
that they would all enroll in the college preparatory course. In doing so one
girl followed her parents instructions, but two did not. The parents of one
of these girls acquiesced in their daughter's decision, but the other girl's
mother, a single parent, rescinded the decision. Hollingshead notes:

> Nellie's mother was explosively angry with Nellie and with the high school
> authorities for allowing Nellie to enroll in the college preparatory course. She
> immediately told Nellie that she must change to the secretarial course. Nellie
> cried most of the night, but her mother went to school the next morning and
> changed Nellie's course herself. Nellie continued in school for a year and a
> half, but dropped out of her old clique, and then left school to work in the
> "dime" store. (p. 171)

Notably, in this particular case school personnel were supportive of the
student's desire for college, while the parent was not, which suggests that
the process of track assignment need not always have worked to hinder
upward mobility. Still, given the outcome, in this passage the explicit overarching programs, their overt power in students' lives, and the link between
social background and placement are all in evidence.

Cicourel and Kitsuse (1963) describe a similar system of explicit overarching programs in "Lake Shore High School," a school chosen for study
because it represented the "most advanced developments in educational theory and practice" (p. 23). Notwithstanding its status as an advanced school,
Lake Shore High continued to have overarching programs.

Despite the widespread practice of formal tracking, researchers are unclear as to whether the system of overarching tracks actually resulted in
differential socialization. For example, Paulsen (1991) reports that 1965 seniors who followed a college preparatory program had greater political effi-

cacy even after social class, race, sex, and grades were controlled. However, Wiatrowski, Hansell, Massey, and Wilson (1982) report no effects of track location on socialization outcomes on 1966 sophomores. Thus, the effectiveness of the track system in personality development remains unclear. Still, the intent behind the design of the system *is* clear—its original aim was to provide a means of differentially socializing students.

This system continued in place for some time. As late as 1965, when the Educational Testing Service collected data for the Academic Growth Study, researchers were able to use school records to classify 93% of students into tracks (Alexander, Cook, & McDill, 1978). Yet, by 1991 National Center for Education Statistics survey data covering a nationally representative sample of 912 public secondary schools revealed that 85% of schools had neither the records nor the practices that would allow school personnel to identify students' track location (Carey, Farris, & Carpenter, 1994). In short, schools no longer enroll students into explicit overarching programs. The stark contrast between 1965 and 1991 raises at least two important questions: What happened? What does it mean?

THE DISMANTLING OF OVERARCHING PROGRAMS

As for what happened, the historical record is incomplete on this point because few historical studies of tracking have been conducted. The evidence, however, strongly suggests that the late 1960s to early 1970s was a period of retreat from the use of overarching programs, at least in some geographic areas. Moore and Davenport (1988) studied placement policies of the New York, Chicago, Philadelphia, and Boston school systems. They found that prior to 1965 these systems assigned students to overarching tracks or programs; for example, Chicago schools used a four-track system composed of honors, regular, essential, and basic programs. All students were assigned to one of the four tracks, and that track assignment determined students' courses.

By 1975 these four urban school systems had disassembled the procedures for formally enrolling students into specific tracks. Instead, Moore and Davenport found that the old track labels—honors, remedial, essential, and basic—were now applied to *courses* in different subjects, and students enrolled into courses, not programs. Thus, the overarching programs were dismantled, but the foundational element of tracking, the differentiated curriculum, remained.

To explain this change in school practice Moore and Davenport note that the civil rights movement of the 1960s heightened equity concerns in education as well as elsewhere. Moreover, during this period a key foundational idea of tracking came under sustained and serious attack. The assumption that a unitary intelligence determined the limits of one's capacity for learning, and the academic fields based on this assumption, had provided a major intellectual support for tracking in earlier eras. As contestation around the assumption of a unitary intelligence occurred, alternative conceptions of intelligence were proposed.

Contestation around these ideas continues (Fischer et al., 1996; Herrnstein & Murray, 1994). However, as the definition of intelligence became unsettled, the articulation of alternative conceptions of intelligence both provided resources that opponents of tracking may have used explicitly in arguing against overarching tracks *and* supplied background assumptions that may have made the position adopted by opponents of tracking appear "reasonable" to some constituencies. It was in this intellectually and politically charged atmosphere that opponents of tracking argued against assigning students to a full program of courses in vastly different domains on the basis of presumed or actual proficiency or deficiency in one or two. Moore and Davenport suggest that many urban school systems retreated from broad program assignments in this environment.

Although the research needed to generalize these causal claims to other urban, suburban, and rural districts has yet to be done, court documents provide evidence to support Moore and Davenport's contention. Ruling in *Hobson* v. *Hansen*, a case that may have had a high profile among educational administrators, Judge Skelly Wright ordered Washington, DC, school administrators to abolish tracking (Hayes, 1990). Although judges have not been consistent in prohibiting tracking, Wright's 1967 decision may have sensitized school administrators to the possibility of litigation. The mere possibility of litigation may have encouraged administrators to alter the institutional structures that had implemented and maintained tracking.

Whatever the mechanism—and more historical work on this point is needed—it is apparent that by 1980 few schools assigned students to overarching programs. Oakes (1981) found that out of 12 secondary schools in her national study of tracking in the United States, only four maintained the traditional form of broad program assignment, and more recent evidence suggests that an even smaller proportion of schools practice the traditional form of tracking.

Thus, unlike most other Western nations, contemporary high schools in the United States do not have clear paths through the curriculum. Instead of assigning students to programs that determine students' courses, most schools in America have dispensed with the overarching programs, and many have assigned the level designations to individual courses. This procedure allows continued stratification within subjects, but breaks the necessary relation across subjects. What remains is a differentiated curriculum within subjects.

RESEARCHER RESPONSE TO THE UNREMARKED REVOLUTION

The ideological origins of the in-school stratification system appear incontrovertible. Although existing evidence of the effect of the pre-1965 tracking system on student efficacy remains equivocal (Paulsen, 1991; Wiatrowski et al., 1982), the historical origins of tracking alone provided a far from neutral backdrop for the 1970s debate concerning whether the primary effect of schools was legitimation of the adult system of stratification. Most accounts of adult stratification accepted the history and research on tracking and therefore made a place for track location in investigations of student attainments (Hauser, Sewell, & Alwin, 1976). Ironically, by that time schools had changed their practice in ways that made the historical origins of tracking less accurate as a description of the actual workings of in-school stratification and that presented new challenges for both theory and research.

Education Researchers

Educational researchers and sociologists of education have responded to the new regime with new concepts and have begun to explore strategies designed with the new regime in mind. These responses can be divided into three groups: elaboration of the *opportunity to learn* (OTL) concept, *reinterpretation* of existing measures, and development of *course-based* approaches.

The cross-national context is the fount of the OTL response to the new regime. The First International Mathematics Survey in the early 1960s introduced the opportunity to learn concept, and it was substantially revised in the Second International Mathematics Survey (SIMS) (McDonnell, 1995). SIMS analysts needed a framework that would allow them to compare curricula cross-nationally. As McDonnell (1995) reports, they viewed the mathematics curriculum as having three aspects: (1) the intended curriculum, (2) the implemented curriculum, and (3) the attained curriculum. The intended curriculum is described in official documents; the implemented curriculum concerns how teachers teach content inside classrooms; and the attained curriculum is manifest in the level of student achievement.

In 1994, as part of the effort to ensure accountability, OTL became part of the law of the land for American education with the passage and signing of President Clinton's Goals 2000: Educate America Act. As expressed in law, OTL concerns not only students' places in the curriculum, but also their access to appropriate instructional materials, well-trained teachers, and physical security on school premises, as well as teachers' access to continuing professional development (cited in Dougherty, 1996). The law provides incentives for school systems to develop OTL standards, with the ultimate aim of furthering schools' success in reaching educational goals established at the national level. This legislative development has prompted researchers to study the general concept, its specific manifestation in policy, and its likelihood of success (Dougherty, 1996).

Despite the possible utility of OTL for policy, the OTL concept presents at least two problems for researcher efforts to understand in-school stratification. One problem is that this framework may lead to the premature abandonment of still-useful concepts for viewing schools and their relation to the stratification order. A second problem is that this concept is so broad that it can encompass practically every feature of students' school experience.

With respect to the first problem, in the move from old frameworks to new ones, it is possible for time-tested and potentially useful concepts, such as the concept of tracking in schools, to become lost. Indeed, Dougherty points out that the legislative definition of OTL ignores tracking in particular and in many ways ignores both in-school stratification as well as the link between wider societal factors, family background, and student success. Some researchers have attempted to bring tracks back into OTL (Stevenson, Schiller, & Schneider, 1994), but owing to data limitations that effort remains incomplete.

A second problem flows from the breadth of the OTL concept. One advantage of OTL for policy makers is that it is a broad and complex concept, and thus multiplies the policy levers for action. However, for research, the breadth of the concept is potentially problematic. With such a broad concept it is easy for researchers to talk past one another, to unwittingly emphasize different aspects of the same concept, and in doing so to reach apparently different conclusions in their research. Indeed, Stevens (1993) reported 12 different operational definitions of OTL in the research literature. This degree of diversity of operational definitions suggests that researchers are still developing a consensus on how to define, let alone measure, the complex concept of opportunity to learn.

A second response to the new regime has been to alter the interpretation of existing measures. The modal measure of students' curricular locations is students' self-reports of them. If the measure is not re-interpreted, then the conceptual foundation of this measurement approach is in contradiction with the on-the-ground reality of school organization as documented by ethnographies (Oakes, 1981), historical treatments (Moore & Davenport, 1988), and survey research (Carey, Farris, & Carpenter, 1994). The conflict occurs because the decline of formal programs and explicit program enrollment procedures raises the question: What programs are students referring to when they respond to the question about high school programs on survey instruments, given that overarching programs have been dismantled? In response, some analysts have re-interpreted the measure in useful ways (Gamoran, 1992b; Rosenbaum, 1980). For example, Gamoran regards student self-reports as indicators of students' *social-psychological* track location. This kind of re-interpretation can preserve much of the large body of research that has shown robust associations between students' reports of track location and important outcomes, for interpreting and using self-reports in this way is to take seriously the Thomas and Thomas (1928) dictum that "if persons define situations as real they are real in their consequences" (p. 572).

The third broad alternative, the course-based approach, is actually based on an important corollary to the Thomases' maxim, to wit: Only misunderstanding can result when what is real in its consequences is taken to be real as such. Track location certainly concerns students' attitudes about whatever courses of study they are engaged in, attitudes that may be tapped with a social-psychological measure. However, track location also has a *structural* dimension, a dimension that must be considered in order for analysts to further develop their understanding of in-school stratification. The course-based approach, focused on the curriculum as a series of places in a differentiated structure, is one means of pursuing investigation of the structural dimension of tracking.

Like OTL, the course-based approach has a long history; Rosenbaum's 1976 analyses, reported in *Making Inequality*, used students' courses to investigate tracking in one school. Other researchers working in this tradition include Hallinan (1996) and Garet and DeLany (1988). The analyses herein are within this tradition of inquiry.

Two advantages of this approach are the specificity of focus and the retention of existing and important frameworks for considering in-school stratification. Without denying the importance of teacher training and students' physical safety, this approach focuses on the curriculum and relates the curriculum to other aspects. The curriculum serves to organize the students' day and therefore provides the structure within which many of the educational and socialization activities occur. The course-based approach focuses on this structural element of schools.

Moreover, in contrast to the OTL approach, in the course-based tradition tracking can be viewed as one possible outcome of curriculum differentiation. That is, tracking may or may not emerge from the differentiated curriculum. Whether tracking does emerge becomes an empirical question in the course-based approach. Thus, previous conceptions of in-school stratification remain important.

Theorizing Schools in the Stratification Order

Schools have a prominent place in theories of social stratification and political stability. Human capital theory (Becker, 1964), the social-psychological model of educational and occupational attainment (Hauser, Tsai, & Sewell, 1983), Marxist theories of capitalist stability (Bowles & Gintis, 1976), cultural theories of legitimation (Bourdieu & Passeron, 1977), theories of ethnic status competition (Collins, 1979), and theories of the institutionalization of mores (Meyer, 1977) all make the school an important institution in the processes they explain. Indeed, even theories that imply a genetic basis for inequality and insinuate that education is irrelevant cannot sustain the claim (Herrnstein & Murray, 1994; contrast pp. 63–89, 96, 394, and 419–435).

One could go on listing additional explanations for the stability and character of societies, but the basic claim would not diminish—from Becker to Bourdieu, every analyst attempting to explain persons' locations in the adult society and/or the structure of places within that society has had to come to grips with the reality of the school. Yet, owing to changes in the way secondary schools work, the vision of schools that figures in the paradigmatic statements of the school/society relation does not match the reality of how schools stratify students in late-twentieth-century America.

Sociologists of education and education researchers responded to the changes in school practice with new research approaches (Gamoran, 1987; Hallinan, 1992; Rosenbaum, 1980; Stevenson, Schiller, & Schneider, 1994). However, prior to this response a disconnect between tracking research and social stratification theorizing emerged, which prevented the new approaches in the former from influencing theory and research in the latter. Thus, it is especially from the perspective of research on the wider stratification order that the changes in school practice constitute an "unremarked revolution," for perspectives on schools' role in the maintenance of society continue to be based on an implicit vision of schools that is inconsistent with how American schools have operated in the last quarter of the twentieth century.

Prior to the unremarked revolution the purpose of tracking was clear. Tracking was designed not only to slot students into positions in the economy, but also to encourage the individual student to resign himself or herself to this lot. Not only should the student become resigned to this fate, but the student should regard the fate as just. In other words, tracking was designed to sort and pacify students. These aims were accomplished even more effectively by placing students into tracks as early as possible, a strategy buttressed by the rhetoric of intelligence testing, and allowing students little chance for mobility, for mobility might call into question the viability of early selection.

However, the unremarked revolution afforded a dramatic break with this past. Surely, between the inception of tracking and 1965 change occurred. For example, it is possible that the teacher's role in track assignment increased over time. Yet, even as such changes occurred, the basic organization of the school into tracks remained intact, and thus school organization continued to reflect self-conscious efforts to further differential cognitive and social training. The unremarked revolution, however, singularly altered the formal organization of secondary schools so that explicitly labeled tracks no longer exist. In the wake of this unremarked revolution, in-school stratification is, therefore, no longer self-consciously and explicitly designed for differential socialization.

Yet, the curriculum is still fashioned with the bricks of the previous order; students still take different classes, many of which have titles that peg them as "college preparatory" or not. However, both the overarching signposts through and the authoritative gatekeepers of the curriculum have been muted. In this new regime the places students occupy may be vastly different than before. If the prior system was constructed for differential socialization, and evidence strongly suggests it was, it follows that transformations in it may have altered students' experience of school.

In and of itself this change is important, but its importance can only increase once one realizes that the prior system was designed to maintain a particular form of social stability, built on fostering either commitment or acquiescence to the prevailing social order. Now that the schooling system has been transformed, one can wonder whether the current structure facilitates, hinders, or is irrelevant to the legitimation of the adult system of stratification. Although an answer to this question is beyond the scope of this work (which focuses only on the school), it is apparent that any effort to answer this question must be based on an accurate description of the new stratification system of the school.

INSTRUCTIONAL, SOCIAL, AND INSTITUTIONAL EFFECTS OF TRACKING AFTER THE UNREMARKED REVOLUTION

Researchers have been concerned both with whether tracks matter and with how the effects of tracking are produced (Dreeben & Barr, 1988; Gamoran, 1989; Pallas, Entwistle, Alexander, & Stluka, 1994). Three different mechanisms through which tracking might have its effects have been identified.

Effects of tracking might be created through *instructional* differences be-twccn tracks. Evidence suggests that students in high tracks are taught more material at a speedier pace. Thus, one explanation for the higher average achievement of high-track students is that, owing to their greater exposure to curriculum content, they learn more over time and outdistance peers in lower tracks.

Alternatively, tracks are also *social* contexts within which students judge themselves and become socialized. As social contexts, tracks have systematically different norms and thus students are socialized differently. One could interpret the research on tracking and students' attitudes toward school as part of this literature (Berends, 1994; Paulsen, 1991).

Third, tracks can be seen as *institutionalized* entities. Drawing on the work of Meyer (1977), analysts have argued that track location conveys information about the student to others that shapes their response to the student. Widespread understanding of what it means to be low track or high track allows members of the wider society to react to the student on the basis of the student's place in this very public stratification system.

Researchers have studied all three of these conduits through which track location may have its effects. Studying elementary school students, Gamoran (1989) found that the effects of tracking were fully explained by differences in content and speed of coverage, lending weight to the instructional argu-ment. However, Pallas, Entwistle, Alexander, and Stluka (1994), while find-ing no support for social effects of tracking, found some evidence of institu-tional effects of track location. They rcport that parents and teachers had higher expectations for students' performance if students were in higher tracks, even when students' performance was controlled.

Research on the mechanism through which track effects come to be is extremely important. However, this research is based on a particular under-standing of how tracks exist. Formerly, tracks were public institutionalized arrangements. For some schools, such as elementary schools, this may still be correct. Yet, most secondary schools changed the way in which they organized for instruction after 1975, such that formal tracks no longer exist. Thus, study of how in-school stratification works after the unremarked revo-lution is necessary to shed light on which, if any, of the instructional, social, and institutional conduits continue to channel advantages to some and disad-vantages to others.

To investigate this issue we need consider two dimensions that are es-sential to determining how any stratification system works. One dimension concerns whether placement within one hierarchy is associated with place-ment in *another* hierarchy. In classical work on social stratification this was considered the question of status crystallization (Lenski, 1954). Lenski (1954) theorized that those in concordant positions in different hierarchies (e.g., income, education) might have more heightened identification with those positions than persons who were in discordant positions. In research on tracking one may regard students' simultaneous placement in two different hierarchies as an issue of scope à la Sørenson (1970). In theorizing dimensions of track systems, Sørenson defined scope as the amount of time students spend with the same set of peers. One may regard the association between students' courses as an indicator of scope, because when students occupy similar levels of courses in different subjects it is plausible to infer that scope is high.

A second dimension essential to investigation of stratification systems is the dimension of mobility. Understanding the system of tracking requires investigation of both dimensions. Both scope and mobility bear on whether the effects of tracking occur through instructional, social, or institutional mechanisms. As long as within-subject curriculum differentiation exists, it is likely that instructional differences will play a part in determining students' learning. Yet, the decline of formal programs may have major implications for whether social or institutional conduits matter for secondary school students.

Students' Courses in Disparate Subjects

Formerly, institutional mechanisms ensured that a student's day would be composed of very similar types of cognitive training and socialization. The social relations and cognitive demands in the math class the student took would be similar to the social relations and cognitive load of the English class, because the student would be in the same level, with virtually the same peers, for both, and because the social relations and expectations in different levels of classes differed systematically.

Courses of different levels still differ systematically (Oakes, 1985). However, absent the overt institutional mechanisms of the past, it is possible, in principle, for students to take vastly disparate levels of courses in different subjects. This possibility makes it necessary to ask whether students actually *do* take disparate courses in different subjects and, if so, what the patterns of course taking are. In other words, are students' courses in different subjects associated or not? And if courses are associated, in what ways are they associated? These questions are important because different patterns of course taking—different forms of association—have different implications.

If, for example, one finds that despite the change in school practice students are still in the same level of course across subjects, then one might surmise that *de facto* tracking works to segregate students. This kind of pattern would facilitate continued differential socialization and suggest that any changes in the school/economy/polity relation are unrelated to changes in the in-school stratification system. Moreover, a finding of continued seg-regation would mean that tracks may continue to provide contexts within which norms differ systematically and that despite the decline of formal programs *de facto* tracks may have institutional effects.

However, if one finds a form of association that highlights discrepant course-levels across subjects, what one might call the educational equivalent of contradictory class locations (Wright, 1985), then students are likely to be exposed to discrepant types of socialization and cognitive demands over the course of a school day. Such a pattern would make socialization more varied and therefore threaten the existence of social effects of track location. Even more stark, if students commonly enroll in disparate courses it may be difficult to discern a student's track location. If so, it is unlikely that institutional effects play a major role in the new environment.

If disparate course taking is common, then the role of schools in differentially socializing students may be hindered or perhaps seriously undermined by changes in school practice. What this would mean for legitimation is unclear, because its implication turns on what in particular is being legitimated. Yet, if the structures inside school have changed this dramatically, any understanding of how schools buttress adult inequality must note this new state of affairs and take it into account in crafting an explanation for how adult inequality is supported by schools.

Thus, in short, what one finds upon investigating students' course taking in disparate subjects is consequential for how to understand the curricular structures within which students experience school. And how one understands the curricular structures within which students experience school is extremely important for how one describes schools' place in the stratification order.

Mobility over Time

As designed, institutional mechanisms ensured that over the course of students' careers the students would encounter very similar, indeed reinforcing, types of socialization and cognitive training. This was arranged by admitting little mobility between tracks. Students in lower tracks fell behind academically, and thus upward mobility was difficult. But researchers have documented that even downward mobility, although more common, was still rare (Rosenbaum, 1976). However, more recent research has suggested that upward mobility is now more common than downward mobility (Hallinan, 1996).

Given the decline of overarching programs that structured explicit sequences of course taking, mobility may be possible, and the possibility of mobility is certainly consequential for how one sees schools. The more rare upward mobility is, the more difficult it becomes to sustain the idea that the school provides an arena where students may transcend not only the disadvantages of birth, but also the disadvantages imposed by early school failure.

If, however, changes in schools have made upward mobility more likely than downward mobility, then one might wonder how schools effected this unprecedented social transformation. For, in most areas of life, analysts find advantages accruing to those who already have them (e.g., the well-known Matthew Effect in science, in which accolades flow to those who already have them; Merton, 1968).

In addition, high mobility rates would undermine the social and institutional mechanisms of tracking. However, low mobility rates might reinforce the social and institutional mechanisms, despite the decline of formal programs.

Whether upward or downward, mobility complicates the socialization students undergo. In the early days of tracking mobility was anathema, and for purposes of socialization and cognitive training it still may be. However, for purposes of legitimation, different patterns of mobility may have different implications; thus, it is important to understand mobility in school in order to comprehend how schools may support the wider system of social stratification, either by helping students or explaining their failure.

Taken together, these questions—questions concerning scope and questions concerning mobility—are extremely important. The answers to these questions may have significant implications both for how scholars come to characterize the in-school stratification system and for how citizens come to judge the stratification of children.

PLAN OF THE BOOK

Existing research suggests how, between 1965 and 1975, institutional actors removed the overarching signposts of the curriculum. The curriculum remained stratified, but the logic of the strata became submerged. This change in school *practice* is nothing short of a revolution.

To assess the aftermath of that revolution I first investigate students' course taking in disparate subjects. The decline of formal programs allows students the logical possibility of taking discrepant courses in different subjects. Moreover, it frees students from being held back by failure in one area, as placements in different fields are not necessarily tied together. Chapter 2 assesses the form of students' course taking, to discern whether students are enrolled in discrepant courses, while Chapter 3 introduces individual-level factors into the analysis of students' placements, to determine whether achievement in some domains is more important than achievement in others.

Chapter 4 examines whether there are discernible differences in the stratification regime across school environments. Researchers have shown that some types of schools have resisted changes in the tracking regime. Some analysts have argued that the history of tracking has not ended—middle-class parents seem to want to segregate their children through tracking just as much as earlier elites sought to maintain segregation. Chapter 4 does not investigate the motives or strategies of different groups, as that is not possible with the data available. Yet, I *can* investigate whether the tracking regime of the school differs by compositional characteristics of the school. Given the arguments analysts have made about the efficacy of the middle class, one would expect to find a residue of their effect in the realized structure of tracking. Chapter 4 searches for this residue.

Chapters 5 and 6 investigate mobility. Chapter 5 is concerned with patterns of mobility, while Chapter 6 examines individual-level factors in students' movement through the curriculum. Earlier research suggested that mobility is rare and universally downward, while more recent research reaches different conclusions. Both chapters address these issues; Chapter 5 focuses on the overall pattern of mobility, while Chapter 6 investigates the correlates of placement over time.

The prior tracking regime was constructed for both cognitive and socialization aims. The bulk of the book investigates the new structure of tracking. Yet, one may wonder whether this new structure has cognitive and socialization effects. Chapter 7 begins to assess the implications of the unremarked revolution for student outcomes by asking whether students' location in the in-school stratification system is associated with their cognitive achievement, interest in school, and college entry.

A concluding chapter summarizes the findings and suggests their implications for different perspectives on the school/economy relation. Appendices describe in detail the measurement decisions (Appendix A) and the analytic strategy used in the study (Appendices B and C).

The analyses investigate students' course taking in math and English only. It is customary for researchers to confine their attention to one or two subjects. Some research has considered math, some research has investigated math and science, other research has studied English, and still other research has investigated math and English (Catsambis, 1994; Garet & DeLany, 1988; Hallinan, 1996; Rosenbaum, 1976; Stevenson, Schiller, & Schneider, 1994). This study focuses on math and English because these are the two central subjects of the curriculum. One difference in the analysis, however, is that for much of it I will be concerned with students' *simultaneous* placement in both curricula. This concern is the basis of the selection of math and English, for these two subjects cover disparate domains. As many of the questions concern whether students' placements in one domain are associated with their placements in a very different subject area, it was important to select subject areas that are truly disparate. For these reasons I focus on math and English.

All analyses are based on High School and Beyond sophomore (HS& B) data. HS&B is a longitudinal survey with base-year data collection in 1980 and follow-ups of respondents in 1982, 1984, 1986, and 1992. A nationally representative data set, HS&B has several features that make it an ideal resource for investigating track structure and effects.

HS&B data are particularly useful for investigating the questions under study here because of the inclusion of information from students' high school transcripts. In earlier work I constructed Course-Based Indicators of track location (CBIs) using HS&B transcript data (Lucas, 1990). These measures classify students according to their actual course taking in each subject for each year of high school. As it is also possible to identify students who do not take a course in the subject in a given academic year, students are categorized as taking remedial, business and vocational, lower college, regular college, and elite college preparatory courses, as well as not taking a course in the subject. These CBIs provide the measures of subject-specific placement used in this study. Accordingly, further information on the construction of the measures and their conceptual relation to other approaches is provided in Appendix A.

HS&B also contains good measures of achievement, social class background, race, ethnicity, sex, and aspirations. And, although more recent data are available, HS&B provides the first nationally representative data on a cohort that completed secondary school soon after the change in school practice. Thus, HS&B is an ideal data set for investigating the issues posed by the unremarked revolution.

Much of the analysis is based on log-linear models, which rarely have been applied to studies of tracking. Thus, Appendix B provides a primer on log-linear modeling and is devised to aid those familiar with regression models or ANOVA to become familiar with log-linear models. Appendix C details the decisions made in modeling and aims to allow those who have used log-linear and similar models in the past to replicate my research.

However, the chapters to come focus on substantive matters. My perspective is that through the use of appropriate statistical techniques certain features in the data, features of the social world, become visible. The body of the book focuses on what questions need be asked and what answers were obtained for a cohort of students who entered high school after the unremarked revolution.

These questions are of paramount importance. Every analyst admits, explicitly or by virtue of attention, that schools are the key institution in persons' entry into the adult stratification system. Given the theoretical centrality of schools to the material and ideological maintenance of stability in Western societies, it is certain that systematic investigation of in-school stratification is required. This need is neither new nor newly recognized.

The enduring motivation for research on in-school stratification has been understanding the production and maintenance of educational, occupational, political, and economic inequality, and understanding has been pursued with a series of analyses of various stages of the schooling process and at various degrees of distance from the classroom. After the publication of Coleman's 1966 report, educational researchers increased their attention to in-school stratification processes. A primary focus of this research was cognitive growth, but other factors were considered as well.

Yet, after a brief period of cross-pollination in the 1970s, stratification research and tracking research went their separate ways. This is unfortunate, for the unremarked revolution has major implications both for the structures inside schools and for the understanding of adult stratification. To begin to unearth these implications we need turn to the questions the unremarked revolution poses. What is the structure of tracking? What is the pattern and prevalence of mobility? What are the correlates of students' placement? What, if any, track effects remain? And, most important, what do the answers to these questions reveal about the workings of American education and the character of American society?

CHAPTER 2

Course Taking After the
Decline of Formal Programs

The unremarked revolution removed the institutional mechanism that linked students' courses in disparate subjects. In the wake of this change students' course selections in one subject are, in principle, no longer constrained by their placements in another subject. Yet students' courses in different subjects still may be associated. Many factors, such as peer pressure, bureaucratic enrollment procedures, logistical scheduling difficulties, incomplete information, informal organizational arrangements, historical factors, and others, may conspire to maintain an association between students' courses.

Students' courses may be associated in a myriad of ways, but these many possibilities may be divided into two broad types. In one type of pattern some small subset of mutually exclusive programs accounts for the association between students' courses. When students enrolled in the college preparatory program, the general program, or the vocational program, these programs accounted for the association between students' courses. Although explicit enrollment in programs is now rare, students' course taking still may reflect these cleavages in the curriculum.

In the second type of pattern students may be so likely to take discrepant levels of courses that the structure of tracking is considerably more complex than before. If this second pattern prevails, one would expect to find many students taking, for example, advanced mathematics while also taking less advanced English courses.

Adjudicating between these two broad patterns is important, for each has different implications for the role of tracking in student socialization and the ultimate efficacy of political agitation that encouraged the retreat from formal overarching programs. With respect to socialization, tracking historically has been described as a means of segregating students and socializing different sets of students for different futures. This characterization hails from a period in which students were assigned explicitly to two or three programs. If one finds the same kind of pattern, even though formal program assignment rarely occurs and schools have changed their course assignment practices, then differential socialization through tracking would seem to remain a strong possibility. Although this historically observed pattern does not *require* that schools socialize students differently, it is clear that this pattern can facilitate differential socialization because students in one environment would rarely or never experience or interact with other students and environments.

However, if one finds that discrepant course taking is either patterned or common, or both, one might start to see in-school stratification in a different light. This alternative characterization would suggest that schools face difficulties in providing targeted socialization. If students take courses of different levels in different subjects, and if the level of any given course is associated with different socialization aims and strategies as many contend, then students are exposed to discrepant and potentially contradictory socialization.

With respect to the political issues surrounding tracking, the political effort to dismantle overarching programs was motivated by the desire to prevent students' difficulty in one subject from limiting their opportunities in other subjects. Thus, if one finds that discrepant course taking is still rare even after the decline of formal programs, then one might infer that despite the success of the effort to end formal programs, the structure of tracking in school remains very much the same. However, if one finds that discrepant course taking is patterned and/or common, then it would confirm that the unremarked revolution had an impact on students' places in school and therefore may have affected students' experience of school. In short, identifying the best way to characterize how courses are associated has implications for how one understands this particular school reform as well as students' experience of schools.

SCOPE

Students' courses can be associated at one point in time or across time. In the tracking literature the second of these, the across-time association, is referred to as *mobility*. If the association is strong, then students are constrained by their prior placements.

In contrast to the across-time association, there is no consensus on what to call the association between students' courses in different subjects. I contend, however, that the association between students' courses in different subjects taken at the same time is actually a measure of *scope*.

Several perspectives and definitions of scope can be found in the tracking literature. As I noted in Chapter 1, in his illuminating delineation of the dimensions of tracking, Sørenson (1970) defined scope as the extent to which student groups are stable over time, and specifically mentioned that scope might be low if students were placed in different vertically differentiated curricula according to differences in their preparation for study in different subjects. By Sørenson's definition, when scope is high, students spend large amounts of their time with the same set of peers. Conversely, when scope is low, students spend time with different sets of peers.

Later analysts have elaborated the concept of scope. Rosenbaum (1976) includes track mobility as a facet of scope. Oakes (1985) views the number of courses that are tracked (i.e., differentiated) as an indicator of scope. In some ways these elaborations are consistent with Sørenson's original formulation. Clearly, one implication of the incidence of track mobility is how much time students spend with the same set of peers. If rates of track mobility are high, groups are likely to be unstable and the amount of time a student spends with the same set of peers will, all else equal, be low. Similarly, schools with several subjects differentiated have more potential to have high scope than do schools with few subjects differentiated. This potential exists because if several subjects are differentiated, then students may spend their entire school day with the same set of homogenous peers. Because the amount of time a student spends with the same set of peers is the definitive feature of scope, finding a school with several subjects differentiated may be very much like finding a school with high scope.

However, there may be costs to regarding track mobility and number of subjects differentiated as aspects of scope. Viewing track mobility as a variant of scope de-emphasizes important differences between scope and mobility. One difference is that mobility necessarily concerns changes in status over time; in contrast, scope can refer to membership in two simultaneously existing groups, such as the groups for English and the groups for mathematics. Moreover, there is no necessary relation between mobility rates and the amount of scope. A system with relatively high mobility (which usually is regarded as a sign of low scope) could still have high scope by Sørenson's definition if, for example, students who are mobile in math are mobile in English to the same degree and in the same direction. Thus, despite the undeniable importance of track mobility and its likely *empirical* relationship to scope, it seems useful to preserve the *conceptual* distinction between scope and mobility.

Similarly, there may be problems in defining scope as the number of subjects that are differentiated. To equate the number of subjects differentiated with the amount of time students spend with the same peers is to assume that the association between students' placements in the different subjects is perfect or very close to perfect. This assumption may not be true.

An alternative approach is to consider the association between courses in different subjects as one appropriate way to measure scope, because an estimate of the association between courses in different subjects reveals the degree to which students are constrained by their simultaneous placement in other subjects.

This issue is not the same as scope, but it is consistent with the concept. Sørenson defined scope in reference to time spent with the same set of peers in different educational subjects. Thus, scope refers to the nexus between subjects. Consistent with this view one can ask to what degree the groups that students occupy in one subject overlap the groups that they occupy in another subject. If the overlap is high, then the association is high, the nexus is tight, and scope is high. Thus, by investigating the association between placements in different subjects, one can determine whether the nexus is tight. This nexus is directly related to scope, and thus the analysis of the association between subjects is one way to analyze scope.

Prior to 1965, scope should have been high. Now that schools no longer explicitly assign students to overarching programs, it is necessary to ask whether the association has changed.

EXISTING EVIDENCE

Evidence suggests that the association between students' courses *has* changed in the wake of the unremarked revolution. Using information drawn from the transcripts of 1,700 students in four California high schools in 1979, Garet and DeLany (1988) estimated the influence of social background factors on students' placements and investigated whether the college/non-college dichotomy described students' course taking in math and science. They found that the college/non-college dichotomy did not adequately summarize the association between students' courses. As the college/non-college dichotomy was a staple basis of the pre-1965 organization of students' programs, Garet and DeLany's finding suggests that something has changed.

The work of Stevenson, Schiller, and Schneider (1994) is consistent with Garet and DeLany's finding. After studying the sequences of course taking from Grades 8 through 10 in science and mathematics, Stevenson, Schiller, and Schneider (1994) report that "many students in the college preparatory track were not in the advanced sequence in mathematics, whereas some students in the general and vocational tracks were" (p. 194).

Ethnographic research also suggests that track structure is more complex than a college/non-college dichotomy, or even a general/vocational/college preparatory trichotomy allows, and thus that matters have changed (Goodlad, 1984; Oakes, 1987). As Oakes reports, stratification of the higher education system in California encourages further differentiation of college preparatory tracks in high schools. Thus, at least two college preparatory tracks may be common in California schools, one slotting students into the more selective University of California system, and another sending students into the less selective California State University system. These kinds of processes support the expectation that the college/non-college dichotomy does not describe students' placements.

However, analysts have yet to establish what pattern *does* describe students' course taking. Determining what pattern describes the association is key to identifying the cleavages of the in-school system of stratification. What the literature tells us is that something has happened. Now that the system has been transformed, it is important to determine what new structure that transformation has created.

METHODS OF INVESTIGATING SCOPE

The primary data for this chapter are four cross-tabulation tables, one for each academic year, that cross-classify students' mathematics course by students' English course. Students fall into one of six categories for math and one of six categories for English. Thus, in any given academic year students can combine math and English course taking in any one of 36 ways. Each particular combination is represented by one of 36 cells of the 6×6 cross-classification table.

Much of the existing research reports on mathematics and science. As I remarked in Chapter 1, for the questions addressed here mathematics and English are better subjects to study because both are central to the high school curriculum and the two subjects represent clearly distinct domains of inquiry. Because the subjects are central, the results reflect core organizational challenges and their resolution. And because the courses represent distinct domains of inquiry, the association between them is more easily regarded as a manifestation of *de facto* tracking.

Table 2.1 contains the cross-classification of ninth graders' math and English courses as an example of the cross-tabulations under study. To discern the pattern of course taking, one must investigate whether certain categories of courses hang together. An appropriate way to do so is to use log-linear levels models (Hauser, 1978). Log-linear models are appropriate for investigating the association between categorical variables, and levels models allow close, even cell-by-cell, consideration of patterns of concentration.

One could, of course, simply inspect the 6×6 tables to see whether students are in different levels of courses for the two subjects. Table 2.1 shows that 385 students take regular college prep English but take no math, 829 students take regular college prep English and also take remedial math, and so on. From Table 2.1 it is apparent that some students *are* in different

Table 2.1. Cross-Tabulation of Mathematics by English, Ninth Grade

	ENGLISH					
MATH	None	Remedial	Business/ Vocational	Lower College	Regular College	Elite College
None	327	39	2	5	385	26
Remedial	74	147	1	26	829	59
Busi/Voc	169	353	5	34	3550	155
Lower Coll	43	169	1	37	1945	122
Reg Coll	98	205	1	67	5266	464
Elite Coll	20	59	0	5	846	160

levels of courses for the two subjects. However, just looking at the table will not answer the research question, because doing so does not subject the assessment to formal statistical tests that can reveal whether the observed pattern is or is not likely to be the result of sampling variation. Thus, the methods followed herein, while more complicated than just inspecting the table, have a real advantage.

For each log-linear model estimated one may obtain several summary statistics. Among other things, these summary statistics allow one to assess whether the association between the variables is adequately captured by the model (i.e., whether the model fits the data) and also may allow one to select a preferred model that provides the most complete description of the association. For making these decisions I will rely on the Bayesian Inference Criterion (BIC) statistic (although other basic summary statistics also are presented). An advantage of BIC is that when analyzing a data set one can use it to compare two models. When BIC is negative, the model provides an adequate description of the association in the table. The more negative BIC is, the better the fit of the model. When comparing models, very small differences in BIC can be ignored, but a difference of 6 or more points is strong evidence in favor of the model with the smaller (i.e., more negative) BIC statistic (Raftery, 1995). Further details on the advantages of BIC and the analysis strategy are available in Appendices B and C.

THEORIES, SUBSTANCE, AND MODELS

Each log-linear model reflects a set of substantive claims about how students' courses hang together, that is, a set of substantive claims about the association between students' courses. For any given set of substantive claims it is possible to identify either mechanisms that might produce or explain the substantive outcome, implications of the substantive outcome for how schools work, or both. These explanations and elaborations may be used to further develop theories about schools, students, and tracking.

Thus, each model is estimated because of its *substantive* and *theoretical* implications. If upon estimation a particular model fits the data, and the parameter estimates from the model are as the substantive claim suggests, then the substantive claim is supported and the theoretical implications are worthy of additional consideration. I will examine seven models: the independence model (Ind), the college/non-college model (CNC), the college/non-college/not-taking model (CNCNT), the parallel placement I model (PP–I), the parallel placement II model (PP–II), the discrepant course-taking I model (DC–I), and the discrepant course-taking II model (DC–II).

Independence and College/Non-College Models

The names of many of the models may be self-explanatory; others are merely suggestive. For example, the substantive claim of the independence model is that students' courses in math and English are *not* associated. If the independence model fits, then one may infer that students' courses in math and English are not associated statistically. This substantive finding might be explained *theoretically* by arguing that overt track assignment practices may have been the only support for an association between students' courses, so that once that support was removed, the association dissolved. Note, however, that the independence model allows assessment of the substantive claim only. If the substantive claim proves true, then the theoretical claim that makes sense of the substantive claim gains a degree of support.

An alternative substantive claim is that the association between students' courses is explained by the college preparatory/non-college preparatory dichotomy. Analysts have shown that this distinction is the most salient one for achievement (Gamoran, 1987). Given the importance of this distinction, investigating whether the complex course taking reduces to this dichotomy is worthwhile. The CNC model tests this idea by translating the claim that the association between subjects is driven by the college prep/non-college prep dichotomy into the claim that the concentrations of students in different combinations of courses is dependent on whether the combination of courses is college preparatory, non-college preparatory, or something else. In essence, the 36 combinations of course taking are partitioned into three sets: (1) both courses are college preparatory; (2) both courses are non-college preparatory; and (3) one course is college preparatory and the other course is not college preparatory. The partition may be conveyed by the *design matrix* in Figure 2.1A.

Figure 2.1. Design Matrices for Six Models of Student Course Enrollment in Mathematics and English

A. College/Non-College

M\E	NT	RM	BV	LC	RC	EC
NT	c	c	c	c	a	a
RM	c	c	c	c	a	a
BV	c	c	c	c	a	a
LC	c	c	c	c	a	a
RC	a	a	a	a	b	b
EC	a	a	a	a	b	b

B. College/Non-College/Not-Taking

M\E	NT	RM	BV	LC	RC	EC
NT	d	a	a	a	a	a
RM	a	c	c	c	a	a
BV	a	c	c	c	a	a
LC	a	c	c	c	a	a
RC	a	a	a	a	b	b
EC	a	a	a	a	b	b

C. Parallel Placement I

M\E	NT	RM	BV	LC	RC	EC
NT	b	a	a	a	a	a
RM	a	c	a	a	a	a
BV	a	a	d	a	a	a
LC	a	a	a	e	a	a
RC	a	a	a	a	f	a
EC	a	a	a	a	a	g

D. Parallel Placement II

M\E	NT	RM	BV	LC	RC	EC
NT	b	a	a	a	a	a
RM	a	b	a	a	a	a
BV	a	a	b	a	a	a
LC	a	a	a	b	a	a
RC	a	a	a	a	b	a
EC	a	a	a	a	a	b

E. Discrepant Course-Taking I

M\E	NT	RM	BV	LC	RC	EC
NT	a	b	c	d	e	f
RM	b	a	g	h	i	j
BV	c	g	a	k	l	m
LC	d	h	k	a	n	o
RC	e	i	l	n	a	p
EC	f	j	m	o	p	a

F. Discrepant Course-Taking II

M\E	NT	RM	BV	LC	RC	EC
NT	a	b	c	d	e	f
RM	b	a	b	c	d	e
BV	c	b	a	b	c	d
LC	d	c	b	a	b	c
RC	e	d	c	b	a	b
EC	f	e	d	c	b	a

Key:

M=mathematics	NT=Not taking	BV=Business/Vocational	RC=Regular College
E=English	RM=Remedial	LC=Lower College	EC=Elite College

Design matrices replace the cells of a cross-tabulation table with symbols. In the design matrix for the CNC model, each letter signifies a level of concentration in the cell of the cross-tabulation table, after marginals are controlled. If the same letter is in two different cells, it means that the model specifies that those cells have the same level of concentration (after marginals are controlled, within sampling error). In the CNC design matrix three levels of concentration are specified: *b*, which pertains to students who are taking college preparatory courses for both subjects; *c*, which pertains to students taking non-college preparatory courses for both subjects; and *a*, which pertains to students enrolled in both college preparatory and non-college preparatory courses. Because the lower college courses resemble the old general track, the lower college preparatory math/lower college preparatory English combination is classified as non-college preparatory. I regard this collection of courses as lower college preparatory rather than as general track because of the vast increase in the diversity of colleges. (For further information on this classification, see Appendix A.)

Returning to the model, note that neither it nor the design matrix specifies which concentrations are greater; the parameter estimates will reveal which concentrations are relatively greater. However, the theoretical motivation for estimating the college/non-college model is the expectation that there are larger concentrations for b and c compared with a. Thus, in order for the model to support the theoretical expectation it must satisfy two criteria. First, the model must "fit." Second, it must produce parameter estimates for a, b, and c whose pattern of greater and lesser concentrations matches the expectation that motivated estimation of the model. If the model does not "fit," it is probably useful to consider alternative models. After describing the other models considered, I will turn to results to see which models provide an adequate description of the patterns of students' course taking.

College/Non-College/Not-Taking Model

The college/non-college/not-taking (CNCNT) model is one alternative to CNC (see Figure 2.1B). CNCNT posits that an adequate summary of the association can be obtained by accounting not only for students in college prep and non-college prep courses, but also for students who do not take a course in the two subjects.

The difference between CNC and CNCNT is that the latter separates students who enroll in neither math nor English (d) from all other students (a, b, and c). The no math/no English combination is allowed to be more or less common than other non-college prep course-taking combinations. Moreover, students who enroll in one subject but not in the other are treated as following a discrepant course-taking pattern. Substantively, CNCNT states that in order to summarize the association between students' courses in math and English, one must account for students who do not take math and English. One cannot simply regard these students as following a "non-college preparatory course" without distorting the on-the-ground reality in important ways.

Based on the work of Garet and DeLany; Stevenson, Schiller, and Schneider; and others, there is already good reason to doubt that the college/non-college model will provide an adequate description of students' course taking. Quantitative research has shown that the college/non-college dichotomy does not describe students' course taking. Ethnographic research has shown that the categories of courses are more varied. CNCNT provides one alternative way to describe the association between courses in disparate subjects.

Parallel Placement Models

Another possibility, however, is that the decline of overarching programs and the elaboration of in-school stratification have created additional categories, but students are invariably in the *same* category for different subjects. An implication of this claim is that although something has changed, course taking remains such that differential socialization is likely because students are in parallel placements across subjects.

Two models, PP–I and PP–II, investigate this possibility. The design matrices for these models are very similar (see Figure 2.1C and D). These two models both focus attention on the main diagonal, the cells that contain students who are taking the same level of course for the different subjects. However, the models differ in that PP–I allows each combination of parallel placements to have its *own* concentration, while PP–II estimates a *common* level of concentration for all parallel placements. Substantively, PP–II implies that the incidence of taking advanced courses in both subjects is about the same as the incidence of taking less advanced courses in both subjects (after appropriate controls), whereas PP–I implies that there may be large differences between these course combinations. I estimate both models to reduce the chance that I will reject the claim of parallel placement just because I was incorrect in my guess as to the relative incidence of the different combinations. (Further elaboration on this point is provided in Appendix C.)

Discrepant Course-Taking Models

So far the explanations for the association between math and English have emphasized the tendency of students to take nominally equivalent courses in different subjects. These explanations imply that when summarizing students' course taking, one may de-emphasize students in disparate levels of instruction for different subjects. Alternatively, one may consider whether the concentrations of students in disparate levels of courses for different subjects appear to be a systematic and important part of course taking.

Focusing on students in discrepant categories is quite important, for several reasons. First, students in discrepant categories have not been the focus of analysis before. Thus, researchers know very little about them—not how common they are, or whether patterns among them exist. Second, the decline of overarching programs *created* the very places these students may occupy. Thus, learning about these students is key to learning whether the association is qualitatively different than one would expect were overarching programs *actually* in place.

Third, symbolically, these locations are potentially extremely important. These students may occupy the educational equivalent of contradictory class locations (Wright, 1985), which I call (to avoid confusion) contradictory *course* locations. These students may demonstrate the *possibility* of discrepant course taking, and thereby serve to legitimate the course assignment process. Clearly, such legitimation is likely a local phenomenon; a necessary but insufficient condition for these students to occupy symbolically important roles in their own schools is that the course offerings in their schools be sufficiently varied to allow them to occupy contradictory positions in the *local* curriculum structure. This analysis cannot address that question; however, the analysis can discern whether there are patterns of students in these discrepant (and potentially contradictory) locations; given the potential importance of these students, investigating the patterning is a worthy, though limited, first step.

To consider whether students in discrepant course locations are important for understanding how students' courses are associated, I estimate two models: DC–I, and DC–II (see Figure 2.1E and F). DC–I, which estimates three times as many parameters as does DC–II, offers a relatively unstructured form for discrepant course taking. In contrast, DC–II specifies a much more structured form for discrepant course taking, for it requires that the prevalence of students depends on the degree of discrepancy in the courses. This is indicated in the design matrices for each model. The design matrix for DC–I includes 15 parameters for discrepant course taking; the design matrix for DC–II includes only five parameters, one for each degree of distance from the diagonal. However, despite differences in the looseness of the structure they allow, both models imply that to understand the association between students' courses in different subjects, one must attend to students in disparate levels of courses in different subjects.

The selection of one model over the others is to state that the substantive claims about the association that are embedded in the selected model provide a better match to the data under study. At present only the ideas have been presented, but the question as to which set of ideas best reflects the pattern of association remains unanswered. It is that question that the next section addresses.

ASSOCIATION BETWEEN MATH AND ENGLISH

Best Explanation

Summary statistics from the models are presented in Table 2.2. In Grade 9 the two most effective descriptions are provided by one of the theories of discrepant course taking (represented by DC–I) and the college/non-college/not-taking model. The BIC statistics for these models are so close (their difference equals 2.5) that I cannot select between them. Future studies may

Table 2.2. Fit Statistics for Models of Mathematics by English Tables

MODEL	L^2	df	BIC	Δ
Panel 1—Ninth Grade (sample size = 15,694, effective *n* = 4,935)				
Independence	553.0	25	340.4	6.96
College/Non-College	437.1	24	233.0	6.16
College/Non-College/Not Taking	115.8	22	−71.3	3.43
Parallel Placement I	107.3	19	−54.2	2.71
Parallel Placement II	367.9	24	163.8	6.61
Discrepant Course Taking I	16.2	10	−68.8	0.66
Discrepant Course Taking II	186.3	20	16.2	5.17
Panel 2—Tenth Grade (sample size = 15,672, effective *n* = 4,928)				
Independence	205.8	25	−6.8	5.59
College/Non-College	108.4	24	−95.7	4.04
College/Non-College/Not Taking	79.0	22	−108.0	3.56
Parallel Placement I	109.0	19	−52.6	3.76
Parallel Placement II	155.2	24	−48.9	4.65
Discrepant Course Taking I	12.4	10	−72.6	0.01
Discrepant Course Taking II	45.6	20	−124.4	2.31
Panel 3—Eleventh Grade (sample size = 14,642, effective *n* = 4,604)				
Independence	341.1	25	130.2	8.38
College/Non-College	221.4	24	18.9	7.07
College/Non-College/Not Taking	113.1	22	−72.5	4.67
Parallel Placement I	89.8	19	−70.5	3.18
Parallel Placement II	170.3	24	−30.2	5.99
Discrepant Course Taking I	23.6	10	−60.7	1.51
Discrepant Course Taking II	65.6	20	−103.1	3.81
Panel 4—Twelfth Grade (sample size = 14,111, effective *n* = 4,437)				
Independence	425.5	25	215.5	10.22
College/Non-College	256.1	24	54.6	8.88
College/Non-College/Not Taking	143.5	22	−41.3	5.92
Parallel Placement I	111.2	19	−48.4	3.99
Parallel Placement II	201.5	24	0	6.88
Discrepant Course Taking I	16.7	10	−67.2	1.43
Discrepant Course Taking II	72.2	20	−95.7	4.35

be able to adjudicate between these two models for ninth grade by investigating which set of parameters estimated on these data make the best predictions on new data. However, what must be remarked here is that both models signify that the change in school practice has had important effects on how students are stratified in school, because both provide further evidence against the college/non-college dichotomy.

For all other grades, one model provides the best description of the pattern of students' placements (as shown by the negative values for BIC), and that model is DC–II. The difference in the BIC statistics between DC–II and the next best model is 16.4, 30.6, and 28.5 for tenth, eleventh, and twelfth grade, respectively. This result provides very strong evidence in favor of discrepant course taking II over other models, suggesting that for the last 3 years of high school, students occupying discrepant course locations are important for understanding national curriculum structure.

Table 2.3 contains estimates for a DC–II model that reflect the pattern of students' concentrations for Grades 10, 11, and 12, after the marginal effects are removed (i.e., these estimates reflect the "pure" association between math and English). Students who are in the same level of course for math and English (the numbers in boldface) provide the baseline. Numbers in other cells signify how much less common it is for students to be in that location in comparison to students who are in any one level of course for different subjects. So, for example, based on the association between math and English, one would expect to find 44.7% as many students taking a combination of elite college preparatory math/remedial English as taking regular college prep math/regular college prep English.

Table 2.3. Parameters from Discrepant Course Taking Model II, for Grades 10, 11, and 12

	ENGLISH					
MATH	None	Remedial	Business/ Vocational	Lower College	Regular College	Elite College
None	**1**	0.777	0.693	0.513	0.447	0.256
Remedial	0.777	**1**	0.777	0.693	0.513	0.447
Busi/Voc	0.693	0.777	**1**	0.777	0.693	0.513
Lower Coll	0.513	0.693	0.777	**1**	0.777	0.693
Reg Coll	0.447	0.513	0.693	0.777	**1**	0.777
Elite Coll	0.256	0.447	0.513	0.693	0.777	**1**

Note: Above coefficients were calculated by re-estimating the DC-II model on the three-way table of math-by-English-by-grade for Grades 10, 11, and 12. The numbers in the cells are the anti-logs of the interaction parameters from the model.

The results in Table 2.3 show that students are more likely to be in the same level of course for math and English than they are to be in any other single combination of courses. Also, the incidence of discrepant course taking declines the more discrepant the courses are, as signified by the declining numbers as the cells move away from the diagonal of ones (i.e., as the cells move away from the main diagonal). Thus, I find that students' courses are associated and that students are more likely to take courses of similar levels, although not necessarily courses of the same level. This is a subtle but important change from the previous tracking regime.

However, Table 2.3 has a hidden implication that bears on the incidence of discrepant course taking. The model shows that discrepant course taking is patterned and thus technically important. But, are most students in exactly the same level of course across subjects? The answer is hidden in Table 2.3, for it shows the number of students in any discordant course combination relative to the number of students in any concordant course combination. What is masked is that although students are more likely to take the same level of course for both math and English than they are to take any other *single* combination of courses, adding up the number of students taking discrepant courses in math and English reveals that students in discrepant courses are numerous. Indeed, once I purge the table of marginal effects and consider the association between students' courses alone, I find that, on the basis of the association, more than 75 out of every 100 students are allocated to discrepant courses in math and English.

This result is obtained by using the relative concentrations of students denoted in Table 2.2 to allocate 100 students to the 6×6 table. This is preferable to using the raw cross-tabulation table because the raw table reflects not only the association between math and English, but also the pattern of course taking in the subjects separately (i.e., the association and the marginal distribution). Still, the raw data table shows that about two-thirds of the students occupy contradictory course locations.

One response to this finding is to question the definition of "same." However, the finding reported above remains even if the definition of "same" is relaxed so that students taking either the same level of course in different subjects or courses that are adjacent (e.g., courses in either of the two diagonals with values of .777) count as "same." Even with this less stringent definition, I still find that 44% of students are in discrepant categories of courses. Thus, contradictory course taking appears to be an important part of students' experience of schools.

Of course, one might be tempted to explain away this finding by noting that there are far more possibilities for discrepant course taking than otherwise. This would be a mistake, for it ignores that the discrepant places in the curriculum are the very places that were created by the decline of over-

arching programs. Whether the average discrepant location has more students than the average concordant location is irrelevant to the issue of
whether discrepant course locations are theoretically or substantively important. What the calculations show is that while concordant positions are important, so are discordant positions.

The numerical result bears on the incidence of discrepant course taking
and has important implications for analysts. In analyzing students' places
in the in-school stratification system, researchers should not de-emphasize
students who are in discrepant courses. Not only are the concentrations *patterned*, but also these students are *numerous*. Taken together, these two findings suggest that de-emphasizing these students is not to silence random
noise, nor is it to overshadow a rare constellation of course taking. It is,
instead, to miss a systematic and numerically important aspect of how in-
school stratification works.

That said, I must reiterate that the association is such that the greater
the discord between two courses, the less likely a student will have them
both on his or her schedule. These results suggest that the way in which
courses are associated is subtly different from what one would expect were
overarching programs in existence. However, even this subtle difference implies that potentially important social change has occurred inside schools
in the wake of the dismantling of mechanisms of program enrollment; the
unremarked revolution in school practice has been efficacious, at least in
some respects.

Adequate Explanation: Implications for Research and Theory

The comments above have outlined some implications of the best-fitting
model. The best-fitting model, a model highlighting the systematic nature
of discrepant course taking, provides a subtly different and more complex
vision of how in-school stratification works. However, before I conclude this
chapter, a few brief remarks concerning some of the models that provided an
adequate (but not preferred) fit are also in order. For these adequately fitting
models imply that simple changes in research practice may improve research, while providing a sufficiently accurate reflection of the complexity
of in-school stratification.

On the basis of the BIC statistics (see Table 2.2), I reject the college/
non-college distinction (the CNC model) for Grades 9, 11, and 12. However,
the CNC model provides an adequate fit to the tenth-grade data. This finding
has a major implication for research practice, for it implies that researchers
who are using tenth-grade data, either as a baseline for longitudinal research
or alone, may continue to categorize tenth graders according to the college/
non-college distinction. This is possible because the college/non-college dis-

tinction provides an adequate (not the best, but an adequate) description of students' course taking in Grade 10. Thus, depending on the purposes of a particular study, it may be sufficient to categorize students in tenth grade as either college preparatory or not.

For other years the college/non-college distinction did not provide an adequate description of the association between math and English courses. Thus, using the simple college preparatory/non-college preparatory distinction may be unwarranted. However, the college/non-college/not-taking model did provide an adequate description of the association. The adequate fit of this model means that analysts may construct a minimally sufficient summary of students' curricular location by adding the taking/not-taking distinction to the existing distinction between college prep/non-college prep. In some cases this distinction will be easier to add than in others. The important point, however, is that one need not go all the way to the DC–II framework in order to conduct analyses based on an expected association between students' courses in different subjects. If one can add the taking/not-taking distinction, then one can ensure that major demarcations in the curriculum have been captured. This strategy should reduce the distorting effects of relying on the college/non-college distinction alone for grades for which it did not provide an adequate description.

Parenthetically, I also estimated four models (four on each academic year) that investigated whether one can dispense with the college/non-college distinction and use only the taking/not-taking distinction. These models (not shown) tended to fit better than the CNC model. This implies that a minimally adequate division for analysts would be to divide students into two groups: (1) those who took math and/or English in a particular grade, and (2) those who did not take math and/or English in the particular grade. In many cases this may be simpler than adding a not-taking demarcation to the college preparatory/non-college preparatory distinction. However, while these models provided an adequate fit to the data, and fit better than the CNC models, they did not fit as well as CNCNT. Thus, CNCNT (and the distinctions it posits) is preferred.

In addition, I must note that by the BIC criterion, the independence model also fits the tenth-grade table. If the independence model fits, then one might maintain that there is no association between math and English, and therefore *de facto* tracking is not occurring. Moreover, the index of dissimilarity (Δ), which signifies the percentage of students misclassified by a model, shows that less than 6% of students are incorrectly classified by assuming that math and English are statistically independent in tenth grade. This means that more than 94% of the cases are *correctly* classified by assuming that math and English are not associated. Why, then, do I still infer that *de facto* tracking is occurring in this case?

Because, even for tenth grade, the independence model is still far worse than any other description of the association between math and English. In other words, an assumption of independence between math and English in tenth grade, while adequate, is the poorest of all the assumptions I tested. Although the adequate fit of the independence model in Grade 10 provides strong evidence that the dismantling of formal programs has been consequential (for when overarching formal programs existed, there was a clear association between math and English), I still conclude that *de facto* tracking *does* exist. Yet, I also must conclude that the pattern of association between courses in different subjects, the evidence of *de facto* tracking, appears subtly different from the association that existed prior to the change in school practice.

I have described the pattern of association and some of its implications. In sum, although the revolution in school practice appears to have gone quite some way toward breaking the relation between courses in different subjects, it did *not* end tracking, it transformed it. That transformation has allowed students to be placed into discrepant courses. The potential implications of this change are large. The present understanding of the change can be only the beginning of the effort to trace the implications of this new state of affairs.

CONCLUSIONS

Existing research from a variety of theoretical perspectives and methodological approaches has suggested that the college/non-college dichotomy no longer provides a proper summary of the in-school system of stratification. Although researchers have accepted this finding, no new vision of the in-school stratification system has arisen to replace the previous one.

The results above confirm that in some ways and for some research purposes no new vision is needed. The college/non-college distinction still serves as an adequate description of how tenth graders are arranged in school. In addition, simple adjustments to the college/non-college distinction (such as adding a category for students taking neither math nor English) provide a satisfactory description for all academic years. Thus, if one's aim is to utilize a simple and adequate description of tracking in order to study track effects or to control for track location, no change, or slight changes, appear sufficient.

However, if the aim is to develop a theory of how in-school stratification works, then the most accurate description of students' course taking in disparate subjects at the same point in time is needed. The most accurate description is quite different from the adequate descriptions, for in contrast to the above approaches, it highlights students' placement in discrepant courses.

The vast majority of students occupy such locations. The concentrations of students in discrepant locations does not bear the signature of random noise but, instead, appears patterned. This vision of how students are placed in two simultaneously acting systems of division evidently confirms a subtle but potentially consequential effect of the unremarked revolution. Prior to the dismantling of overarching programs, it was virtually impossible for students to take discrepant courses; after this revolution, the vast majority of students occupy discrepant locations.

The change implies that tracking, often regarded as a mechanism that facilitates schools' efforts to socialize students for different futures, may work less well than it did in the past. For the majority of students are now taking course patterns that expose them to different levels of coursework; to the extent that different levels of coursework are associated with different styles of instruction and socialization efforts, then the task of differentially socializing students must at best be more difficult.

The potential failures of tracking as a socializing tool may have serious implications for the legitimacy of the adult system of stratification. These serious implications become evident once one contrasts the claims about how schools worked in the past with how schools appear to work now. If earlier analysts were correct that highly segregated track structure supported the status quo at the time, then one must ask whether the current status quo is equally supported by the new regime.

However, to state that this is a new regime is to assume that the findings provide evidence of social change. An alternative interpretation is that the findings simply may identify the long-standing nature of the association between students' courses that was hidden by earlier assumptions about how courses would be associated. Although this is quite possible, I know of no data that would allow one to ascertain the association between students' courses for the 1950s and 1960s. Moreover, researchers have described a process by which social change appears to have occurred. This research is coupled with ethnographic evidence on how schools worked in the past (Cicourel & Kitsuse, 1963; Hollingshead, 1949). Given this evidence, and unless and until further analyses of earlier data reveal differently, I regard the results presented here as evidence of how matters have changed since 1965, rather than as evidence of the enduring patterns of course taking.

One may wonder how it could be that something researchers *know* to have effects does not seem to be key to the allocation process. After all, the college/non-college demarcation has been shown to be the most achievement-related distinction in the curriculum (Gelb, 1979). Some researchers have shown this division to be more important for achievement than the division between students who graduate and those who drop out of school (Gamoran, 1987). Students identified as college track outscore their non-college track peers on tests of achievement, are less likely to drop out, are more likely to enter college, and more (Gamoran & Mare, 1989; Natriello, Pallas, & Alexander, 1989; Rosenbaum, 1980). How, then, can the college/non-college dichotomy fail to summarize students' programs of study?

Although the answer to this question may be complex, one word must be present in any answer, and that word is *information*. Information, or the lack thereof, certainly can provide a plausible explanation as to how the most salient distinction for achievement might *not* be the most salient distinction when it comes to how students are allocated to courses in different subjects. This explanation goes as follows: First, other researchers have shown that the high school curriculum has been elaborated in part to match a diverse set of collegiate institutions and in part for other reasons (Oakes, 1987; Powell, Farrar, & Cohen, 1985). One may posit that the more elaborate curriculum differentiation is, and absent clear signposts through the curriculum, the more obscure the demarcation that is most relevant for achievement may be, especially to students. In other words, in a world with lots of lines, finding the line that matters and getting oneself onto the "right" side of that line may not be easy. Indeed, some students may be unaware that there is a "right" side of the line.

Thus, the key achievement-related distinction may concern the college/non-college divide. But an elaborate set of options and confusion as to where different courses lead may allow students to enroll themselves in courses with only a hazy awareness of how the courses map onto the college/non-college dichotomy. There is certainly evidence that students register for courses with only a faint awareness of the long-term implications of their decisions, owing in part to reluctance on the part of counselors to interfere with students' aspirations (Powell, Farrar, & Cohen, 1985; Rosenbaum, Miller, & Krei, 1995). As students are central actors in the registration process, and as they may not be responding to good information about the implications of their decisions, they may allocate themselves (or acquiesce in their allocation) to courses using criteria other than the college/non-college divide. If criteria other than the college/non-college distinction are used to make course enrollment decisions, then it is quite likely that the association between subjects may not be captured by the college/non-college dichotomy.

This chapter has shown again that the college/non-college categorization is incomplete for most academic years. Moreover, a minimally adequate categorization would add a not-taking category to the common college/non-college divide. But the most accurate summary of the association between students' courses highlights students taking discrepant courses. To be sure, students are most likely to enroll in courses of similar levels. This pattern of association provides evidence of continued *de facto* tracking. Even so, the possibility of taking discrepant courses, and its emergence as a key feature of in-school stratification, is arguably a direct result of the revolution in school practice and signals subtle but potentially important social change within schools.

Amid this changed set of circumstances, new opportunities arise for students to construct schedules that are uniquely suited to their own situation. Given these new opportunities, it is important to ask what factors are associated with students' placements. Does social class continue to matter, or will controls for specific achievement erase the putative social class effect? Will achievement in the domain be more important than achievement outside the domain for placement? Answers to these questions are key to a fuller understanding of this regime of tracking. Chapter 3 takes up these questions.

CHAPTER 3

Merit and Track Placement

Chapter 2 ignored individual-level factors, but students do not enter schools as blank slates; they come with, among other things, all of the attributes research has shown to be important in the stratification system (e.g., race, class, gender, and ethnicity). Thus, it is important to consider correlates of students' placement to more clearly understand curricular stratification. To that end, this chapter investigates the role of background and achievement.

Researchers have investigated the correlates of placement using a variety of conceptions of placement. They have studied summary track location as an outcome, usually dichotomized as college prep/non-college prep (Alexander, Cook, & McDill, 1978; Gamoran & Mare, 1989; Lucas & Gamoran, 1991; Rosenbaum, 1980); have investigated students' level of placement within one subject alone (Catsambis, 1994); or have analyzed students' placements in two subjects *separately* (Garet & DeLany, 1988; Hallinan, 1992; Stevenson, Schiller, & Schneider, 1994). As I have distinguished between curriculum differentiation (the division of students into different groups for instruction in one subject) and tracking (the association between two differentiated curricula), I will investigate correlates of students' simultaneous placement in two subjects, rather than correlates of students' placements in one subject.

FINDINGS FROM EXISTING RESEARCH

Previous research on correlates of track placement has shown that social class, measured student achievement, race, and sex are important determinants of track location (Gamoran & Mare, 1989; Garet & DeLany, 1988; Hallinan, 1992; Jones, Vanfossen, & Ensminger, 1995; Rehberg & Rosenthal, 1978; Rosenbaum, 1980; Useem, 1992).

Evidence exists that blacks and Latinos are far more numerous in the non-college track than are whites and Asians (Oakes, 1985). These gross enrollment differentials suggest that tracking may maintain racial and ethnic segregation in the wake of judicially mandated desegregation (Oakes, 1994a,

1994b). However, studies of race- and ethnic-linked disadvantages in assignment that control for achievement have been more equivocal, and some have even shown black advantages in assignment.

Garet and DeLany's study of four California high schools found that black students were *more* likely to be enrolled in a math course than were white students, once achievement was controlled (i.e., net of achievement), and more likely to be enrolled in advanced math than were white students. Asian students were also more likely to take advanced mathematics than were whites. This finding is consistent with the Gamoran and Mare (1989) conclusion that blacks are more likely to be in the college track, net of measured achievement and social background factors. However, using more structural measures of track location, Lucas and Gamoran (1991) found that blacks and whites were equally likely to be in the college track.

Notably, if differential placement occurs in elementary school, one should expect racial differences in secondary school placement to disappear once achievement is controlled, because early differential placement may have created lower achievement for blacks and Latinos. Yet, some evidence suggests that differential placement by race does not occur in elementary schools (Pallas, Entwistle, Alexander, & Stluka, 1994) or in middle schools (Hallinan, 1992). Thus, whether racial and ethnic status is an advantage, a disadvantage, or irrelevant to secondary school curricular location remains unclear.

Gender differences in placement are also a concern. Once again, the findings are unclear. Gamoran and Mare (1989) found that girls were more likely to be in the college track than were boys, while Lucas and Gamoran (1991) found no effect of sex on track placement. Similar to Lucas and Gamoran, Garet and DeLany (1988) found no effect of sex on students' high school mathematics placements. Focusing on younger students, Catsambis (1994) found that middle school girls equaled boys in mathematics achievement and mathematics placements. But for English placements, Hallinan (1992) found that middle school girls were disadvantaged. The thrust of these findings is net gender equality in high school placements, but enough discrepancies exist to make the conclusion unclear.

The complexities surrounding the effects of race, ethnicity, and sex are not mirrored in the results concerning socioeconomic status and measured achievement. Consistently, researchers find that higher social status is associated with placement in more advanced courses or the college preparatory track. Just as consistently, measured student achievement is positively related to enrollment in advanced courses or college preparatory tracks. Historically, researchers have regarded social class status as an inappropriate factor for track placement (Hallinan, 1994a). Conversely, the positive effects of measured achievement are regarded as evidence that students are matched to curricula for which they are prepared and that they deserve, that is, that tracking is to some extent meritocratic (Rehberg & Rosenthal, 1978).

The interpretation for social status is sound. However, now that schools have dismantled formal programs, the interpretation for measured achievement is no longer sound. It was sound when summary measures of achievement were used to assess the meritocratic nature of students' placements in a system with overarching tracks. Yet, students typically have strengths in some areas and weaknesses in others, and the decline of formal programs means that students may be matched to courses on the basis of their achievement in specific domains. Thus, any summary measure of disparate areas of achievement may obscure the specifics that are essential to uncovering whether students are matched to courses in ways that reward achievement in the domain of inquiry the course represents. For one to conclude that students are placed according to their achievements, the evidence must show that students' achievement matters for the subject in which the achievement has been made. However, if achievement in unrelated areas is associated with students' placement in a particular subject, net of achievement in the particular subject, then the meritocratic claim is unwarranted.

Why is this discussion of the domain-specific nature of achievement important? Because some contend that the pedagogical advantage of tracking is that it allows the creation of homogenous groups for instruction (Hallinan, 1994a). Analysts find that teachers prefer to teach students with similar levels of preparation (National Education Association, 1968); and, as Wells and Oakes (1996) show, many parents fear their children will be slowed by less-prepared peers in heterogenous classes. It is in part on the basis of this fear that many middle-class parents agitate to maintain tracking. Yet, if achievement in unrelated domains can gain students admission to courses in domains in which they lack achievement, then this particular pedagogical argument for tracking is dissolved. Thus, much rides on whether the pattern of achievement effects is consistent with meritocratic matching.

ANALYSIS PLAN: INDIVIDUAL CORRELATES OF JOINT PLACEMENT

The foci of the analyses are two 3×3 cross-classifications of students (based on the CNCNT model). To produce these tables I first recoded the math and English course-taking variables separately. The recoded variables combine regular college preparatory and elite college preparatory categories into a college preparatory category, and lower college, business and vocational, and remedial categories into a non-college preparatory category. Students not enrolled in a course for the subject form a third category. I then cross-tabulated the two 3-category variables to produce the 3×3 table under investigation here. This new table reflects the CNCNT model from Chapter 2, which did fit the data. Because the collapse of the table conforms to a model that fit the data, as well as for other reasons elaborated in Appendix C, this collapsed version does not distort the findings.

These 3×3 cross-tabulations are shown in Table 3.1. Panel 1 shows the number of eleventh graders taking each combination of math and English, while Panel 2 shows the course taking of twelfth graders. Like Chapter 2, this chapter provides an analysis of students' joint placement in two differentiated curricula. Unlike the previous chapter, however, this analysis emphasizes the individual-level correlates of placement. Thus, instead of modeling the gross pattern of association, students' locations in each 3×3 array are modeled as a response, and individual-level variables are used as regressors. An appropriate model in these circumstances is the multinomial logit model.

The multinomial logit model is similar to the binary logit or logit model. The logit model often is used to investigate dichotomous outcomes. For example, the logit model has been used to investigate the correlates of high school graduation. In this example, the dependent variable has two categories—drop out of school (often coded 0) and graduate from school (coded 1). Estimating this logit model produces one set of coefficients that capture the association between the independent variables and the probability of completing high school. But what also must be noted is that what one has obtained is an estimate of the association between the independent variables and the probability of completing high school *in comparison to the probability of dropping out*. The dropout category serves as a baseline with which the graduates are compared. Only one set of coefficients is needed to describe the difference between these two groups.

Here, however, there are nine rather than two possible outcomes. Yet,

Table 3.1. Cross-Tabulations of Mathematics and English Enrollment

		ENGLISH		
	MATHEMATICS	None	Non-College	College
Panel 1—	None	767	715	3117
Grade 11	Non-College	259	856	3271
	College	250	631	4776
Panel 2—	None	1853	1300	3539
Grade 12	Non-College	583	860	2080
	College	267	689	2940

one may use one of the nine outcomes as a baseline (just as one implicitly uses one of the two outcomes as a baseline in the binary logit) and estimate the multinomial logit model. Instead of one set of coefficients, the model will produce eight sets of coefficients, one for each outcome minus the baseline. These coefficients will compare eight of the outcomes with the baseline outcome. In this case I use the group of students who are college prep for both math and English as the baseline. Note that substantive results are not sensitive to the baseline selected, but using a theoretically or substantively interesting group as the baseline does aid interpretation of the results.

Table 3.2 shows the same cross-tabulations listed in Table 3.1. The difference is that Table 3.2 reflects the number of students in each category relative to the number of students in the college prep math/college prep English combination. For example, Panel 2 of Table 3.2 shows that 860 fewer students combined college prep English with non-college prep math than combined college prep math and college prep English. The college prep math/college prep English combination provides a baseline with which all other combinations are compared. One may see how more or less common any other combination is when compared with the baseline category. The multinomial logit model will make essentially the same kind of comparison. The difference is that whereas Table 3.2 lists the number of students in each category in relation to the baseline category, the remainder of the tables have the same format but contain regression-like coefficients. These coefficients are analogous to the numbers in Table 3.2, except that they reflect how the concentrations of students in the cell differ *relative to the baseline category*, as the values of the explanatory variable change.

Just as in Chapter 2, I obtain fit statistics for the multinomial logit

Table 3.2. Cross-Tabulations of Mathematics and English Enrollment (All comparisons with the mathematics/English college prep category)

		ENGLISH		
	MATHEMATICS	None	Non-College	College
Panel 1—	None	−4009	−4061	−1659
Grade 11	Non-College	−4517	−3920	−1505
	College	−4526	−4145	0
Panel 2—	None	−1087	−1640	599
Grade 12	Non-College	−2357	−2080	−860
	College	−2673	−2251	0

model. In this case I use BIC*.[1] The interpretation of BIC* is much the same as the interpretation of BIC; if BIC* is negative, the posited model provides an adequate fit to the data, and the more negative BIC* is, the better the fit of the model. Further detail on the selection of the multinomial logit model is provided in Appendix C.

While Chapter 2 analyzed data from Grades 9 through 12, this analysis focuses on students' placement in Grades 11 and 12. This will allow the measures of tenth-grade factors, such as measured achievement and aspirations, to reflect pre-existing differences between students.

Figure 3.1 contains information about the independent variables. One brief comment regarding them will be helpful. Three dichotomous variables categorize students as black, Latino/a, and other non-white. The other non-white category is used in the models to ease comparisons between whites, blacks, and Latinos. However, there are so few students in the other non-white category, and the category is so racially and ethnically heterogenous, that I will not discuss the parameter estimates for that category.

DETERMINANTS OF CURRICULAR PLACEMENT

A Role for Graduation Requirements?

In Chapter 2 I suggested that information, or the lack of it, might explain why students' course taking does not appear to follow the traditional college prep/non-college prep demarcation. The decline of formal programs removed important information on the implications of course taking, but it did not remove all available information. In the wake of the decline of formal programs, one important set of informational items that remains available to every student is the set of graduation requirements. Although some students receive information about what is required for college, many students are not so informed. Thus, the decline of formal programs has left a substantial proportion of students with only the graduation requirements as a guide. Graduation requirements, however, typically concern *time* studying a subject, not particular levels of mastery. Thus, students who have only the graduation requirements to go by are at a distinct disadvantage.

There are at least two ways graduation requirements might matter for

---

[1]BIC, used in Chapter 2, implicitly compared every model with the saturated model. BIC*, which will be used here, implicitly uses the null model, the model with no regressors, as the baseline (Raftery, 1995). The formula for BIC* $\approx -\chi^2 + ((df)(\ln(N))$ where χ^2 is the design-effect adjusted X^2 statistic for the comparison between the null and the posited models, df is degrees of freedom, and N is the effective sample size (Raftery, 1995).

Figure 3.1. Independent Variable Descriptions
_____

All variables are recoded to the midpoint for missing cases. With the exception of the graduation requirement variables, a control for missing on each particular variable is used. The indicators of missing on graduation requirements were perfectly correlated; thus, one indicator for missing is used to signify missing on the graduation requirement variables.

Social Background
    Socioeconomic status is measured with a composite formed by students' reports of mother's education, father's education, father's occupational status, family income, and a household items index.
    Male—students' self-report of sex was used.

Race/Ethnicity
    The omitted category for three dichotomous race/ethnicity indicators is white.
    Black—students' self-report of black or not
    Latino/a—students' self-report of Latin ancestry
    Other non-white—students' self-report of Asian, Native American, Alaskan Native, or Pacific Islander.

Achievement
    Five tenth grade tests are used to measure achievement:
        Vocabulary (range 0–21), Reading (0–19), Writing (0–17), Math I (0–28), Math II (0–10).
    Mathematics achievement is measured by the sum of the two mathematics subtests, normed to range between 0 and 10, and centered on 0.
    English achievement is measured by the sum of the writing, reading, and vocabulary tests, normed to range between 0 and 10, and centered on 0.

Aspirations
    In tenth grade, students were asked to report the minimum level of education with which they would be satisfied. This measure, dichotomized as less than college graduate and college graduate or more, indicates student aspirations.

Graduation Requirements
    Schools' graduation requirements in math and English were taken from school principals' reports for the class of 1982. Approximately half of the schools were surveyed in 1982; thus, approximately half of the students have data for these variables, while half do not.
_____

students' course taking: (1) requirements compel students who want to graduate to take a certain number of courses, and (2) requirements provide information about what is and what is not important. There is no direct way of determining what portion of course taking reflects student response to compulsion and what portion reflects student response to information. Compulsion is probably extremely important. However, some students may take courses not because they feel compelled to do so, but because the information they have implies that the course is important. Thus, while compulsion is an extremely significant aspect of graduation requirements, it is also fair to say that for many students the requirements may serve to communicate what is important and what is not—in short, to provide information.

It is impossible with the data here to assess the relative strengths of those factors, but I can assess whether requirements seem to matter overall. Table 3.3 presents two multinomial logit models, one for Grade 11 and one for Grade 12, that aid assessment of this question.

Consider the first set of results, a cross-tabulation table of eleventh grade math and English placements. However, the cells of the table do not contain the numbers of students in each category. Instead, the cells contain the coefficients from the multinomial logit model, which reflect whether the concentrations of students in the cell are associated with a given explanatory variable. Thus, the coefficients that compare a student's chance of taking neither math nor English with a student's chance of taking both college prep math and college prep English are .177 (for the constant), −.107 for math requirements, and −.440 for English requirements. Only the coefficient for English requirements is statistically significant at $\alpha = .05$. (Standard errors are available from the author.) This cell tells us that the more years of English required for graduation, the less likely that students will take neither English nor math (in comparison to their chance of taking both college prep English and college prep math).

One difficulty with the multinomial logit model is that very simple models quickly become cumbersome. The number of β coefficients equals $k \times (j - 1)$ [where k equals the number of explanatory variables plus 1 (for the constant), and j equals the number of categories in the dependent variable]; the models in Table 3.3 have only two explanatory variables (plus a constant), but also have nine outcomes, making a total of $3 \times (9 - 1) = 24$ β coefficients. This proliferation of coefficients can make interpretation a challenge. This common difficulty is exacerbated in the current case because the outcome variable actually is defined by two variables, math and English. Thus, every coefficient reflects what might be termed a double comparison, as it reflects the likelihood of following one course pattern defined by two variables in comparison to following another course pattern defined by two variables. This means that discussion of coefficients can become quite com-

Table 3.3. Multinomial Logit Model 1 of Mathematics and English Enrollment (All comparisons with the baseline mathematics/English college prep category)

	MATHEMATICS	ENGLISH		
		None	**Non-College**	**College**
	None	0.177	0.237	0.355
	Math Requirement	−0.107	−0.369*	−0.509*
	English Requirement	−0.440*	−0.373	0.042
Panel 1-	**Non–College**	−0.704	−0.158	0.781
	Math Requirement	−0.150	−0.141	−0.261*
Grade 11	English Requirement	−0.535	−0.362	−0.158
	College	−0.916	−2.026*	Baseline
	Math Requirement	−0.125	−0.191	Category
	English Requirement	−0.513	0.086	
	None	4.202*	1.074	0.185
	Math Requirement	−0.383*	−0.609*	−0.528*
	English Requirement	−1.054*	−0.215	0.267
Panel 2-	**Non-College**	3.825*	1.784*	−0.503
	Math Requirement	−0.462*	−0.581*	−0.553*
Grade 12	English Requirement	−1.210*	−0.521*	0.328
	College	2.857*	−1.118	Baseline
	Math Requirement	−0.005	−0.562*	Category
	English Requirement	−1.441*	0.192	

Grade	Effective *n*	Null Model L^{2*}	Model 1 L^{2*}	df	BIC*
11	4604	−8257.3	−8229.4	24	146.6
12	4437	−8781.8	−8687.7	24	13.3

Note: A control for missing data on requirements (56% in Grade 11, 56% in Grade 12) is also included in the models; *= parameter estimate discernibly different from zero at or below $\alpha = .05$

plicated, especially for dummy variables. In order to facilitate the discussion, then, I will suppress the obligatory "in comparison to students in college prep math/college prep English" phrase. Unless otherwise noted, all reported findings are in comparison to students who follow college preparatory courses for both subjects.

Considering Table 3.3, I find that requirements seem to be more important in Grade 12 than in Grade 11. More coefficients are discernibly different from zero for Grade 12 than for Grade 11. The direction of the coefficients suggests that the more math and English that is required, the more likely the students will be in the college prep course for both math and English.

These results suggest that course requirements do matter in allocating students to courses for both subjects. Moreover, requirements appear more important in twelfth grade than eleventh grade. This is as one might suspect, because seniors are likely to have more prior coursework than juniors, and thus for any given level of "exposure" requirements, juniors are less likely to have satisfied the requirement. Thus, it is in senior year that one would expect to see larger differences based on requirements in the school. The evidence suggests that for two seniors who have the same number of prior courses, but attend schools that require different numbers of completed courses in a subject, the student attending the school with more requirements is more likely to take a course in the subject, and more likely to take a college preparatory course in the subject, than her peer at a school that requires fewer courses.

Although I cannot partition this effect into that owing to compulsion and that owing to information, both factors are potentially important for students' course taking. Still, the positive BIC* statistics suggest that this model is not an adequate description of track placement. In other words, other factors besides graduation requirements are associated with individual students' placements.

Sociodemographic Factors

Table 3.4 contains coefficients describing the association between sociodemographic factors and curricular placement. (I removed the requirements variables from this model to focus on the gross association of social background and placement.) The particular perturbations are there for the interested reader to see. The main story with respect to race and ethnicity is that blacks and Latinos are less likely to be in college preparatory math/college preparatory English than are whites in eleventh grade. However, blacks and whites have similar chances of enrolling in college preparatory math/college preparatory English in twelfth grade. In contrast, the Latino disadvantage persists into twelfth grade.

With respect to sex the patterns are complex. Boys are more likely to take neither math nor English in eleventh grade. However, girls are more likely to combine college prep English and non-college prep math than are boys.

In twelfth grade the sex difference in chances of not taking both subjects goes away. But girls are still more likely to combine non-college prep math with college prep English, and they are also more likely to not take math while taking college prep English. In addition, they are more likely than boys to combine non-college prep math and not taking English. These findings identify potentially important complexities in the sex differences in patterns of course taking.

Turning to social status, in both grades higher social status is associated

Table 3.4. Multinomial Logit Model 2 of Mathematics and English Enrollment
(All comparisons with the baseline mathematics/English college prep category)

| | MATHEMATICS | ENGLISH | | |
		None	Non-College	College
Panel 1—	**None**	−2.306*	−1.911*	−0.275*
Grade 11	Male	0.347*	0.068	−0.027
	Black	0.845*	0.033	0.123
	Latina	0.801*	0.537*	0.373*
	Other Non-White	0.694*	0.095	−0.418
	Social Class	−1.086*	−1.050*	−0.915
	Non-College	−3.205*	−1.851*	−0.255*
	Male	0.286	−0.037	−0.237*
	Black	0.309	0.636*	0.538*
	Latina	0.428	0.881*	0.635*
	Other Non-White	0.571	0.245	0.005
	Social Class	−1.182*	−0.797*	−0.757*
	College	−2.877*	−1.965*	Baseline Category
	Male	−0.141	0.148	
	Black	−0.492	−0.450	
	Latina	−0.090	0.002	
	Other Non-White	0.385	−0.524	
	Social Class	−0.101	−0.238*	
Panel 2—	**None**	−0.217*	−0.541*	0.500*
Grade 12	Male	−0.096	−0.033	−0.251*
	Black	−0.283	−0.257	−0.115
	Latina	0.620*	0.467*	0.418*
	Other Non-White	0.199	−0.572	−0.340
	Social Class	−0.971*	−0.768*	−0.831*
	Non-College	−1.097*	−0.980*	−0.068
	Male	−0.404*	−0.241	−0.383*
	Black	−0.410	−0.090*	0.312
	Latina	0.318	0.559*	0.689*
	Other Non-White	−0.517	−0.355	−0.317
	Social Class	−0.972*	−0.814*	−0.751*
	College	−2.302*	−1.433*	Baseline
	Male	0.126	0.182	Category
	Black	−0.270	−0.331	
	Latina	0.039	−0.205	
	Other Non-White	−0.200	0.041	
	Social Class	−0.096	0.024	

Grade	Effective n	Null Model L^{2*}	Model 2 L^{2*}	df	BIC*
11	4604	−8257.3	−7961.5	48	−203.7
12	4437	−8781.8	−8567.3	48	−36.7

Note: A control for missing data on social class (12% in Grade 11, 12% in Grade 12) is also included in the models; * = parameter estimate discernibly different from zero at or below $\alpha = .05$

with higher placements. This replicates the findings commonly produced. The negative BIC* statistics suggest that, by themselves, sociodemographic factors provide a useful explanation of students' placements.

The Role of Prior Achievement in Specific Domains

In investigating the role of achievement in curricular location, it is important to control for two potentially confounding factors. First, low aspirations might make some high-achieving students have lower placements than expected. Thus, controlling for aspirations is important. Second, schools typically require more English than math for graduation; thus, partialing out the effect of graduation requirements is necessary to facilitate comparison of math and English achievement effects.

Before assessing the effects of achievement, it is possible to consider whether race, ethnicity, gender, and social class effects are altered once controls for prior achievement and requirements are introduced. Making these changes turns out to change the net effect of race and ethnicity (see Table 3.5). Once achievement is controlled, Latinos do not appear to differ from whites in Grade 11 or Grade 12. In addition, blacks appear advantaged in their placements in comparison to whites; if two students are of the same sex, have the same social status, have the same test scores, and attend schools with the same graduation requirements, but one is black and the other white, the black student will be more likely to be in college prep math/college prep English. Thus, adding aspirations, achievement, and requirements to the model allows a black advantage to emerge.

Introducing controls for achievement alters the findings for race/ethnicity. In contrast, gender effects and social status effects appear as they did in the sociodemographic model; thus, the conclusions remain apt even after achievement and several achievement-related factors are controlled. This implies that the sex differences detailed above are not explained away by differences in aspirations or prior achievement. Instead, girls and boys similar on these attributes still combine courses in different ways, ways that disadvantage girls.

Given the dismantling of mechanisms for enrolling into overarching programs, the social status effect is also particularly notable, given that aspirations are controlled. In a world lacking overarching tracks, differential aspirations might maintain *de facto* tracks. In addition, differential aspirations might explain the association between socioeconomic status and course enrollment. However, the evidence suggests that the second claim is untrue; net of aspirations and achievement, social status continues to be associated with college preparatory course enrollment. This finding, that two students who differ only on social background are likely to follow divergent course

Table 3.5. Multinomial Logit Model 3 of Mathematics and English Enrollment (All comparisons with the baseline mathematics/English college prep category)

	MATHEMATICS	ENGLISH		
		None	**Non-College**	**College**
Panel 1—	**None**	−0.055	0.380	0.699
Grade 11	Male	0.321*	0.017	−0.036
	Black	0.234	−0.570*	−0.385*
	Latina	0.253	−0.001	0.080
	Other Non-White	0.499	−0.019	−0.511
	Social Class	−0.621*	−0.531*	−0.477*
	Math Achievement	−0.458*	−0.392*	−0.418*
	English Achievement	−0.242*	−0.303*	−0.155*
	College Aspirations	−0.640*	−1.396*	−1.015*
	Math Requirement	−0.210	−0.440*	−0.568*
	English Requirement	−0.411	−0.296	0.102
	Non-College	−0.802	−0.134	1.164*
	Male	0.254	−0.051	−0.233*
	Black	−0.333	−0.051	−0.003
	Latina	−0.143	0.311*	0.165
	Other Non-White	0.373	0.072	−0.117
	Social Class	−0.716*	−0.359*	−0.340*
	Math Achievement	−0.386*	−0.491*	−0.457*
	English Achievement	−0.292*	−0.182*	−0.122*
	College Aspirations	−0.579	−0.362	−0.786*
	Math Requirement	−0.228	−0.231	−0.332*
	English Requirement	−0.498	−0.308	−0.118
	College	−0.849	−1.948*	Baseline
	Male	−0.157	0.133	Category
	Black	−0.353	−0.514	
	Latina	−0.007	−0.053	
	Other Non-White	0.403	−0.519	
	Social Class	−0.100	−0.158*	
	Math Achievement	0.091	0.000	
	English Achievement	0.015	−0.087	
	College Aspirations	−0.229	−0.149	
	Math Requirement	−0.074	−0.170	
	English Requirement	−0.527	0.097	

Table 3.5, *continued*

MATHEMATICS	ENGLISH		
	None	**Non-College**	**College**
Panel 2— **None**	4.682*	1.572*	0.852
Grade 12 Male	−0.170	−0.075	−0.270*
Black	−0.985*	−0.922*	−0.698*
Latina	0.048	−0.040	−0.042
Other Non-White	0.063	−0.674	−0.461
Social Class	−0.450*	−0.307*	−0.411*
Math Achievement	−0.364*	−0.347*	−0.359*
English Achievement	−0.288*	−0.233*	−0.160*
College Aspirations	−0.828*	−0.621*	−0.639*
Math Requirement	−0.438*	−0.633*	−0.547*
English Requirement	−1.046*	−0.183	0.274
Non-College	4.555*	2.431*	0.228
Male	−0.455*	−0.279	−0.411*
Black	−1.016*	−0.673*	−0.262
Latina	−0.171	0.080	0.222
Other Non-White	−0.579	−0.465	−0.449
Social Class	−0.494*	−0.349*	−0.325*
Math Achievement	−0.356*	−0.356*	−0.317*
English Achievement	−0.220*	−0.194*	−0.200*
College Aspirations	−0.880*	−0.956*	−0.756*
Math Requirement	−0.498*	−0.618*	−0.590*
English Requirement	−1.181*	−0.503*	0.326
College	2.728*	−1.088	Baseline
Male	0.031	0.146	Category
Black	−0.448	−0.421	
Latina	−0.073	−0.271	
Other Non-White	−0.279	0.009	
Social Class	−0.039	0.088	
Math Achievement	0.158	0.102	
English Achievement	−0.208	−0.198*	
College Aspirations	0.109	0.049	
Math Requirement	0.021	−0.485*	
English Requirement	−1.444*	0.145	

Grade	Effective n	Null Model L^{2*}	Model 2 L^{2*}	df	BIC*
11	4604	−8257.3	−7536.6	128	−375.8
12	4437	−8781.8	−8187.2	128	−125.5

Note: Controls for missing data on social class (12% in Grade 11, 12% in Grade 12), course requirements (56%, 56%), college aspirations (29%, 30%), math achievement (16%, 15%), and English achievement (17%, 17%) are also included in the models; * = parameter estimate discernibly different from zero at or below $\alpha = .05$

patterns that tend to advantage those of higher social class, questions whether tracking is meritocratic.

Although this finding is important, it is not news; researchers routinely find social status effects and routinely regard those effects as signs of non-meritocratic matching. Here, however, it is possible to push the question of meritocratic tracking one step further. It is possible to ask whether the evidence suggests that students are matched to courses according to achievement in the particular domain of inquiry. From Table 3.5 it is apparent that in nearly every comparison, for both junior and senior years of high school, the effect of mathematics achievement is larger than the effect of English achievement. The basic invariance of the pattern of effects is extremely important. Some have argued that curricular differentiation allows students of varying abilities to be placed in courses that match those abilities (Hallinan, 1994b). This argument is true, for dividing students could allow students to be placed in groups that match their abilities. However, the evidence suggests that this does not seem to be occurring.

If curricular differentiation served to place well-prepared students in challenging courses for which they were prepared, one should find no effect of mathematics achievement on English placements once English achievement is entered in the model. Even if there is some effect of math achievement (as one might expect given that math achievement measures may pick up some effect of omitted variables), under a regime of meritocratic placement one should find *higher* effects for English achievement in comparison to mathematics achievement for placements in demanding English classes. But I do not.

Using eleventh-grade results from Table 3.5, I estimated the probabilities of college prep course enrollment for middle-class white males with college aspirations but varying mathematics or English achievement, and attending a school that requires 2 years of math and 4 years of English (the modal requirements). The probabilities for college prep math enrollment appear in Figure 3.2; those for college prep English enrollment appear in Figure 3.3.

These figures are striking. Figure 3.2 shows that the math achiever, the student who obtained the highest possible math score (and who is at the mean in English achievement and is represented by the solid line), has nearly a 90% chance of taking college prep math, while the English achiever, the student who obtained the highest possible English achievement score (and who is at the mean for mathematics achievement and is represented by the dashed line), has about a 60% chance of taking college prep math. Thus, by achieving in the domain of mathematics, the math achiever has a 30-point advantage in chances of enrolling in college prep math. Contrast this arguably appropriate domain-specific achievement advantage with the results in

Figure 3.2 College Preparatory
Math Enrollment by Math and
English Achievement

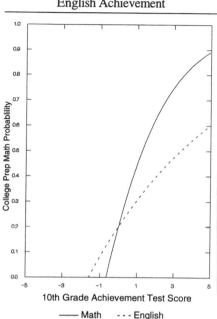

10th Grade Achievement Test Score

—— Math   - - - English

Figure 3.3. The English achiever (again represented by the dashed line) has about a 78% chance of being in college prep English. However, the math achiever (who is at the mean in English achievement) has a higher chance of being in college prep *English*.

These results are quite inconsistent with students' obtaining entry to courses in the domains of inquiry in which they have achieved. The association between courses—that is, tracking—actually appears to work *against* the creation of homogenous instructional groups, by heavily weighting achievement in some domains even when those domains appear less relevant. Consequently, it appears that tracking does not accomplish what many teachers and middle-class parents say they desire, namely, the construction of groups of homogenous preparation so as to facilitate instruction and speed learning.

One could argue that this exercise is irrelevant because students really have very similar levels of achievement across different domains. But the evidence suggests this is untrue. Even after 10 years of schooling, during which course assignment practices may have increased the relation between mathematics and English achievement, less than half of the variance of the

Figure 3.3 College Preparatory
English Enrollment by Math and
English Achievement

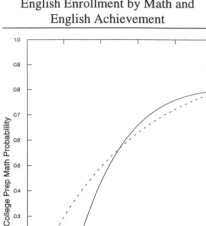

math and English tests is shared in common. The orthogonal other half of
the variance in domain-specific achievement may be enough to allow domain-specific achievement matching. School-level analyses, with much
larger within-school samples, would be needed to determine whether this is
true.

Two other possible explanations for the finding above are that greater
reliability or larger variance in the math tests lies behind the larger effect of
mathematics achievement. These explanations are inadequate as well. Indeed, the effects of math achievement might be even larger were one to
adjust for measurement error, because the math subtests have reliabilities of
.85 and .54, while the vocabulary, reading, and writing subtests have reliabilities of .81, .78, and .80, respectively (Heyns & Hilton, 1982). Nor is this
pattern likely to be explained by larger variances in measured mathematics
achievement, as the variances on the renormed 10-point tests are approximately equal (math = 3.0; English = 2.7).

A third dismissive explanation of the finding is that schools use grades
in courses to determine course assignments, and the standardized test scores
available in the data set are not the achievement measures schools use to

aid enrollment decisions. This is true. However, the grades recorded in the HS&B data set are problematic to use in this analysis. The categorization of students into levels of courses is standardized across schools in this study (see Appendix A). And researchers have documented that many schools give students enrolled in advanced classes a boost in grading (Rosenbaum, 1976). The data set does not identify which schools engage in this practice, so that the grade data cannot be made comparable. Yet, in order to assess the claim of meritocratic assignment, one must use a variable that is comparable across institutions. If one uses incomparable measures, one will not know whether students are of equal levels of achievement in different schools (or even of equal levels of achievement in different courses in the same school), and thus one cannot determine how achievement matters or does not matter for chances of obtaining advanced instruction. Thus, only the standardized HS&B test is appropriate for this analysis because the grade data, adjusted in different schools and in different courses in different ways, may not be commensurable across institutions or levels of coursework. Yet, this eventuality is not problematic, because the HS&B tests are associated with the types of achievement measures school personnel do have at their disposal. Thus, even if the measure of achievement were different, it is unlikely that the findings would change, provided the measure of achievement was appropriately standardized.

There is at least one other interpretation of the result I obtain. It is possible that the coefficient for the math test reflects the effects of other factors that are omitted from the model. The standard "fix" for this possibility is to introduce additional factors into the model that explicitly measure what the included variable might measure artifactually owing to the omission of important variables. However, even if one or two additional variables are identified and included, one will still be able to posit additional factors that are absent from the new model. Thus, there is no ironclad defense against the claim that some omitted variable would reverse the findings.

Rather than lengthening the list of variables that are in the model in order to protect against the chance of omitted variable bias, it is worth considering the features that an omitted variable would need to have in order for its inclusion to reverse *not only* the statistical findings obtained but also the *qualitative inference* of nonmeritocratic matching. This omitted variable would need to be associated with math achievement, be less associated with English achievement (or have no association with English achievement), and be a demonstrably "appropriate" criterion for placing students into English courses. As I know of no such variable or concept, I have concluded my analysis of this question at this juncture.

Of course, there may be alternative explanations of the finding. But, at present, the differences in the effect of math and English achievement appear large and consequential, even after controlling for social class, race, gender, aspirations, ethnicity, and course requirements. The effect of equal increments of measured achievement in math and English appears quite different, and this pattern points to the primacy of mathematics achievement in course enrollments, suggesting that tracking does not serve to match well-prepared students to courses for which they are well prepared.

CONCLUSIONS

The aim of this analysis was to consider the role of individual-level factors in students' curricular placements and to examine in particular whether the association between achievement and placement is actually a sign of meritocratic matching. In the process I investigated whether requirements seem to matter, theorizing requirements as both a coercive and an informational mechanism for students. Course requirements were associated with students' placements, and course requirements appeared more important for twelfth grade than for eleventh grade.

The analysis centered on whether race, ethnicity, gender, social status, and achievement mattered for placements. With respect to race and ethnicity, I found enrollment disadvantages for blacks and Latinos, although the black disadvantage disappeared in Grade 12. However, once aspirations, achievement, and requirements were controlled, an enrollment advantage emerged for blacks, while the enrollment disadvantage disappeared for Latinos, vis à vis whites. This finding is consistent with the work of both Oakes (1985) and Gamoran and Mare (1989). The finding concerning sex differences suggests that more study is needed, because when these findings are compared with other work, the results appear very sensitive to the strategy of analysis.

As expected, social status appears to play a pivotal role in students' course locations, even after several factors, such as aspirations and achievement, are controlled. Although this social class effect may reflect unmeasured differences between students that are associated with social class (e.g., achievement in civics) and thus may be benign, there is ample evidence that the analysis is capturing some of the more pernicious effects of social class advantage. Ethnographers have supplied extensive evidence that middle-class parents often act individually to ensure that their children are placed in advanced classes for as many subjects as possible. Research at many different educational levels has shown this process at work.

So, for example, Lareau (1989) shows how middle-class parents, regarding elementary school teachers as equals or subordinates, refuse to accept teacher judgments and go around, over, and through the teacher to secure what the parents regard as in the best interest of their child. In contrast, lower-middle-class parents, many of whom lag behind teachers in education and nearly all of whom lag behind teachers in comfort with the institution of the school, accept (with frustration, perhaps) teacher evaluations of their child.

Further, Useem (1992) documents how better-educated parents are more likely to have more and more detailed knowledge about the stratification system of the school and its impact on their children's future. Moreover, Useem found that these parents were more likely to intervene for their children and were known to make efforts to override teacher recommendations for courses. Given that the social class effect remained even after achievement in specific domains, aspirations, race, and requirements were controlled, it is quite possible that the remaining effect of socioeconomic status is owing to the kinds of processes Useem and Lareau identify.

The resilience of the social status advantage in curricular location, however, is not new. What was new was the evidence bearing on the meritocratic or nonmeritocratic implications of the effect of measured achievement in specific domains.

Measured achievement in English does not "pay off" as well as does measured achievement in mathematics. When it comes to placement in English courses, the returns to math achievement are *larger* than the returns to English achievement. Notably, the larger advantage of math achievement appeared even though the measurement of math achievement was less reliable and even after several other important factors were controlled. Thus, this finding seems solid at present.

Despite the unremarked revolution, this regime remains unmeritocratic in important ways. Not only does social class continue to have effects that resemble unfair advantage, but even the most likely positive effect of the dismantling of formal programs—the ability of achievement in the specific domain to dominate other achievements—has not been found. Clearly, whether a particular situation is meritocratic turns not only on *what* is rewarded, but also on whether the *match* between specific achievement and specific reward is apt. The results here suggest that, despite the changes in school practice, a mismatch between achievement and reward exists in American secondary schools.

The unremarked revolution in school practice bore directly on the extent to which students could be placed into similar levels of study for disparate subjects. Chapter 2 documented that the majority of students occupy contradictory course locations. This chapter has shown that even with the change in school practice, inequities related to achievement continue. Yet, Chapters 2 and 3 paid little attention to school-to-school differences. But schools vary. Oakes, Wells, and others have investigated how tracking differs across schools and how different types of schools have political landscapes that may protect tracking. The next step for the investigation of the scope of tracking is to broaden the analysis to consider some school-level factors that might be associated with its strength. Chapter 4 takes up this set of issues.

CHAPTER 4

Socioeconomic Diversity, School Environment, and Track Structure

Chapter 2 provided a detailed investigation of several theories of students' course taking, and Chapter 3 focused on individual-level determinants of students' placements. These two chapters identified a best description of the association between students' courses in math and English, and found little sign of meritocratic matching in course assignment. Notably, Chapter 3 reported important effects of social class location on student course enrollment. This chapter takes up where the previous ones left off, and investigates whether social class may determine not only a student's placement, but also the very structure of tracking in the school.

Traditionally, sociologists and education scholars have debated whether the environment of school matters. More recently, research on the politics of de-tracking has identified school characteristics that seem to hinder de-tracking. These two factors combine to make the question of whether environmental factors matter for the strength of tracking an important one.

POTENTIAL CORRELATES OF TRACK STRUCTURE

Tracking and Social Class Segregation

Tracking rose in concert with the promulgation of compulsory schooling laws, the expansion of schooling, and the construction of comprehensive schools. Documents suggest that in many locales compulsory schooling laws were passed to force immigrant children into state-run institutions in which they could be socialized or, in the word of the time, Americanized ("Immigration," 1851/1974; Kelley, 1903). Yet, a serious debate raged as to what to do with these new students once they were deposited at the schoolhouse door. Should the institution continue to teach as if it faced the same set of students it had faced before? Would steadfast adherence to the classical curriculum ensure equal opportunity even for the children of immigrants, or would such stubbornness make school irrelevant to its new matriculants? If the latter, should schools elaborate the curriculum to provide a place for everyone? Or would this effort either incidentally or purposely serve to keep everyone in their place? What emerged from this debate was the differentiated curriculum, which prepared some students for higher education, and others for (at best) other opportunities (Kliebard, 1995).

Many critics of tracking have drawn on its origins to maintain that tracking is based in an ideology of paternalism and brazen desire to maintain class and/or race segregation. In her *Sociology of Education* exchange with Hallinan (1994a, 1994b), Oakes (1994a, 1994b) argued that historical evidence suggests that a race- and class-coded curricular hierarchy reinforces stereotypes and perpetuates disadvantage. Oakes points to the historical origins of tracking during a period of high immigration and nativist hostility. The rise of tracking coincided with the effort to make schools compulsory, an effort that succeeded in placing immigrant children into schools, while segregating immigrant and nonimmigrant children through tracking. Oakes has maintained that continuing political support for tracking appears to have many of the same motivations that characterized the inception of tracking.

In generalizing from the historical basis of tracking to its maintenance in many contemporary institutions, Oakes implies that the strength of tracking one finds in a school may be associated with factors about the school. She argues that middle-class parents work to maintain tracking when they fear that if tracking ends, their children will be lumped with lower-class children and receive an inferior education. If Oakes is correct, when one compares schools one should find that schools with more socioeconomic diversity have a higher association between students' placements in disparate subjects. Other researchers have already assessed whether the mix of black and white students in a school is associated with more pronounced tracking and have found that it is (Braddock, 1990). Yet, no published research has assessed the role of class diversity on track structure using nationally representative data. The issue of class diversity is addressed in this chapter.

Sector, Size of Place, and Curriculum Structure

Debate about the effect of school environments on students has a long history, animated by political, technical, and theoretical disagreement. Indeed, the issue of whether class diversity matters for track structure can be encompassed within the general discussion of whether school differences matter.

But the specific issues that have engendered much of the debate about school effects turn on sector and size of place. A principal work in this debate was that of Coleman, Hoffer, and Kilgore (1982), in which they argued that private schools are better at teaching, reducing social class-related disparities, keeping students engaged, and more. However, critics such as Goldberger and Cain (1982) correctly pointed out that students are not randomly assigned to public and private schools. Instead, students (and their parents) assign themselves to these institutional types. Because the assignment of students to one or the other sector is not random, one cannot so easily regard outcome differences as a reflection of the greater capability of one or the other institution. Indeed, the process of assignment to public or private schools may be driven by factors that analysts do not observe, so that the standard approach of statistically controlling for observable differences does not work. Thus, what Coleman, Hoffer, and Kilgore label an effect of school sector on achievement actually may be the result of nonrandom selection.

Chubb and Moe (1988) countered with the assertion that private schools are successful because they are driven by the logic of the market. In contrast, public schools are driven by politics, and politics produces a vampire bureaucracy that constrains on-site educators and oversees from afar the production (or underproduction) of knowledge. The worst cases can be found in urban settings, where the educational bureaucracy is most advanced. Thus, in Chubb and Moe's view, one should not worry about unobserved differences because whatever these differences may be, they are part and parcel of the bundle of differences that distinguish public and private schools. Even if selection effects really explain the difference between the performance of public and private schools, these selection effects exist because many parents do not have the *option* of making a selection. Thus, Chubb and Moe claim, public and private school differences reflect different institutional environments and lead to different student outcomes, and if the public wants to equate these environments for students, then citizens must expose public schools to the market forces that have made private schools perform better.

This debate about sector and size of place has taken place amid an implied understanding of how the two sectors work. Compared with private schools, and with suburban schools, urban public schools are regarded as disorganized, necessarily attendant to discipline, and therefore less effective educational environments. Where does tracking fit in this vision?

Clearly, researchers have attended to differences in tracking across school environments. Ethnographies by Valli (1990), Camarena (1990), and Gamoran (1993) report that Catholic school low-level classes are more rigorous than their public school counterparts. Also, statistical analyses by Gamoran (1992b) have demonstrated convincingly that the effects of track location vary by school sector. Moreover, Riehl, Natriello, and Pallas (1992) show that course assignment procedures in urban public schools are chaotic, a finding that is consistent with some aspects of the Chubb and Moe perspective. Yet, it remains unclear whether these differences occur in concert with track structure differences or despite track structure similarities.

This limitation remains because at present it is not known whether curricular stratification in private schools is the same as it is in public schools. Perhaps it is incorrect even to speak of tracking in private schools; private schools may have low-level classes, but no association between students' placements in different subjects. Or, given that Riehl, Natriello, and Pallas (1992) show that public school assignment procedures are chaotic, they may be so chaotic that tracking does not emerge from the differentiated curriculum in urban schools, while the better-organized private schools may have tracking. The existing research showing differences in outcomes by sector and size of place does not resolve the issue because it is still not clear whether outcome differences between public, private, urban, suburban, and rural schools are based on different stratification regimes or whether apparent differences in outcomes are produced *in spite of* structural similarity.

Adjudicating between these two circumstances is important because if track structure differences lie behind the observations of Valli, Camarena, and others, then perhaps changing the structure of tracking can close the performance gap that appears to exist between private and suburban schools on the one hand, and urban public schools on the other. Yet, if the structures do not differ by school environments, then one must look elsewhere—perhaps to instructional differences or perhaps to resource differences—to explain sector differences in the reports of how schools seem to work.

Thus, despite existing and useful research, an important question remains. Do courses hang together very similarly in public, private, urban, suburban, and rural schools, or are these environments so different that they give rise to starkly disparate course-taking regimes? This question as to whether the same degree of association will be found in different school environments is specific to tracking, but it serves also as one specific instance of a general question, namely, what, if any, are the differences between public and private schools, and urban, suburban, and rural schools?

ANALYSIS STRATEGY

The primary data for this facet of the investigation are a four-way cross-tabulation table of three-category math by three-category English by academic year by school type. The three categories of math are not taking a math course, non-college prep math, and college prep math; the categories for English are the same—not taking, non-college prep, and college prep.

There are 12 school types, reflecting combinations of sector, size of place, and extent of socioeconomic diversity (high vs. low). For example, one school type is public, urban, and low on socioeconomic diversity; another school type is private, suburban, and low on socioeconomic diversity.

To analyze these data, I use Goodman's RC Model II (Goodman, 1979). RC Model II is not a log-linear model, but it is similar to a log-linear model in that it provides a way to measure the association between two categorical variables. The advantage of using RC Model II is that, unlike the models used in Chapter 2, it produces one statistic—ɸ—that measures the association between two different subjects. Using this model, therefore, allows one to determine the association between students' courses in each type of school for each academic year. These association parameters may be analyzed to determine whether the strength of association varies systematically with each of the school characteristics.

The levels models, used in Chapter 2, could be used to address this question, but RC Model II is better because it concentrates all of the differences between the academic years and school types into one parameter, ɸ. Thus, using RC Model II reduces the chance that one will miss a real difference between school types or grades.

As before, summary statistics from RC Model II will reveal whether the model adequately describes the association. If the model *does* provide an adequate description of the association (as signified by a negative BIC statistic), then the ɸ's that summarize the association between math and English for each school type may be compared to discern whether school factors are related to the strength of association in students' course taking. The sum of the squares of the ɸ coefficients equals 1; the ɸ coefficients thus reveal the relative magnitudes of the association between subjects for different school types. However, no absolute scaling of the ɸ coefficients is possible. Further details on RC Model II are provided in Appendix C.

RELATIVE MAGNITUDE OF SCOPE IN DIFFERENT TYPES OF SCHOOLS

The summary statistics from RC Model II are $L^2 = 58.40$, with 144 degrees of freedom, for a BIC statistic of -1155.79. RC Model II provides an adequate description of the association in the four-way table under consideration. Thus, the parameters that reflect the association between math and English, which are shown in Table 4.1, are worthy of consideration.

Some findings are conspicuously evident. For example, regardless of size of place, and regardless of the degree of class diversity, the public schools all appear to follow the same pattern. Ninth grade has a stronger

Table 4.1. Measures of Association (ϕs) between Mathematics and English Enrollment for 12 School Types Over Four Academic Years

	ϕs			
SCHOOL TYPE	Grade 9	Grade 10	Grade 11	Grade 12
Panel 1—Schools with Low Socioeconomic Diversity				
Public Urban	0.2168	0.1479	0.1071	0.0901
Public Suburban	0.1919	0.0703	0.0879	0.0643
Public Rural	0.1469	0.0438	0.0633	0.0381
Private Urban	−0.4068	0.0595	0.0663	0.0472
Private Suburban	0.0325	0.0236	0.0328	0.0381
Private Rural	0.2590	0.0930	0.1422	−0.0300
Panel 2—Schools with High Socioeconomic Diversity				
Public Urban	0.1608	0.0620	0.0937	0.0851
Public Suburban	0.2236	0.0946	0.0532	0.0727
Public Rural	0.1389	0.0544	0.0723	0.0575
Private Urban	0.2997	−0.3943	0.1591	0.1494
Private Suburban	0.2387	0.0966	0.1110	0.0909
Private Rural	0.0884	0.1176	0.0425	0.0742

association than tenth grade, and tenth, eleventh, and twelfth grades are virtually indistinguishable. Private suburban schools with high social class diversity also follow the same pattern as public schools.

This is consistent with students ending their formal study of subjects once they complete the requirements. The modal graduation requirement for math during this period was 2 years, while the modal graduation requirement for English during this period was 4 years. Given this set of requirements, one might expect many students to end their study of mathematics once they satisfy the graduation requirements for math, yet continue to study English because it is still required. If this course-taking pattern is common, then the association between math and English would be lower for later academic years, because in later academic years many students, regardless of their placement in English, would not take math. Thus, the relationship between math and English placements should weaken. Indeed, I find that the association between math and English is higher in Grade 9 than in later years, which is somewhat consistent with the effect of course requirements reported in Chapter 3. Yet, the association is virtually the same in Grades 10, 11, and 12. Given that most schools require 2 years of math, requirements are unlikely to be the whole story behind the drop-off in the math/English association between Grade 9 and Grade 10. Instead, the difference may be that high schools have a weaker association between courses than do junior high schools, and many ninth graders are in junior high schools. This supposition can be explored in future research.

While the finding for academic years is fairly conspicuous, some questions of concern are difficult to address on the basis of Table 4.1. For example, is high social class diversity associated with higher ϕ coefficients, as Oakes proposes? On the basis of Table 4.1 it appears that for some types of schools the answer is yes (e.g., private suburban schools), while in other cases the answer appears to be no (e.g., public urban schools). To provide a summary determination of whether school factors are or are not related to the strength of association between students' course taking, I estimated a multiple regression model using the ϕ coefficients as a dependent variable on school characteristics and academic years (see Table 4.2). However, I deleted two observations from the regression analysis because they were extreme outliers (studentized residuals of −5.69 and −4.39 and Cooks' Distance statistics of .42 and .33, respectively) and swamped all effects. The deleted observations were private urban ninth grade with low social class diversity, and private urban tenth grade with high social class diversity.

Table 4.2 is illuminating. It replicates the finding that in tenth, eleventh, and twelfth grade, the association between math and English tends to be smaller than it is in ninth grade, which is consistent with students completing requirements and ending their formal study of subjects with fewer requirements, such as math. Moreover, I find that social class diversity is associated with the strength of association between math and English. (For this analysis

Table 4.2. Regression of Measures of Association (ϕs) between Mathematics and English Enrollment on Characteristics of Schools

Variable	Coefficient	Absolute T-Value
Constant	.186	8.169
Grade 10 (vs. Grade 9)	−.091	4.154
Grade 11 (vs. Grade 9)	−.087	4.065
Grade 12 (vs. Grade 9)	−.108	4.920
High Socioeconomic Diversity (vs. Low)	.027	1.750
Public (vs. Private)	.000	0.012
Rural (vs. Urban)	−.041	2.121
Suburban (vs. Urban)	−.040	2.069
R^2	.494	

n = 46 because of removal of two extreme outliers

I have used $\alpha = .10$ as a cutoff to treat the parameter as statistically significant, because of the small sample size ($n = 46$). All other instances in the book use $\alpha = .05$.) Schools with higher social class diversity have a stronger association between courses. This finding is consistent with Oakes's contention that social class diversity is a factor in the maintenance of tracking.

Given the way in which the analysis has been conducted, the magnitude of the social class effect is not directly estimable. Social class diversity ranges from very high to very low, but given the within-school sample sizes, it was necessary to dichotomize the socioeconomic diversity variable. Thus, the regression coefficient does not reflect the difference between schools that are one unit apart on the socioeconomic diversity variable. Instead, the magnitude reflects the mean difference between low and high diversity schools. Yet, the full range of the effect (the difference between the school with the lowest socioeconomic diversity and the school with the highest socioeconomic diversity) is not estimable. Such estimates must await further analysis. Still, on the basis of the results presented here, the conclusion that social class matters for the strength of tracking regimes finds support.

I also find that urban schools differ from both rural and suburban schools. Urban schools have a higher association between students' placements in math and English, even though socioeconomic diversity is controlled. This may reflect the higher degree of bureaucracy in urban schools, which may limit the ability of courses of study to be tailored to particular students, or it may reflect the tendency of urban schools to have other kinds of diversity (e.g., racial and ethnic diversity) that might evoke the same kinds of response from parents that socioeconomic diversity appears to elicit.

However, I find no net difference between public and private schools. Thus, the documented difference in how public and private schools use tracking provides further evidence of how the *same* structure leads to *different* outcomes. Analysts must, therefore, continue efforts to look to something other than structure—perhaps instructional differences, resource differences, or resource allocation differences—to explain sector differences.

These other factors are not part of this analysis, but their absence is not meant to indicate their presumed irrelevance. This analysis has focused and continues to focus on the structure of positions and persons' location within the existing positions. It is clear that the structure of positions may be important; one reason structures are important is that they provide the channels through which pedagogically useful resources flow. Yet, district- and school-site actors make decisions as to which curricular locations obtain which resources. As an example, Gamoran (1993) notes that private schools tend to allocate experienced teachers with high expectations for their students to both high- and low-level classes. In contrast, Finley's (1984) analysis of a public school revealed that teachers sought to teach the high-level classes and that the process of assigning teachers to classes reinforced the idea that low-level classes are undesirable. Finley documents how teachers assigned to low-level classes see their skills and motivation atrophy over time.

These kinds of resource allocation processes and decisions and potential differences between these processes and decisions at successful and unsuccessful schools deserve more attention, for the evidence presented here suggests that the structure of the tracking systems in public and private schools does not differ. Understanding whatever performance differences there are between these two sectors therefore requires closer inspection of factors other than the structure of tracking.

PLACEMENT, STRUCTURE, AND THE
MECHANISMS OF CLASS ADVANTAGE

Considering how scope, the association between students' courses, varies by school characteristics has revealed that a common factor under consideration—the public/private division—has no net association with the degree to which students' courses in disparate subjects are associated. It also has provided support for Oakes's contention concerning the maintenance of tracking in contemporary schools. I find that school environments with more socioeconomic diversity have discernibly higher levels of association between students' placements in different subjects.

Oakes has posited what one might term a social class conflict explanation for this pattern. Her research on the efforts of middle-class parents to undermine de-tracking initiatives suggests that middle-class parents are key actors in the maintenance of tracking. Middle-class parents provide the political legitimacy school administrators need in order to remain in office and schools need in order to remain in business. Middle-class parents are able to provide these resources because they have the political and economic wherewithal to make real any threats to retaliate or abandon the school. This is one way in which the patterns observed above may come to be—parents may agitate politically and collectively for the maintenance of tracking, especially in schools where its demise would throw their children into contact with students from lower-class backgrounds.

Chapter 3, however, reported that students from advantaged socioeconomic backgrounds had placement advantages, even after race, sex, achievement, aspirations, and graduation requirements were controlled. I noted that this finding is consistent with ethnographic evidence showing that many middle-class parents push their children into classes over the objections of school personnel (Useem, 1992).

The patterns observed in this chapter are consistent with small, individual actions to obtain advantaged places in the curriculum that Useem identifies, as well as with the collective class-based actions to preserve the overall system of in-school stratification that Oakes documents. Thus, both explicit agitation for the status quo, and use of information that has value within that system, may make the system of in-school stratification more pronounced in schools with greater socioeconomic diversity. If so, one may wonder whether both the collective and individual forms of middle-class parents' agitation for their children may crowd more deserving students out of higher-level classes.

To this point, I must conclude that the impact of the unremarked revolution appears to have been uneven. On the one hand, it appears that the locations in the curriculum have multiplied tremendously. The majority of students take courses of discrepant levels. This means that students seem to be putting courses together in unprecedented ways. Even though students are still likely to take courses that are of similar but not exactly the same level, this new structure of in-school stratification is still likely to make it more difficult for tracking to work to socialize students for different futures.

Yet, the rise of discrepant course taking occurs even as I find evidence of a major failure of the change in school practice. Students do not appear to be assigned to courses on the basis of their success in the domain of inquiry. Thus, the pedagogical rationale of tracking is undermined. This failure signals also a key failure of the decline of formal programs. In principle this change in school practice allowed one to break the power of students' performance in unrelated domains over their other placements. Yet, the analysis indicates that the power of unrelated domains remains strong.

Moreover, despite the burgeoning diversity of structural places in the in-school stratification system, I seem to find two ways in which social class continues to matter for tracking. First, it appears that individual middle-class parents continue to secure their children's advantage in the existing in-school stratification system. Second, heightened socioeconomic diversity at the school level is associated with more pronounced divisions in the curriculum, which is consistent with Oakes's claim that tracking is maintained by the collective political action of middle-class parents in environments where tracking is threatened by de-tracking initiatives. Both the individual and the collective activities are based in middle-class parents' access to more extensive information about the stratification system of the school, an information advantage that was only exacerbated by the decline of formal programs.

The unremarked revolution removed the signposts of the curriculum, weakened the power of gatekeepers, and attempted to destroy the power of unrelated achievement on students' opportunity. At this juncture, after considering students' placements at one point in time, I find a more variegated curriculum that is likely to lead to less effective differential socialization, continued school environmental differences consistent with both collective middle-class agitation and individual middle-class proactivity, and enduring power for unrelated achievement for students' placements. Truly, the success of the dismantling of formal programs appears paradoxical. Its focal promise of subject-specific meritocratic placements remains unrealized, and in its wake information, disproportionately available to children of middle-class parents, has become, if anything, even more important and more disproportionately allocated.

Through three chapters the scope of tracking has been the focus. Scope was the central dimension addressed by the change in school practice, and so it is the appropriate starting point for an analysis of the implications of the unremarked revolution. But another key dimension of stratification systems, mobility, is also a potentially important determinant of students' experience, and the analysis would be remiss to ignore this important dimension.

However, completeness is not the only motivation for analyzing mobility. The foregoing analyses of scope have unearthed apparently unintended consequences of the change in school practice for the course taking of students. Thus, it is quite apparent that the aims of reform do not necessarily limit the effects of reform. While it is possible that the decline of formal programs most directly affects students' course taking at one point in time, it is also important to discern the patterns and correlates of mobility now that the mechanisms organizing in-school stratification have changed.

To be sure, the unremarked revolution, which affected scope in particular, may have had little sway with respect to the dimension of mobility. Yet, absent an empirical analysis of mobility in the more recent period, this expectation must remain tentative. Therefore, to understand tracking and student experience after the unremarked revolution, investigation of mobility is required. It is this dimension of tracking systems that the next two chapters address.

CHAPTER 5

Is Tracking a Tournament?

There are at least two dimensions relevant to understanding the implications of the in-school stratification system for students' experience of schools and for discovering whether the stratification system is meritocratic. One dimension, scope, concerns the extent to which placements in one subject limit students' options in other subjects. The unremarked revolution in school practice sought specifically to break the link between students' placements in disparate subjects. To the extent that students achieve at different levels in different subjects, breaking the necessary link between placements in different subjects may allow the meritocratic nature of students' placements to increase, while at the same time permitting students to be exposed to discordant types of socialization. However, having assessed the extent to which the unremarked revolution was successful in this regard, it appears that the success was uneven. Students now commonly occupy discrepant locations in the curriculum, and thus there is no necessary link between courses in disparate subjects. Each student may be exposed to different types of socialization. Yet, achievement in unrelated domains still confers advantage. Moreover, social class remains an important determinant of students' assignments, further dissipating the meritocratic thrust of schools.

A second dimension, mobility, also bears on the meritocratic nature of the stratification system. One of the pedagogical justifications for curriculum differentiation is that it allows students to be taught according to their prior preparation. If this teaching is successful, then at least some students should improve enough to be prepared to move up over time. Yet, research suggests that prior to the unremarked revolution mobility was rare, and when students did move they tended to move downward (Rosenbaum, 1976). More recent research, however, has found that mobility is not rare, and some evidence suggests students are more likely to move up than down (Hallinan, 1996). This contradiction has raised doubt as to how to describe students' mobility chances in school.

Doubt as to how to characterize mobility translates into doubt as to how to characterize the school, because analysts' understanding of how in-school stratification works, and its implications for students' experience and socialization, depends in part on mobility just as it depends on scope. The incidence and pattern of mobility together may determine the ease or difficulty schools encounter in socializing different sets of students for different futures, because while scope concerns students' exposure to different types of socialization at one point in time, mobility concerns students' exposure to different types of socialization over time. Moreover, analysts' understanding of whether schools are meritocratic or not depends in part on mobility, because if mobility is universally downward, it becomes difficult to regard schools as engines of upward mobility. Clearly, then, different patterns and directions of mobility may lead to different implications for our understanding of schools. This chapter thus concerns a question bearing on each of the above issues: What is the pattern of mobility in school after the unremarked revolution in school practice?

UNDERSTANDING IN-SCHOOL MOBILITY

Tournament Mobility: Speculation and Evidence

In his illuminating case study of "Grayton High," Rosenbaum (1976, 1978) reported how tracking decisions are made, what the structure of tracking is, and what mobility patterns prevail. Upon finding an extremely low probability of upward mobility between high school tracks and a comparatively high incidence of downward mobility, Rosenbaum (1976) offered a compelling metaphor to describe the pattern he observed—the metaphor of tournament mobility. According to Rosenbaum (1978), tournament mobility is easily understood: "When you [students] win, you win only the right to go on to the next round; when you lose, you lose forever" (p. 252).

Rosenbaum's research made several important contributions to the tracking literature. Methodologically, Rosenbaum used the kind of data most useful for analyzing patterns of mobility—cross-tabular arrays of students' courses. Using cross-tabular arrays, one can investigate inflows and outflows to particular discrete locations, hypothesize barriers to movement (as Rosenbaum did by hypothesizing a barrier dividing the two college-track levels from the three non-college-track levels), consider whether some categories can be combined (because their relation to other categories is the same), and make the order of categories an empirical question. Thus, Rosenbaum illustrated many of the necessary elements of a thorough analysis of the patterns of track mobility. Theoretically, in his discussion of mobility, Rosenbaum revised Turner's (1960) concept of contest mobility by identifying a particular kind of contest that might structure secondary school mobility.

Despite these important contributions of Rosenbaum's analysis, the metaphor of tournament mobility is not secure. The Grayton data that

Rosenbaum used allowed him to demonstrate the existence of asymmetric downward mobility, but not tournament mobility. The central idea of tournament mobility is not only that winners win only the right to go on to the next round, but also that losers can never win again. In order to test whether losers in one round can win in subsequent rounds, one must observe the move from time point 1 to time point 2, identify "losers," and then observe the "losers" moving *from* time point 2 to a subsequent time point. Thus, at least three time points are required to test the tournament mobility speculation. As both of Rosenbaum's analyses covered only two time points, the jury is still out on whether tournament mobility described the pattern of students' movement in the past.

Doubting Tournament Mobility: Recent Evidence

For nearly 20 years Rosenbaum's metaphor of the tournament provided our best understanding of secondary school track mobility. There is good reason to suspect that the metaphor may remain an apt one. Although the dismantling of formal programs dissolved the formal link between students' placements in disparate subjects, it did not directly address the issue of mobility. Thus, upward mobility may still be extremely rare.

However, as yet no research has demonstrated the existence of tournament mobility. Wilson and Rossman (1993) found no support for the presence of tournament mobility. More recently, Hallinan (1996, pp. 990–993) reports that students actually are more likely to move *up* than down. Both findings seriously question Rosenbaum's speculation of tournament mobility.

Yet, recent studies also have used designs that preclude a straightforward test of tournament mobility, as they have not, for example, covered at least three time points. These limitations mean that the compelling metaphor of the tournament has not been subjected to appropriate examination.

Assessing a Metaphor

Before proceeding, however, an important question to ask is, Do researchers or practitioners care whether the metaphor is "correct enough?" After all, metaphors are not meant to be read literally and therefore, in a sense, it is obvious that metaphors are never entirely correct. Although this observation is true, I believe that it is important to learn whether the data support the tournament mobility metaphor. A metaphor may be more or less illuminating; there are better and worse metaphors. In addition, determining whether a metaphor is accurate is important because metaphors have power. People respond to the resonance of a metaphor and may even develop strategies based on faith in a metaphor. Thus, while it is true that no metaphor, or model, is completely accurate as a description of the world, for all the reasons above it is important to determine whether the tournament mobility metaphor is an apt description—a good metaphor—or an overstatement. Subjecting a metaphor to empirical test is not to judge those who proposed the metaphor. It is, instead, to determine whether the metaphor has utility in the new environment of schools.

Other analysts have already questioned the metaphor, and some have reached diametrically opposed conclusions. However, the tournament mobility metaphor has not yet been subjected to appropriate tests. Reconsideration of it will allow determination of whether the mobility regime in school is summarized accurately by the stark metaphor of the tournament.

Alternative Patterns of Track Mobility

So far I have focused on tournament mobility. However, there are many other possible alternatives to a tournament mobility pattern, and at least some research suggests alternative patterns may prevail. For example, De-Lany (1991) and Riehl, Natriello, and Pallas (1992) show that students' schedules are often the result of efforts to solve logistical problems rather than the product of concerted efforts to match students to appropriate instruction. This focus on logistics may serve to check the rise of asymmetries of movement because high mobility in one direction might produce very unequal-sized groups.

Further, the ethos engendered by the decline of formal programs may allow students to zig-zag across the subject-specific curriculum in quite complicated ways. These movements may make later location statistically independent of prior location, or may make students as likely to move up as they are to move down. Thus, it is important to investigate these alternative possible patterns of mobility as well.

ANALYZING IN-SCHOOL MOBILITY

The basic data analyzed here are two cross-classifications of students' course taking in sophomore, junior, and senior year. One cross-tabulation is for mathematics and one is for English. The variables for Grade 11 and Grade 12 have seven categories—elite college, regular college, lower college, business and vocational, remedial, not taking a course, and dropped out. The tenth-grade variables have all of those categories except dropouts, for the data do not show tenth-grade dropouts moving to subsequent tracks. Thus, the tables under investigation have seven rows, seven columns, and six layers, and are thus $7 \times 7 \times 6$.

These junior by senior by sophomore year cross-tabulations contain the cases that had no missing data on mathematics (14,981 cases) or English (14,799 cases) placements. Generalities covered earlier about model selection procedures all apply directly here.

DO PRIOR PLACEMENTS CONSTRAIN LATER PLACEMENTS?

The first issue to consider is whether there is any association between students' locations in different years. If there is no association, then early placements do not constrain later placements, and one can conclude that when it comes to mobility through the curriculum, schools are "open" institutions in the extreme.

To assess whether there is an association between students' courses in different years, I estimate the independence model.[1] The independence model asserts that there is no association between placements; if the independence model fits, then the assertion of independence between placements is defensible.

For mathematics the independence model had $L^2 = 3970.69$, df $= 240$, $\Delta = 34.85$, and BIC $= 1940.85$. In contrast, for English the independence model had $L^2 = 1476.80$, df $= 240$, $\Delta = 18.59$, and BIC $= -550.10$. Thus, the independence model does not fit mathematics, but the negative BIC statistic suggests that the independence model does fit mobility in English! This finding is both consequential and unexpected.

A very simple model provides an adequate description of mobility in English, but more complex descriptions are required for math; thus, mobility patterns in the English curriculum differ from mobility patterns in mathematics. This particular difference may follow from the relatively more hierarchical nature of mathematics instruction. Compared with English, mathematics courses are more likely to build on each other. This feature may partially explain why independence fits for English, but not for math. The important implication of this claim is that investigating mobility in only one

---

[1]In Chapter 2 I analyzed two-way tables. In this chapter I analyze three-way tables. There is only one independence model for two-way tables, but there are three versions of the independence model for three-way tables; the particular version estimated on these data is mutual independence. (For a discussion of types of independence for three-way tables, see Agresti, 1990; for a justification of my use of mutual independence as a baseline for the analysis in this chapter, see Appendix C.)

subject may lead analysts to misunderstand within-subject mobility broadly considered.

However, although one may *adequately* describe mobility within English by asserting that students may move freely across the curriculum, to accept this description is to accept the misclassification of approximately one-fifth of the students (as shown by the index of dissimilarity, Δ). One may, therefore, wish to further explore the patterns within English, even though independence is an adequate characterization of the relation between students' placements.

CONTESTING TOURNAMENT MOBILITY

There is an association between mathematics placements over time, and although independence provides an adequate description of mobility in English, a sufficiently large proportion of students are misclassified by an assumption of independence between English placements over time to motivate further investigation of mobility in English. It is now necessary to consider whether tournament mobility provides a cogent description of within-subject mobility.

To pursue this line of inquiry, I estimate two variants of a tournament mobility model. Both variants partition students' sequences of course taking into nine mutually exclusive patterns of mobility. Students may move up, down, or remain in the same level in moving from Grade 10 to Grade 11, and they also may move up, down, or remain in the same level in moving from Grade 11 to Grade 12. Thus, there are nine distinct paths: (1) stable, stable; (2) stable, up; (3) stable, down; (4) up, stable; (5) down, stable; (6) down, down; (7) up, up; (8) up, down; and (9) down, up. If patterns of mobility resemble a tournament, then paths 2, 4, 7, 8, and 9 should be far less likely than the others.

Obviously, rigid tournament mobility would make paths 2, 4, 7, 8, and 9 impossible, but one need only look at the raw tables to conclude that this is not the case. However, assessing the tournament mobility metaphor based on a quick look at the tables ignores an important fact: Tournament mobility was a *metaphor*. No one ever stated it would be completely true in every case. As in every description of the world, metaphor or model, the expectation is that it highlights important patterns. In such situations, a less stringent and more appropriate (i.e., a probabilistic) test flows from reasoning that under the metaphor or model, certain patterns should be rare. For these reasons, modeling may be used to address the issue. Thus, to support a conclusion of tournament mobility, a model must fit the data, *and* the parameters from that model must be such that patterns 2, 4, 7, 8, and 9 are rare.

The two models estimated differ only in what counts as movement. In the model of tournament mobility (TM), any change is regarded as either an upward or a downward move. In the four-category tournament mobility model (TM4C), the cells first are partitioned into college preparatory, non-college preparatory, not-taking, and dropout categories. Only moves that cross the boundaries of these categories are considered upward or downward moves.

The results (see Table 5.1) suggest that some form of tournament mobility may describe mobility in mathematics as well as English. For mathematics, the BIC statistics suggest that TM does not fit the data but that TM4C does. For English, the BIC statistics show that both versions fit the data, but TM fits better. The BIC statistics indicate that the pattern specified by the model is an adequate summary of within-subject mobility, but to discover whether the tournament mobility metaphor is apt requires consideration of the parameter estimates for the relevant models.

Table 5.2 presents, from the best-fitting tournament mobility model for mathematics and English, respectively, the parameters that describe the pattern of students' concentrations (the λs). The "For 100 Students" columns are probably most useful because they translate the interaction parameters into the number of students, out of 100, one would expect to follow each pattern, after marginals are controlled, for each subject. Considering mathematics first, the three patterns that include upward movement (but not downward movement) account for about 11.8 out of 100 students, while the three patterns that include downward movement (but not upward movement) account for about 43.9 students. Thus, asymmetric downward movement appears to characterize mobility in mathematics. Making a similar calculation for English leads to a somewhat muted but still qualitatively similar conclusion: approximately 21.3 students are expected to be upwardly but not downwardly mobile, compared with about 33.6 expected to be downwardly but not upwardly mobile. Thus, findings for both math and English stand in contrast to descriptive findings that upward mobility is more prevalent than downward mobility.

Table 5.1. Fit Statistics for Models of Tournament Mobility

MODEL	L^2	df	BIC	Δ
Panel 1—Mobility in Mathematics (effective $n = 4,711$)				
Tournament Mobility (TM)	2505.78	232	543.60	26.85
Four-Category Tournament Mobility (TM4C)	1913.56	232	−48.62	21.76
Panel 2—Mobility in English (effective $n = 4,654$)				
Tournament Mobility (TM)	439.36	232	−1519.98	7.83
Four-Category Tournament Mobility (TM4C)	766.21	232	−1193.13	11.98

Table 5.2. Interaction Parameter Estimates from Four-Category Tournament Mobility Model for Mathematics and Tournament Mobility Model for English

Pattern from Grade		Mathematics Results			English Results		
10–11	11–12	Coeff.	e^λ	For 100 Students	Coeff.	e^λ	For 100 Students
Stable	Stable	Basis	1.000	33.134	Basis	1.000	36.251
Up	Up	−2.744	0.064	2.131	−2.394	0.091	3.308
Stable	Up	−1.962	0.141	4.658	−1.217	0.296	10.735
Up	Stable	−1.880	0.153	5.056	−1.610	0.200	7.246
Down	Up	−1.446	0.236	7.804	−1.842	0.159	5.746
Up	Down	−2.310	0.099	3.289	−2.171	0.114	4.135
Stable	Down	−0.737	0.479	15.856	−0.990	0.372	13.470
Down	Stable	−0.590	0.554	18.367	−1.105	0.331	12.007
Down	Down	−1.228	0.293	9.704	−1.630	0.196	8.083

Asymmetric downward mobility seems a fair description for both subjects, but do the model results support the tournament mobility metaphor? This will of necessity be a judgment call. Analysts can produce numbers summarizing the flows of students, but some may regard the proportion of students who rise after falling as so high that tournament mobility seems an overstatement, while others may regard the very same numerical figures as supporting the tournament mobility metaphor. This is, in the end, the controversy of how to determine whether an effect is big or not in another guise. The controversy is made stronger here because the tournament mobility metaphor was not meant to be read literally. That said, it is still potentially useful to provide the statistics on student flow. With these statistics, it is possible to determine how likely it is that students can come back to "win" after "losing."

Students who lost may be represented by those who were downwardly mobile in the transition from Grade 10 to Grade 11. The question, then, is how many of those downwardly mobile students were able to move up in their transition from Grade 11 to Grade 12? Combining appropriate figures from the last column of results for math in Table 5.2 shows that, once marginals are controlled, about 35.875 students out of 100 are expected to be downwardly mobile between Grades 10 and 11. Of these, 7.804 are expected to be upwardly mobile between Grades 11 and 12; about one-fifth of the students who "lose" come back to "win" again. For English the results are similar—about 25.836 students are downwardly mobile in moving from Grade 10 to 11, and of these, 5.746 are expected to move up in the next academic year. Thus, about one-fifth of the students who "lose" in English come back to "win" again. This finding suggests that although the majority of downwardly mobile students do not experience later upward mobility, enough do to regard the distinctive claim of the metaphor of tournament mobility—one loss removes one from the tournament—as an overstatement.

That is not to deny the consequential nature of a downward move; approximately 4 out of 5 students who move down *do not rise* again (net of marginals). A downward move appears extremely disadvantageous in these terms. However, the single-elimination tournament is an even more severe selection regime, and it is important to reject the metaphor because it is overly severe compared with mobility in school. This is necessary because of the potential power of metaphors. Students and parents who know that a student has moved downward may, taking the tournament metaphor to heart, become resigned to the lower placement. Yet, changes in school practice likely have increased the chance that protest of low placements might be effective. Moreover, the data suggest that upward mobility after downward mobility, while rare, *does* occur. Thus, in terms of empowering parents, it is important to reject the metaphor in a very visible way, even while acknowledging that students who move downward appear to be battling relatively long odds if they seek to move upward.

ALTERNATIVE DESCRIPTIONS OF MOBILITY

The above is not the only research to question the tournament mobility metaphor; some research has even shown exactly the opposite, that students are more likely to move up than down (e.g., Hallinan, 1996). The findings above suggest that tournament mobility is an overstatement. But at this point the provisional conclusion, that asymmetric downward mobility prevails, rests only on the tournament mobility models, and therefore the basis of the conclusion may be shaky. The tournament mobility model for math misclassifies one-fifth of the students, enough to ask whether the analysis is headed down the wrong path entirely. Perhaps mobility is asymmetric, but asymmetrically upward. Or perhaps owing to the decline of overarching programs, students may be equally likely to move up or down. Rather than rely on the results of the tournament mobility model to make inferences concerning other patterns, a better way to test these possibilities is to estimate models that are targeted to these ideas.

Considering Symmetric and Asymmetric Mobility

I investigated additional possibilities by estimating the following four models: asymmetric mobility (AM), heterogenous asymmetric mobility (HAM), quasi-symmetry (QS), and conditional quasi-symmetry (QS–C). Schematic design matrices for asymmetric mobility, heterogenous asymmetric mobility, and quasi-symmetry are shown in Figure 5.1. The design matrices are schematic in that they do not reflect the full specification of the model. Instead, the design matrices reflect the pattern of the parameters linking two academic years. A full representation of the model would show all of the parameters linking Grades 10 and 11, Grades 11 and 12, and Grades 10 and 12. In the present case it is not necessary to show the full pattern because the main ideas can be conveyed by illustrating the link between any 2 years. However, full equations for the models are provided in Appendix C.

The design matrix for the AM model shows that for a given pair of years, two contrasts are estimated: (1) the contrast between immobility (*a*) and upward mobility (*b*), and (2) the contrast between immobility (*a*) and downward mobility (*c*). Thus, for any two academic years, the AM model produces two parameters that capture the incidence of upward and downward mobility. As students may be mobile from Grade 10 to 11, Grade 11 to 12, and Grade 10 to 12, the AM model produces six parameters that capture the incidence and direction of mobility. If the AM model provides

Figure 5.1. Schematic Design Matrices for Asymmetric Mobility, Heterogenous Asymmetric Mobility, and Quasi-Symmetric Models

A. Asymmetric Mobility

M\E	DO	NT	RM	BV	LC	RC	EC
DO	a						
NT	c	a	b	b	b	b	b
RM	c	c	a	b	b	b	b
BV	c	c	c	a	b	b	b
LC	c	c	c	c	a	b	b
RC	c	c	c	c	c	a	b
EC	c	c	c	c	c	c	a

B. Heterogenous Asymmetric Mobility

M\E	DO	NT	RM	BV	LC	RC	EC
DO	a						
NT	a	a	b	c	d	e	f
RM	a	B	a	g	h	i	j
BV	a	C	G	a	k	l	m
LC	a	D	H	K	a	n	o
RC	a	E	I	L	N	a	p
EC	a	F	J	M	O	P	a

C. Quasi-Symmetric Mobility

M\E	DO	NT	RM	BV	LC	RC	EC
DO	a						
NT	a	a	b	c	d	e	f
RM	a	b	a	g	h	i	j
BV	a	c	g	a	k	l	m
LC	a	d	h	k	a	n	o
RC	a	e	i	l	n	a	p
EC	a	f	j	m	o	p	a

Key:

M = mathematics
E = English
DO = Dropout

NT = Not taking
RM = Remedial
BV = Business/Vocational

LC = Lower College
RC = Regular College
EC = Elite College

the best fit to the data, then some kind of asymmetry characterizes students' mobility in school.

However, determining whether mobility is asymmetrically upward or asymmetrically downward requires comparison of the three sets of mobility parameters. The Grade 10 to 11 set can be compared to reveal the incidence of upward and downward mobility across Grades 10 and 11, the Grade 11 and 12 set can be compared to reveal the incidence of upward and downward mobility across grades 11 and 12, and the Grade 10 to 12 set can be compared to reveal the incidence of upward and downward mobility across Grades 10 and 12. Thus, if the AM model fits the data, these six parameters from the model can allow investigation of whether the prevalence of mobility is downward or upward.

The AM model provides only one test of asymmetric mobility. Assessment of asymmetric mobility should not depend entirely on one specification of this phenomenon, for there are at least two reasons that AM could fail to fit. Clearly, AM might fail to fit because mobility is not asymmetric. Alternatively, the asymmetric mobility model may not fit the data because the asymmetries might depend, in part, on the student's curricular location in preceding academic years (i.e., curricular location in Grade 10 for the Grade 10 to 11 transition as well as the Grade 10 to 12 transition, and curricular location in Grade 11 for the Grade 11 to 12 transition). AM does not take into account the student's "point of departure" and thus may fail to fit if the likelihood of upward and downward moves differs appreciably depending on the student's origin location. Thus, an alternative specification of asymmetric mobility is required in order to guard against rejecting asymmetric mobility because the model is too strict.

An alternative specification is provided by the heterogenous asymmetric mobility model. HAM differs from AM in that HAM allows every preceding origin to have its own implications for the direction of movement. Thus, HAM produces 15 upward mobility parameters and 15 downward mobility parameters for each pair of academic years.

However, like the AM model, if HAM fits best, one may consider whether the prevalence of asymmetries is upward or downward. Yet, given the greater flexibility of HAM, investigating the prevalence of mobility requires perusing 90 parameters rather than six.

Both AM and HAM allow investigation of asymmetric mobility. An alternative possibility is that there is no asymmetry in movement. Instead, upward and downward flows may be equal. This might occur owing to institutional arrangements that might check the rise of large asymmetries of movement, for such asymmetries might lead to very unequal-sized groups (Riehl, Natriello, & Pallas, 1992). Thus, although neither Rosenbaum nor more recent researchers have focused on symmetry, there is reason to test for some pattern of symmetric mobility. In addition, as equal flows provide the logical contrast with asymmetry, consideration of equal flows is important.

Two models will test the possibility of equal flows. The quasi-symmetry model is diametrically opposed to asymmetric mobility because it says that upward and downward moves are equally likely, once marginals are controlled. The design matrix for this model also is shown in Figure 5.1. Its contrast with both models of asymmetric mobility is readily apparent; whereas the AM model asserts that upward and downward mobility differ, and HAM asserts that the degree of difference depends on the origin, QS asserts that upward and downward mobility are equal for any origin–destination pair. That is, the parameter describing the net incidence of movement from, say, lower college origins to regular college destination (*n* that is to the right of *a*) equals the parameter describing the net incidence of movement from regular college origins to lower college destinations (*n* that is just below *a*).

A second variant of quasi-symmetry, QS–C, conditions the eleventh grade by twelfth-grade parameters on tenth-grade origins. The design matrix for this model is not provided because its only difference from QS is that the QS parameters are allowed to differ depending on the category of course taken in Grade 10. (For further discussion of the models estimated and exact equations for each model, see Appendix C.)

Prevalent Asymmetric Mobility

Summary statistics from the models are presented in Table 5.3. For mathematics the finding is clear; while three of the four models fit the data (as

Table 5.3. Fit Statistics for Some Models Testing Asymmetric Mobility

MODEL	L^2	df	BIC	Δ
Panel 1—Mobility in Mathematics (effective *n* = 4,711)				
Asymmetric Mobility	2326.36	234	347.27	25.49
Heterogenous Asymmetric Mobility	210.19	150	−1058.46	5.21
Quasi-Symmetry	842.04	195	−807.21	12.95
Conditional Quasi-Symmetry	485.08	120	−529.84	9.56
Panel 2—Mobility in English (effective *n* = 4,654)				
Asymmetric Mobility	373.24	234	−1602.99	7.41
Heterogenous Asymmetric Mobility	71.62	150	−1195.19	2.88
Quasi-Symmetry	239.25	195	−1407.61	5.88
Conditional Quasi-Symmetry	163.75	120	−849.70	3.83

shown by the negative BIC statistics for those models), the BIC statistics suggest that heterogenous asymmetric mobility is the most complete description of the pattern of mathematics mobility. For English the findings are equally clear; in this case all four models fit the data, but BIC statistics suggest that asymmetric mobility provides the most complete description of the pattern of mobility in English.

Note that HAM fits the mathematics data better than the tournament mobility model did. The BIC statistic for HAM is appreciably lower than the BIC statistic for any tournament mobility model. Also, even though the TM4C model fit, it misclassified approximately 22% of the students. In contrast, HAM misclassifies only about 5% of the students for math.

In the same vein, the AM model misclassifies only 7.4% of the students' English placements. This is a substantial improvement in prediction over the independence model. Moreover, by the BIC criterion, the AM model fits better than both the independence model and the tournament mobility models.

To learn whether asymmetric mobility is *downward*, the parameter estimates need to be considered. English, with only six parameters to consider, is more straightforward than math. Each parameter reflects the prevalence of mobility in one direction as a proportion of students in any one of the baseline categories; the higher the proportion, the more prevalent is movement in that direction. I find that downward mobility in the move from Grade 10 to 11 relative to the baseline is $e^c = .505$, which is greater than upward mobility in the move from Grade 10 to 11 (relative to the same baseline), $e^b = .414$. Similarly, downward mobility between Grades 11 and 12 is greater than upward mobility between Grades 11 and 12 ($e^c = .452 > .307 = e^b$). Between Grades 10 and 12 I also find more downward than upward mobility ($e^c = .794 > .483 = e^b$). Thus, the results suggest that mobility in English is asymmetrically downward.

For mathematics the picture is a bit more complex. The simple version of asymmetric mobility provides a very poor description of students' mobility for math. One-fourth of the students are misclassified by the model, and the AM model fails to fit by the BIC criterion. However, each of the other three models fit the data, and on the basis of the BIC statistic it appears that the heterogenous asymmetric mobility is the most complete description of the pattern of mathematics mobility.[2] Table 5.4 contains the parameters from

---

[2]The baseline categories were all students in the same category across any 2 years or who dropped out in the move from one year to the other. Dropouts are included in the baseline to facilitate translating the concept of symmetry into nonsquare tables. However, results will show that substantive claims about which is greater, upward or downward mobility, are not affected, because taking dropouts out of the baseline would only add to the incidence of downward mobility.

Table 5.4. Estimates from Heterogenous Asymmetric Mobility Model for Mathematics

	Grade 11						
Grade 10	Dropout	None	Remedial	Business/ Vocational	Lower College	Regular College	Elite College
Dropout	**1**						
None	1	**1**	.811	.755	.278	.121	.061
Remedial	1	.899	**1**	.656	.440	.045	.018
Busi/Voc	1	.857	.787	**1**	.323	.076	.087
Low Col	1	1.203	.859	.910	**1**	.430	.120
Reg Col	1	1.143	.600	1.088	.416	**1**	1.031
Elite Col	1	.729	.207	.824	.071	.686	**1**

	Grade 12						
Grade 11	Dropout	None	Remedial	Business/ Vocational	Lower College	Regular College	Elite College
Dropout	**1**						
None	1	**1**	.605	.554	.333	.061	.009
Remedial	1	.543	**1**	.346	.571	.034	.013
Busi/Voc	1	.824	.748	**1**	.596	.068	.019
Low Col	1	.669	.551	.453	**1**	.293	.044
Reg Col	1	1.723	1.322	1.647	1.366	**1**	.321
Elite Col	1	2.484	.626	2.085	1.225	1.043	**1**

	Grade 12						
Grade 10	Dropout	None	Remedial	Business/ Vocational	Lower College	Regular College	Elite College
Dropout	**1**						
None	1	**1**	.826	1.023	.535	.153	.042
Remedial	1	.674	**1**	.619	.287	.050	.054
Busi/Voc	1	.890	.728	**1**	.654	.170	.112
Low Col	1	.965	.484	1.133	**1**	.344	.132
Reg Col	1	1.767	.905	2.646	.748	**1**	.439
Elite Col	1	2.000	.654	2.071	.414	.707	**1**

the HAM model for math. The numbers in the table reflect the concentration of students. The higher the number, the more students follow that pattern. The numbers in bold divide each panel into two sections—above the diagonal students are upwardly mobile, below the diagonal they are downwardly mobile. There are three panels in Table 5.4 because one set of parameters is needed to describe mobility between each pair of academic years.

As an example, consider which is more likely, the move from elite college math in tenth grade to business/vocational math in eleventh grade, or the opposite move from business/vocational math in tenth grade to elite college math in eleventh grade. The number capturing downward mobility is .824; the number capturing upward mobility is .087. Downward mobility is far more common.

Perusing these estimates reveals a dominance of downward mobility. Of the 45 comparisons between above and below diagonal concentrations, only eight show more upward than downward mobility. Moreover, of these eight only two span the non-college prep/college prep divide. (As explained before, I have treated lower college prep as non-college because the courses resemble the old general track.) When proposing the tournament metaphor, Rosenbaum highlighted this very distinction between college preparatory and non-college preparatory locations. Given the pattern evident in Table 5.4, and the finding for English as well, it appears that Rosenbaum's finding of asymmetric downward mobility continues to describe students' course-taking patterns, especially across the college/non-college divide.

INCIDENCE OF MOBILITY

In his study of Grayton, Rosenbaum found students were unlikely to move up or down. Hallinan found that mobility was more common than Rosenbaum did. These results support Hallinan's (1996) finding on the incidence of mobility. The implications of the best-fitting model for English are that approximately half of the students change categories in moving from Grade 10 to Grade 11, and about half also change categories in moving from Grade 11 to Grade 12. The findings for math are the same, although there is a slightly higher incidence of mobility from Grade 11 to Grade 12. However, in summary, a high proportion of students are mobile throughout their careers.

The high incidence of mobility means that throughout their careers students are exposed to different kinds of socialization treatments. This means that even within a subject, students will be unlikely to receive consistent socialization. This is an important difference between the previous regime of tracking and the current one. Yet, the finding above—that most mobility is downward—matches the best understanding of the previous organization of schools.

CONCLUSION

Changes in school practice that demonstrably affected scope may have spilled over to alter students' mobility through the curriculum. Rosenbaum's research, which covered a cohort of students completing school during the period in which schools seem to have been changing their practices, led him to speculate on the existence of a single-elimination tournament in which upward mobility was nearly impossible. However, more recent research has found that students are more likely to move up than down.

Unfortunately for analysts' efforts to understand tracking systems, many reasons other than social change might explain the discrepancy between Rosenbaum's findings and more recent research. Although the studies differed in time by 20 years, they also differed in sampling procedure (Rosenbaum's and Hallinan's probability samples vs. Wilson & Rossman's non-probability sample), analytic method, and the heterogeneity of the student bodies (low vs. high). Any one of these differences, in addition to real social change, might explain the different findings. Under these conditions a clear comparison with the past is not possible.

However, analysts, using more recent data, may test *ideas* that were generated in the past. Although these tests will not allow a direct comparison with earlier cohorts, they will allow assessment of whether more recent students' experience is captured by the theories developed in the past, theories that still matter in discussions of tracking regimes. And drawing on findings from recent research, analysts may theorize the implications of the patterns of mobility for students' experience of schools. In so doing, analysts may lay the foundation for cross-time comparative analyses by conducting detailed studies using existing data, and continuing to collect data on later cohorts.

How should this research be conducted? Rosenbaum provided a potentially useful illustration by collecting data on the courses of Grayton students. His analysis of this cross-tabular array yielded many important insights. Unfortunately, analysts seem not to have taken Rosenbaum's lead, and thus no literature has followed through with detailed analysis of the patterns of mobility in schools. What can be found in the literature are analyses of individual-level correlates of placement. Important as these analyses are, they do not allow detailed study of the relationship between discrete locations, and such detailed studies are essential to deepening analysts' understanding of the structure of opportunity in schools. The neglect of the kind of analysis Rosenbaum conducted presents a major puzzle for the sociology of knowledge, for three reasons.

First, by definition, secondary school tracking stratifies students, and in-school stratification is an enduring interest in the sociology of education. Thus, one might expect detailed analyses of students' patterns of movement through the in-school stratification system to be more common than they are at present.

Second, the research literature on a comparable stratifying process (i.e., social mobility) is one of the most methodologically and theoretically well developed areas of sociological research. Accordingly, to the extent that track mobility is movement through a series of discrete locations, one might expect track mobility research to draw at least some of its insights (methodological and/or theoretical) from social mobility research.

Third, the effect of track location on important outcomes (e.g., measured achievement) is well documented (Gamoran & Mare, 1989). Given the importance of track location for outcomes of interest, one might expect sustained attention to be given to studying whether the (potentially) complex patterns of mobility through discrete structural locations constrain or create opportunities for students to reach different places in the curricular structure, places that have demonstrably different implications for adult attainments.

In short, neglect of the trail that Rosenbaum opened cannot be traced to researcher or practitioner disinterest in in-school stratification in particular, disinterest in patterns of mobility through systems of stratification in general, nonexistent theories or methods for addressing the questions that would form the agenda of track mobility research, or the irrelevance of track location for outcomes of interest.

Whatever the reason for its earlier neglect, the trail must be taken up again. By studying the patterns of mobility, analysts may describe them and consider their implications for students' experience of schools. By establishing a solid baseline and collecting additional data, analysts will make it possible to discern the changing nature of the channels of opportunity in schools.

The solid baseline probably will need to be built from this point forward, because past data are problematic for detailed analysis. Rosenbaum learned practically all that could be learned from the Grayton data, but even they appear unequal to the task of providing a solid baseline for cross-time comparative research.

Some of the problems with the Grayton data are that they reflect one school alone, exclude dropouts, and lack racial, ethnic, and class diversity. Although these features may have advantages for some research questions, they present problems if the aim is to provide a secure baseline against which social change may be observed. Despite these difficulties, the Grayton data appear to be the best data from the earlier period; thus, unless more and better data on earlier periods are unearthed, comparisons between previous and more recent periods must remain tentative.

The primary aim of this chapter was to investigate an important theory from the past in order to discern whether it reflects the state of schools in the more recent period. It must be noted, however, that even setting aside the difficulties of making comparisons with the past, assessing the veracity of the tournament mobility metaphor remains difficult. If the tournament mobility model fits, one needs a way to judge whether the number of students who rise after falling is low enough to preserve the tournament metaphor as a pithy and accurate description of in-school mobility. I rejected the tournament mobility metaphor because it seemed to me that the proportion of students who rise after falling was too high to sustain the key claim of the metaphor. The estimate I obtained for the proportion of "losers" who come back to "win"—about one out of five—is approximately twice the proportion of native-born blacks in the United States population. Because we are unlikely to deny the existence of blacks in the United States, even though blacks are relatively rare, it is my view that we also should be unwilling to de-emphasize the existence of a possibility of upward mobility after downward mobility, even though such movement is relatively rare. Thus, when the incidence of upward mobility after downward mobility is compared with other kinds of social and demographic phenomena, it is apparent that one may reject the single-elimination tournament mobility metaphor as a description of mobility.

Yet, in reality there are many different kinds of tournaments. I have focused on the type of tournament described in the original formulation of tournament mobility, which was a single-elimination tournament. However, further analyses may yet salvage the insight reflected by the *idea* of the tournament, perhaps by retheorizing the characteristics of the competition ongoing in schools. Perhaps rather than a single-elimination tournament, it may be that double elimination pertains. Still, at this juncture, it is fair to say that single-elimination tournament rules do not seem operative. This provides a major revision in the draconian idea of a single-elimination tournament process as an allocation mechanism in secondary schools.

Even with this change, however, downward moves are both common and extremely consequential—the vast majority of persons who move downward do not rise again. Thus, although the tournament metaphor is undermined, the idea of asymmetric downward mobility appears appropriate. This directly contradicts the more recent research suggesting greater upward than downward mobility.

One may speculate as to the implications of these general patterns for students' experience of schools. Compared with earlier cohorts, the higher incidence of mobility is likely to reduce the consistency of socialization over a student's high school career.

Recent research showing that upward mobility is common implies that students will see many of their peers moving upward. Seeing this occur, students may learn that upward mobility is possible. If students learned this lesson from seeing more upward than downward mobility, then their experience of school might provide support for one of the key legitimating myths of Western societies, the myth that those who do well can gain upward mobility.

Yet, the data do not support the contention of greater upward than downward mobility. Instead, downward mobility predominates. This larger downward flow reduces the chance that students will have many peers who have experienced upward mobility. Thus, if students' conclusions as to the character of the society they will inherit are drawn from their own experience and the experience of nearby peers, it is unlikely that they will find support in the in-school stratification system for this particular legitimating myth.

This chapter has assessed the patterns of mobility. Upward mobility seems rare, and downward mobility common. Although these particular patterns may have implications for students' experience of schools, I have not assessed these implications; I have only suggested them. Yet, before turning to whether scope and mobility patterns matter, it is important to consider the role of individuals' attributes in determining their chances of upward mobility.

The role of individual attributes in securing mobility is extremely important to the evaluation of in-school mobility. For example, the evaluation of the tracking regime might depend on whether advantages in the curricular hierarchy confer advantages in later placements. If they do not, educators might want to rethink the pedagogical role of tracking; if they do, researchers might want to rethink its relation to processes ongoing in the wider society. Similarly, the role of measured achievement or social class in securing upward mobility may affect the evaluation of tracking. Thus, individual-level factors must be brought into the analysis of track mobility. Chapter 6 takes up that task.

CHAPTER 6

Individual-Level Factors
in Curricular Mobility

So far the investigation of mobility has ignored students' characteristics, but adding individual-level factors will round out the analysis. The analysis of patterns of mobility in Chapter 5 revealed the furrows and dams that channel or constrain upward mobility. By adding individual-level attributes to the analysis, it becomes possible to identify the factors associated with advantageous and disadvantageous negotiation of the terrain.

At least three additional reasons make within-subject mobility an appropriate locus of attention and the investigation of individual-level factors a necessary extension of the analysis. First, students in secondary school are not isolated; they are, instead, embedded within a much larger process of academic training and advancement that extends from preschool and kindergarten through to the awarding of named chairs and Nobel prizes. Studies of virtually every stage of this process have shown advantages accruing to those who already have them. Upon reflecting on advancement in the latter stages of this process, Merton (1968) dubbed this phenomenon the Matthew Effect, after a passage in St. Matthew in which Jesus is quoted as saying:

> For whosoever hath, to him shall be given, and he shall have more abundance: but whosoever hath not, from him shall be taken away even that he hath. (Matthew 13:12)

Students in secondary schools are early in the journey of obtaining academic credentials and awards, but their journey may share much with that of older scholars. Hence, investigating the correlates of success in school can shed light on the process of advancement in academic life. It will be important to ask whether the Matthew Effect operates in secondary schools, or whether those who have little have as much chance to attain high positions over time as those who start out advantaged. Within-subject mobility is an appropriate arena within which this question may be investigated.

This is an important question because recent research has suggested that the Matthew Effect is not evident in secondary school. Instead, the lower a student is in the tracking hierarchy, the more likely the student is to move up. It is important to interrogate this finding, for its implications go far beyond the issue of secondary school tracking.

Second, a comparative study of within-subject mobility for two subjects can reveal both how open different subjects are and whether subject-specific achievement is associated with attaining advantaged positions. If achievement in the domain is not relevant to mobility, then there is more reason to question the validity of curriculum differentiation.

Third, existing debate and potential policy changes make study of within-subject mobility essential. Many de-tracking advocates are calling for the end of the differentiated curriculum (Ascher, 1992; Wheelock, 1992). Yet, research and everyday in-school experience suggest that the differentiated secondary school curriculum has both on-the-ground backing in the form of, for example, well-off and politically well-placed parents (Wells & Oakes, 1996) *and* systemic institutional support in the form of, for example, the differentiated nature of higher education. These and other factors make the withering away of the differentiated secondary school curriculum not only unlikely but also potentially politically and pedagogically unwise. Removing the differentiated curriculum may increase incentives for parents to abandon local schools, and this may lead to further erosion of political support for public schools. Pedagogically, forcing teachers to teach in ways they doubt will be effective may undermine teacher effectiveness and thus student learning. Given this landscape, it is important to understand how within-subject mobility works, in order to determine whether and to what extent the critique of tracking becomes also and necessarily a critique of subject-specific curriculum differentiation.

IN-SCHOOL PLACEMENTS OVER TIME

Although several analysts have investigated correlates of students' placements (Alexander, Cook, & McDill, 1978; Gamoran & Mare, 1989; Garet & DeLany, 1988; Hallinan, 1992; Lucas & Gamoran, 1991), few studies have used prior location as a predictor of later location. Of the studies that have used prior location, many do not concern the high school years, or are analyses of mobility in nations with different tracking regimes. So, for example, in a study of six elementary schools, Gamoran (1989) found that second-grade reading group placement was positively associated with first-grade reading group placement in four of the schools, even though social class and achievement were controlled. Dauber, Alexander, and Entwistle (1996) found that sixth-grade placements in math or English were positively associated with eighth-grade placements in the same subject. In a study of four districts and one Catholic diocese, Gamoran (1992a) found that placement in honors English in eighth grade was positively associated with ninth-grade English placements. Rehberg and Rosenthal (1978) found positive effects of ninth-grade curriculum placement on tenth-grade placement. Similarly, Yogev (1981) studied track mobility in Israel and found that placement in eighth grade had positive effects on tenth grade placement.

Although the analyses above find positive effects of prior location, none of the above analyses investigated placement in the latter high school years as a function of prior placement in high school. One prominent analysis that does investigate this portion of students' careers is the work of Hallinan (1996).

To investigate mobility within English and mathematics, Hallinan (1996) used three logistic regressions to predict upward, downward, and "outward" (i.e., not taking a course in the subject) mobility. Although Hallinan was interested in the effects of race, sex, and social class on later placement, an important aspect of "Track Mobility in Secondary School" concerned the role of prior placement on later placement. Despite common sociological observations to the contrary, Hallinan (1996, pp. 994–996) found that the *lower* one's curricular location, the more likely one is to move up, and the *higher* one's curricular location, the more likely one is to move down. These findings remained even though students in the highest curricular location were removed from the analysis of upward mobility, because they could not move up further.

Hallinan's findings are provocative and potentially extremely important for ongoing debate about the role and usefulness of tracking in America's schools. In the debate between those who favor and oppose de-tracking, Hallinan correctly has attempted to draw attention to the technical aspects of track systems (Hallinan, 1994a, 1994b). Critics of tracking have focused on the political aspects of the maintenance of tracking (Oakes, 1994a, 1994b; Wells & Oakes, 1996; Wells & Serna, 1996; Wheelock, 1992). Clearly, both the technical and the political aspects of tracking are important and worthy of attention, if not for policy, then certainly for sociology.

However, the result Hallinan reports in her analysis of track mobility, that those who begin with low curricular origins are actually more likely to move up than others, could, if true, provide a crucial turning point in this debate. This is so because the vast majority of discussions of tracking presume that the lowly placed are less likely to attain high positions than others. If Hallinan's analysis is correct, it would provide an important example of how political rhetoric uninformed by technical analysis may be based on an incorrect assessment of who wins and who loses when it comes to tracking. It would provide support for a view that de-tracking advocates have paid insufficient attention to the possibly productive way in which tracking works to allocate variably prepared students to different curricula. Thus, Hallinan's

provocative finding is of extreme importance to ongoing debate about tracking, regardless of the other findings with respect to race, sex, and social
class. Its importance only increases when it is juxtaposed to studies of different levels of American education and of secondary schools in other countries, all of which find continued operation of Merton's Matthew Effect.

Hallinan is right—those who pay insufficient attention to the technical
aspects of tracking systems imperil their analysis and the policy prescriptions that might flow from the analysis. However, important theoretical and
methodological questions raised by Hallinan's analysis must be addressed
before the findings of the analysis can be accepted. Moreover, these questions must be faced before further analysis of mobility takes place, for these
questions go to the heart of what is meant by mobility and opportunity.
Thus, before investigating the potential role of individual-level factors in
mobility, it will be useful to discuss the theoretical and related methodological issues that are inherent in the investigation of mobility processes.

RESEARCH ON THE MOBILITY PROCESS:
CHALLENGES AND RESPONSE

Theoretical Questions

There are at least two ways to state the central question posed by research
on the mobility process. One way is to ask: Is there an association between
placement in one hierarchy (origins) and placement in subsequent hierarchies (destinations)? If so, then origins constrain destinations, and if the
association is positive, then the Matthew Effect is found anew.

In contrast, one may investigate mobility by stating the question another
way: Do those at the bottom of one hierarchy have a better, equal, or worse
chance of moving up to higher places in a subsequent hierarchy than do
others? Of course, one may ask a similar question concerning downward
mobility of those at the top of the hierarchy, and similar questions of those
in the middle as well. Yet, the theoretical implications are the same whether
one focuses on those at the bottom, those in the middle, or those at the top,
and so I will attend only to those at the bottom and their prospects for
upward mobility.

The first question concerns persons' chances of reaching advantaged
positions, while the second question concerns persons' chances of reaching
positions *more advantaged than the positions they currently occupy*. This is
a crucial distinction, and it has important substantive and methodological
implications.

The implications follow from one definitive feature of any hierarchy of positions: The lower a position is in the hierarchy, the greater the number of more advantaged positions there are.

Given this truism, the two different questions concerning mobility raise two very different issues. The first asks whether there is an association between where one starts and where one finishes. The second asks whether there is an association between where one starts and one's chances of experiencing upward mobility. These two very different questions may have very different substantive implications. To make plain the different substantive implications of the questions, I will consider the challenge of advising a student who is about to decide where to begin the process of his or her training.

If one considers the first question, then one will base the advice on whether there is an association between origins and destinations. Advice based on this question focuses on where the student finishes, not on whether the student is mobile or not. For the student interested in the final destination, this is the appropriate question to ask, and the appropriate criterion for advice.

However, if the student is interested in selecting an origin that will maximize the chances of experiencing upward mobility over time, the second question is the appropriate question to ask. For such a student, advice must be based on whether origins are associated with the chance of experiencing upward mobility.

Thus, a student faced with asking either of these two questions is actually faced with using one of two different criteria. The first question is concerned with ultimate attainments. A student who wants to maximize the ultimate level of attainment will need to heed the advice that is based on the first question. However, a student who wants to choose an origin category that will maximize the chance of experiencing upward mobility needs to attend to the answer to the second question.

Hence, two ostensible phrasings of the same research question—is there an association between origins and destinations on the one hand, versus is there an association between origins and the likelihood of experiencing upward mobility on the other—actually raise two very different substantive questions. As one might expect, then, translating these questions into statistical models may lead to dissimilar results. However, as I show below, the difference is such that only one of these questions produces illuminating results when pursued through empirical research.

Statistical Challenge

Table 6.1 contains information on 60 hypothetical students. These data show students' origins (as low or middle) and their destinations (low, middle, or

Table 6.1 Origin, Destination, and Mobility Experience of Hypothetical Students

Student	Origin	Destination	Upwardly Mobile?	Student	Origin	Destination	Upwardly Mobile?
1	Low	Low	No	31	Middle	Low	No
2	Low	Low	No	32	Middle	Low	No
3	Low	Low	No	33	Middle	Low	No
4	Low	Low	No	34	Middle	Low	No
5	Low	Low	No	35	Middle	Low	No
6	Low	Low	No	36	Middle	Low	No
7	Low	Low	No	37	Middle	Low	No
8	Low	Low	No	38	Middle	Low	No
9	Low	Low	No	39	Middle	Low	No
10	Low	Low	No	40	Middle	Low	No
11	Low	Middle	Yes	41	Middle	Middle	No
12	Low	Middle	Yes	42	Middle	Middle	No
13	Low	Middle	Yes	43	Middle	Middle	No
14	Low	Middle	Yes	44	Middle	Middle	No
15	Low	Middle	Yes	45	Middle	Middle	No
16	Low	Middle	Yes	46	Middle	Middle	No
17	Low	Middle	Yes	47	Middle	Middle	No
18	Low	Middle	Yes	48	Middle	Middle	No
19	Low	Middle	Yes	49	Middle	Middle	No
20	Low	Middle	Yes	50	Middle	Middle	Yes
21	Low	High	Yes	51	Middle	High	Yes
22	Low	High	Yes	52	Middle	High	Yes
23	Low	High	Yes	53	Middle	High	Yes
24	Low	High	Yes	54	Middle	High	Yes
25	Low	High	Yes	55	Middle	High	Yes
26	Low	High	Yes	56	Middle	High	Yes
27	Low	High	Yes	57	Middle	High	Yes
28	Low	High	Yes	58	Middle	High	Yes
29	Low	High	Yes	59	Middle	High	Yes
30	Low	High	Yes	60	Middle	High	Yes

high). By construction, none of the students have high origins. Moreover, the table is constructed so that students who are in the middle for both origins and destinations experience no mobility, and students with low origins and low destinations also experience no mobility.

Table 6.1 also contains a column denoting whether the student was upwardly mobile or not. I often will refer to this dichotomous variable as UM. Using a logistic regression model to regress the variable UM on students' origins is to ask whether origins are associated with whether the students will obtain destinations that are higher than their origins, that is, whether origins are associated with the likelihood of upward mobility.

When I regressed UM (coded so that UM = 1 if the student is upwardly mobile and UM = 0 otherwise) on origins (coded so that the medium origin category = 1 and the low origin category = 0) using a logistic regression model, I obtained a constant (α) of .6931 and coefficient (β) of −1.3863 (with a standard error of .3871). In other words, the logistic regression of the upwardly mobile dichotomy reveals that the higher the student's origins, the less likely the student will experience upward mobility. Using the formula that translates logit coefficients into predicted probabilities (Neter, Wasserman, & Kuttner, 1989, p. 582):

$$P(U = 1) = \left(\frac{e^{\alpha + \beta X_i}}{1 + e^{\alpha + \beta X_i}} \right)$$

I estimated the probability of upward mobility for a person with a low origin and the probability of upward mobility for a person with a middle origin. The probability of upward mobility for those with low origins is .667, while the probability of upward mobility for those with middle origins is .333. This approach mirrors Hallinan's, and so does the result: The lower one is in the hierarchy, the more likely one is to move up.

However, the data in Table 6.1 can be written in several equivalent ways. One equivalent way is to cross-tabulate origins by destinations; Table 6.2 contains this cross-tabulation. The numbers in bold represent students who are upwardly mobile. Perusing Table 6.2 it is apparent that there is no association between origins and destinations. This is apparent because the distribution of destinations is exactly the same for both origin categories. Because the distribution of destinations does not vary by origin category, there can be no association between origins and destinations. Put another way, knowing a student's origins does not increase one's ability to correctly predict his or her destination.

Even though there is obviously no association between origins and destinations, the logistic regression of the upwardly mobile/not upwardly mobile dichotomy estimates a negative association between origins and the

Table 6.2. Origin by Destination with No Association Between Origins and Destinations (numbers in bold are upwardly mobile students)

Origin	Destination		
	Low	Middle	High
Low	10	**10**	**10**
Middle	10	10	**10**

likelihood of upward mobility. Moreover, the logistic regression finds that low-origin students have a 66.7% chance of upward mobility, while middle-origin students have only a 33.3% chance of upward mobility. Inspecting Table 6.2 makes it clear why origins are negatively associated with the likelihood of upward mobility, and why the predicted probabilities are as they are: Students at the bottom of the hierarchy have two categories to which they may move to be upwardly mobile, while students in the middle have only one.

Thus, the logistic regression of UM (for Table 6.1) is driven by the basic fact of hierarchies: The lower the position, the more positions there are above it. Because the logistic regression of the upwardly mobile/not upwardly mobile dichotomy is biased by this basic fact of hierarchies, there is usually little to be gained by exposing to empirical analysis the question of whether those at the bottom of a hierarchy have a better chance of experiencing upward mobility than others. That is one reason why the alternative question—is there an association between origins and destinations?—is a better substantive question to ask.

Table 6.3 presents another set of hypothetical data arranged this time in a cross-tabulation table. In Table 6.3 only one student falls from a middle origin to a low destination, while 19 students rise from middle origins to high destinations.

Summary indices that dimly reflect the positive association in the table do not go far enough in detailing how much worse those of low origins fare compared with those of middle origins in Table 6.3, but they do confirm that there is a positive association between origins and destinations. The Pearson correlation coefficient for these data is .395; it is well known that Pearson correlations understate the association between categorical variables (Muthén, 1984). Monte Carlo studies have shown that the polychoric correlation is more accurate for measuring the linear association between categorical variables (Bollen, 1989); the polychoric correlation for these data is .545. Thus, it is clear that there is a positive association between origins and destinations in Table 6.3. In cross-time research, analysts commonly regard a (usually smaller) positive association as evidence of an advantage for those who start out advantaged.

Table 6.3. Origin by Destination with Positive Association Between Origins and Destinations (numbers in bold are upwardly mobile students)

	Destination		
Origin	Low	Middle	High
Low	10	**10**	**10**
Middle	1	10	**19**

Yet, when I conducted the logistic regression of the upwardly mobile dichotomy on the data in Table 6.3, I obtained a constant (α) of .6932 and coefficient (β) of -0.147 (with a standard error of .542). In other words, the correlation coefficients show a positive association between origins and destinations, but the logistic regression analysis of Table 6.3 shows no discernible association between the likelihood of upward mobility and origins. Why? Because 20 students in the low-origin category were upwardly mobile, while almost 20 students in the middle-origin category were upwardly mobile. Although the logistic regression of UM on origins produces a technically correct answer to the question of whether the likelihood of upward mobility is associated with origins, this example illustrates why this question is such a poor one to ask. In case after case, one obtains a correct answer to the question of whether upward mobility is associated with origins, yet the answer reveals little about the underlying distribution of opportunity.

Inspection of Table 6.3 shows that students of middle origins have a 19/30 chance of reaching the top, and a 29/30 chance of avoiding the bottom destination. In contrast, students with low origins have a 1/3 chance of ending up on the bottom, a 1/3 chance of ending up on top, and a 1/3 chance of ending up in the middle. More disparate life chances between origins and destinations are rare in real data. Yet, if one used the data in Table 6.3 and an analysis of the variable "upwardly mobile or not" to advise a student, one would be forced to advise the student that prospects for upward mobility do not depend on origins. Although this is technically correct, it is poor advice, for the student's prospects for attaining high positions depend directly on origin. This advice would be even more ironic given that the likely motivation for the quest for upward mobility is to attain a high position, not to experience mobility per se. Because the logistic regression of the upwardly mobile dichotomy for this extremely inegalitarian table obscures the dramatic difference in outcomes that are a direct function of origins, it should be clear that this analysis strategy fails to reveal the underlying structure of opportunity.

It should be noted that when I added other covariates, such as race, to these hypothetical data, I obtained a correct parameter estimate. However, it is quite possible that one might obtain an incorrect result on real data, because regressing the upwardly mobile dichotomy on origins often necessitates removing from the analysis those whose origins preclude upward mobility. Removing those persons may imperil estimation of other relationships.

A Solution to the Statistical Challenge

The above section has demonstrated that one should not analyze the upwardly mobile dichotomy because the results will not reveal the underlying distribution of life chances. This section suggests an additional reason—namely, that better alternative analytic approaches are available.

A very simple approach to address the question of whether origins are associated with destinations (given an *a priori* ordering such as the one Hallinan uses) is to use the ordered probit model (McKelvey & Zavoina, 1975). The ordered probit model posits that a latent variable with a standard normal distribution (i.e., the bell curve) underlies the observed categorical variable. The observed categorical variable marks which threshold has been crossed.

This model has been applied to the study of track placement (Hallinan, 1992); it is equally appropriate for the analysis of track mobility. For the data in Table 6.1, in which there is no association between origins and destinations, I estimated the ordered probit model using destinations as an ordered variable and origins as a dummy variable. The results were as expected; the estimate for the constant is .431 (standard error = .221) and the coefficient for origins is equal to $.289 \times 10^{-5}$ with a standard error of .289, or, in other words, there is no discernible association between origins and destinations for the data in Table 6.1.

Considering the data in Table 6.3, the ordered probit model produced the expected result once again—the estimate for the constant is .531 (standard error = .222) and the coefficient for origins is equal to .945 with a standard error of .333. Thus, the ordered probit analysis shows a positive association between origins and destinations for the hypothetical students in Table 6.3. This matches the inference one would draw on the basis of both the Pearson correlation coefficient and the polychoric correlation coefficient.

Mobility Process Meta-Theory and Methods Revisited

The aim of this rather detailed methodological discussion is not to turn the analysis into a purely technical exercise. Rather, the methodological issues are discussed because they are the operational reflection of often hidden theoretical divisions. Therefore, both the theoretical and the methodological implications of the different questions require attention.

Hallinan (1996) raises a series of potentially important questions about the extent to which prior track location determines later placement. The findings she obtains are provocative to sociology generally and to sociology of education especially.

Juxtaposing Hallinan's findings to those of others reveals that deep and unstated differences in the questions under study may underlie the differences in findings. Given this, I have detailed the reasons behind my preference for studying the association between origins and destinations rather than the association between origins and the likelihood of upward mobility.

Using the former question, I re-investigate the processes of secondary school track mobility. It is important to do so, for if those at the bottom not only are more likely to move up, but also are actually more likely to obtain high positions than are others, then I suspect that at the very least the points in the de-tracking debate, if not the very policy preferences and sociological conclusions discussants adopt, might change appreciably. For this reason, as well as the others provided earlier (investigating whether the Matthew Effect operates, comparing the openness of math and English), it is important to further investigate secondary school within-subject mobility.

MOBILITY PROCESS ANALYSIS PLAN

In order to study within-subject mobility, I capitalize on the order of the categories for the three-category classification of courses and use the ordered probit model. The move from Grade 10 mathematics to Grade 11 mathematics will illustrate the modeling strategy. There are three origin categories—none, non-college prep, and college prep—and *four* destination categories—dropout, none, non-college prep, and college prep. The ordered probit model posits that a latent variable with a standard normal distribution underlies the observed categorical variable. In essence each person has a latent score on the variable of interest, but the data reveal only which of a few categories the person falls into. The thresholds map the observed categorical onto the latent variable such that the observed categorical variable marks which threshold has been crossed. Figure 6.1 illustrates how the ordered probit model maps students' destination categories onto the standard normal distribution. For this analysis the ordered probit model has three thresholds, one threshold separating dropouts from those who do not take a course in the subject, one threshold separating those who do not take a course in the subject from those who take a non-college prep course, and one threshold separating non-college prep students from those taking a college preparatory course.

The values of the thresholds are estimated from the model and are typically of little interest. However, one may express the differences between two or more groups as differences in thresholds. Thus, instead of capturing group differences in a set of intercept-shifts and interactions, one may capture them by estimating different sets of thresholds for different groups. This model, the ordered probit model with stratification, will estimate thresholds for seven strata identified as follows: (1) white males, (2) black males, (3) Latino males, (4) white females, (5) black females, (6) Latina females, and (7) others. For each stratum I obtain three thresholds. This model will produce one set of coefficients that apply to all strata, concentrating all differ-

Figure 6.1 Illustration of Standard Normal Distribution and Thresholds

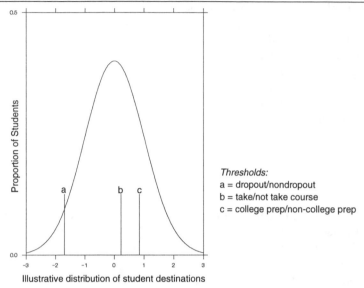

Illustrative distribution of student destinations

ences by strata in the thresholds. Hence, this approach allows full interactions by race and sex, but still provides parsimonious results. Moreover, one may graph the thresholds to easily illustrate the net implications of race and gender for curricular mobility, in a way that focuses on substantive significance.

The ability to obtain separate thresholds for different groups is extremely important in the present case. Evidence suggests that blacks are less likely to drop out of school than are whites once social class is controlled (Lucas, 1996). Yet, the evidence bearing on the upward mobility chances of blacks inside schools is unclear. Some research shows that blacks are more likely to be in higher locations (Gamoran & Mare, 1989; Garet & DeLany, 1988), while other research suggests no racial difference in assignment (Hallinan, 1992; Lucas & Gamoran, 1991). The ordered probit model with stratification is flexible enough to allow a group to have an advantage in reaching some destinations and a disadvantage in reaching other destinations. Thus, using this model will allow for the possibility that blacks are more likely to graduate from school, without constraining the results to show that blacks are more likely to enter advantaged locations. If I find that blacks are more likely to enter advantaged locations, this finding will not be driven by their performance in other parts of the distribution.

Using this model I investigate within-subject mobility, first considering the impact of earlier location on later placements. Then I add social class, measured achievement in both English and math, requirements in the subject, sector, size of place, and indicators of early adult role taking and in-school delinquency.

These last two concepts have been important in considerations of dropping out (Velez, 1989). Here dropping out is treated as a potential destination to which students may move; in the language of demography, dropout is treated as an absorbing state. Other than its character as an absorbing state (i.e., a state from which students do not leave), dropout is just another potential location in the educational careers of students.

However, two remarks—one theoretical and one statistical—need be made about the implications of this treatment of dropouts. Theoretically, the treatment implies that whatever affects one's propensity to drop out also affects one's propensity to reach any of the other potential destinations. Moreover, the coefficient for any given variable is the same across destinations, once the thresholds are scaled appropriately. Note, however, that the *same* coefficient will imply *different* effects on the probability of being in different categories. Basically this occurs because the ordered probit is a nonlinear model.

How students who drop out in Grade 11 are treated in the analysis of mobility to Grade 12 also must be noted. In short, they are dropped from the analysis. The assumption behind dropping them is that they may return to school after dropping out, but if they do they will return to a different grade, or they may pursue a GED or follow any of a number of other possible paths. Yet, fundamentally they no longer will be engaged in obtaining formal schooling with their cohort. Moreover, there are so few dropouts in the HS&B data that it is unlikely that useful estimates of their future track trajectories can be obtained. Thus, I model students' movement into dropout status, but once students drop out, they are removed from the analysis.

MOBILITY PROCESS RESULTS

Investigating the Matthew Effect

First I reconsider the finding of a negative association between curricular origins and destinations. Table 6.4 contains estimates of the association between origins and destinations. The comparison category is non-college prep origins. Thus, those who did not take a course in the subject the previous year are compared with those who enrolled in a non-college prep course, and those took a college preparatory course in the subject the previous year also are compared with those who enrolled in a non-college prep course.

Table 6.4. Simple Within-Subject Mobility Models

	MODEL 1 OUTCOMES							
	Math 11		Math 12		English 11		English 12	
INDEPENDENT VARIABLES	Coeff	S.e.	Coeff	S.e.	Coeff	S.e.	Coeff	S.e.
Math 10								
None	−0.125*	.037						
College	0.957*	.027						
Math 11								
None			−0.285*	.032				
College			0.855*	.029				
English 10								
None					−0.223*	.072		
College					0.740*	.040		
English 11								
None							−0.400*	.052
College							0.474*	.035
Effective n	4531		4281		4531		4281	
L^2 Null Mod	−5624.53		−5123.90		−3791.19		−4521.70	
L^2 Model	−5169.50		−4667.92		−3711.01		−4575.79	
df	20		20		20		20	
BIC*	−741.69		−744.71		7.99		275.41	

The negative coefficient for Math 10 None signifies that students not taking a math course in tenth grade are less likely to enter college prep math in Grade 11 than are other students. Moreover, they are more likely to move downward, that is, drop out of school. Conversely, the positive coefficient for Math 10 College signifies that students taking college prep math in tenth grade are more likely to enter college prep math in Grade 11 than are other students, and less likely to drop out by Grade 11 than others. These findings generalize to mobility between Grade 11 and Grade 12 math; but although prior location is statistically significant for English, the BIC statistics suggest this model is inadequate for English.

What about students' probabilities of not taking a course in the subject or of taking a non-college prep course in eleventh grade? As for these middle destinations, Greene (1993) notes that, for ordered probit models, changes in probability of reaching middle destinations that are associated with changes in an independent variable depend on both the normal curve and the thresholds. Thus, panes A–D in Figure 6.2 graph the probability of different destination categories for a white male with different origins; the area under the curve and bounded by the relevant thresholds represents the probability of landing in any given destination category. In the figure vertical lines mark the thresholds that divide categories; the leftmost threshold (a) divides students who drop out (to the left) from those who take no course in math in the destination grade, the middle line (b) divides students who take no math from those who take non-college prep math in the destination grade, and the rightmost line (c) divides students who take non-college prep math from those who take college prep math in the destination grade (to the right).

These thresholds hold for any normal distribution with a standard deviation of one. By construction, the thresholds map onto a standard normal curve, which has both a standard deviation of one and a mean of zero. Because I used students who took a non-college prep course as the baseline with which other students are compared, the standard normal curve (with a standard deviation equal to 1 and a mean of 0) reflects the experience of students who took a non-college preparatory course in the destination grade.

The coefficients in Table 6.4 indicate that students who did not take math in Grade 10 fared worse in their Grade 11 placements, and students who took college prep math in Grade 10 fared better in their subsequent placements. These coefficients essentially draw different normal curves for students who did not take math in Grade 10 and students who took college prep math in Grade 10 (see Figure 6.2, pane A). (Thus, these curves still have a standard deviation of 1, but do not have a mean of 0.) The coefficients indicate that the curve for those who took no math course in Grade 10 is shifted to the left of the curve for non-college prep students, while the curve for students who took college prep math is offset to the right.

Different sets of students have different curves, yet *the thresholds remain fixed*. These thresholds may be thought of as hurdles a student must surpass in order to enter the next highest curricular position. Thus, it is the thresholds that mark the points that must be reached. The normal curves superimposed above the thresholds show the distribution of three categories of students: (1) those who took no course in the subject the previous year; (2) those who took a non-college preparatory course in the subject the previous year; and (3) those who took a college preparatory course in the subject the previous year. When combined with the fixed thresholds, each curve shows how likely it is that a student with a particular curricular origin will enroll in a particular category of course the next year. Thus, taken together,

Figure 6.2 Probability Distributions of White Males in 11th and 12th Grade College Prep Mathematics and English by Prior Year Curricular Origins

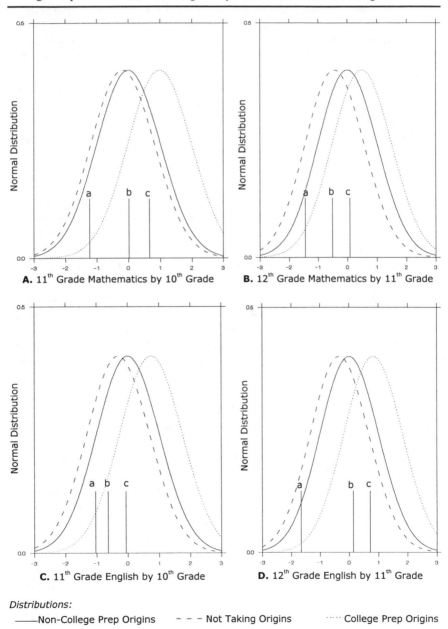

A. 11th Grade Mathematics by 10th Grade

B. 12th Grade Mathematics by 11th Grade

C. 11th Grade English by 10th Grade

D. 12th Grade English by 11th Grade

Distributions:
——Non-College Prep Origins   – – – Not Taking Origins   ⋯⋯ College Prep Origins

Thresholds:
a = dropout/nondropout   b = take/not take course   c = college prep/non-college prep

the one set of thresholds and the three curves show how likely it is for different sets of students to reach different curricular locations.

Figure 6.2A suggests that compared with students not taking math in tenth grade, students taking non-college math in Grade 10 are less likely to not take math in Grade 11, more likely to take non-college prep math in Grade 11, and (as mentioned above) more likely to take college prep math in Grade 11. In summary, the higher a student's origin, the higher the student's destination. Although the consistency between results reported in Chapter 5 and Figure 6.2A is evident, an important additional inference can be made. Figure 6.2A shows more downward than upward mobility for students whose origins are middle, and less upward mobility than the sum of immobility and downward mobility for low-origin students. But students starting from high curricular places are more likely to keep those places than to move downward. Parenthetically, this last finding is the kind of finding that will be missed if students at the top are deleted from the analysis.

These results, which extend to the remaining years for math and will apply to Grade 11 English once controls are added, can be summarized concisely: The higher one's curricular origins, the greater the chance one's destination will be high. Thus, it seems necessary to reject the finding of higher chances of upward mobility for those of lower curricular origins, and to conclude that the Matthew Effect, shown to operate in scientific careers and shown to operate by other names in other spheres, appears also to operate in secondary school careers.

A Full Model of Mobility

Table 6.5 presents a full model of mobility. As expected, early adult role taking (signified by heavy dating) and delinquency are associated with lower destinations. College aspirations tend to be associated with higher destinations as well. Achievement in the specific subject is more important for mobility in that subject than is achievement in the opposite field. This finding does not change when requirements in both subjects are included in the model (model not shown).

How can one make sense of this finding once one contrasts it to the finding, presented in Chapter 3, that achievement in math was more important than achievement in English, even for placements in English? Quite simply. The analyses in Chapter 3 investigated the determinants of placement in Grade 11 and Grade 12, and two of the determinants were tenth-grade mathematics achievement and tenth-grade English achievement. Noticeably missing from the analysis was placement in the previous grade.

The analysis in this chapter adds placement in the previous grade to the models. This change transforms the effect of achievement. In Chapter 3

Table 6.5. Full Within-Subject Mobility

INDEPENDENT VARIABLES	MODEL 2 OUTCOMES							
	Math 11		Math 12		English 11		English 12	
	Coeff	S.e.	Coeff	S.e.	Coeff	S.e.	Coeff	S.e.
Math 10								
None	−0.083*	.036						
College	0.618*	.029						
Math 11								
None			−0.278*	.033				
College			0.545*	.034				
English 10								
None					−0.212*	.075		
College					0.672*	.042		
English 11								
None							−0.394*	.054
College							0.412*	.036
SES	0.151*	.023	0.118*	.023	0.101*	.028	0.061*	.023
Math Ach	0.107*	.012	0.101*	.012	0.027*	.014	0.028*	.011
Math Req	0.096*	.028	0.072*	.027				
English Ach	0.051*	.012	0.025*	.012	0.039*	.015	0.056*	.012
English Req					0.043	.051	0.447*	.035
College Aspirations	0.386*	.041	0.228*	.038	0.032	.063	0.110*	.044
Heavy Dating	−0.283*	.065	−0.290*	.070	0.007	.077	−0.203*	.058
Cut Classes	−0.238*	.035	−0.149*	.035	−0.199*	.040	−0.192*	.036
Suspended	−0.234*	.051	−0.206*	.052	−0.244*	.056	−0.208*	.050
Disciplined	−0.188*	.042	−0.133*	.043	−0.211*	.046	−0.108*	.041
Private	0.216*	.054	0.240*	.050	0.220*	.067	0.286*	.049
Suburban	0.054	.030	0.004	.032	0.169*	.018	−0.068*	.033
Rural	−0.115*	.032	−0.007	.037	0.147*	.036	−0.260	.038
Effective n	4531		4281		4531		4281	
L^2 Null Mod	−5624.53		−5123.90		−3791.19		−4521.70	
L^2 Model	−4874.21		−4508.81		−3589.94		−4422.96	
df	41		41		41		41	
BIC*	−1155.46		−887.35		−57.35		145.35	

the coefficients reflect the association after demographics, requirements, and aspirations are controlled. In this chapter, however, intervening coursework is also controlled. Thus, the Chapter 3 analysis can be interpreted as revealing an association between achievement and placement in a grade that is nearer the total association between achievement and placement. The analysis in this chapter reveals an association that is nearer the *direct* effect of achievement on placement. Thus, the Chapter 3 analysis showed that the total association between math achievement and placement was larger than the total association between placement and English achievement for any given grade. Yet, once I compare two students who, for whatever reason, occupy the same track location in a given grade, then achievement in the specific domain is more important for subsequent placement. What this implies is that mathematics achievement has its effect by virtue of its role in determining early placements. This finding is analogous to the finding that early foreign language study is a key determinant of placements in later years (Alexander & Cook, 1982).

Given this reasoning, the Chapter 3 conclusion, that students who achieve in math are better placed in the subject of English than are students who achieve in English, remains true. The analysis here, however, explicates the process by which this occurs. It does not appear to be the case that year in and year out, students are evaluated and those who do well in math are enrolled into English courses that are above the English courses in which those who do well in English enroll. Instead, it appears that early placements advantage mathematics achievement, and those who do not achieve in math early on remain disadvantaged throughout their secondary school careers.

Referring to Chapter 3 again, I find that, even though many of the behavioral factors that might be relevant to mobility are controlled, socioeconomic status matters as well. This matches the finding from the investigation of students' joint placement in math and English. The results in Table 6.5 indicate that students with socioeconomic advantages are more likely to attain high positions than are others.

The coefficients in Table 6.5 apply to all students. The thresholds obtained from the full model capture differences between blacks, whites, and Latinos/as and between males and females. The sample size for the other non-white category is so small and the groups included in that category are so heterogenous that threshold estimates for them are not reported. The thresholds that are reported are simply z-scores, which can easily be transformed into percentiles. Thus, I use the z-scores to partition students into four destinations—dropout, no course, non-college prep, and college preparatory. These partitions apply to students who were zero on the variables in the full model: middle-class students with mean math and English achievement, who were non-college preparatory the previous year, did not have college aspirations, were not heavy daters, did not cut classes often, were not suspended or disciplined in the tenth grade, and attended public urban schools with mean math and English requirements. Changing any one of these values would be to graph another distribution of destinations. However, if instead I graphed the distributions of, for instance, the students with college aspirations, all the distributions for each race/ethnicity/gender category would slide in the same direction. Thus, none of the race/ethnic and gender comparisons would change. As the major point of estimating different thresholds was to capture potentially important race/ethnic and gender differences, it is appropriate to use this particular set of students to make the comparisons of interest.

Figure 6.3A suggests that white males are most likely to enroll in college preparatory math in eleventh grade. However, both white males and white females are most likely to not enroll in math, even if they do not drop out. Black males are least likely to enroll in eleventh-grade college preparatory math. Taken together, the three thresholds for white males indicate the advantage of using the ordered probit model with stratification. White males are advantaged in reaching top positions, but they are disadvantaged in reaching middle positions, so that white males are more likely to not take math or drop out of school than are blacks or Latinos/as. This finding would be obscured if one used a model that forced the race/ethnic and gender differences to be constant across destination categories.

Another way to express the findings above is to state that some students, even if they have a score on the latent variable "math course" (a score that is based on their achievement, social class, aspirations, and other variables in the model) that is equal to the score of a white male, sometimes will not be in the college prep math course while the white male student will be.

However, Figure 6.3B shows that by twelfth grade the white male advantage in college prep math enrollment no longer holds. Indeed, in Grade 12 black males are most likely, all else being equal, to enroll in a college preparatory math course. White males and females are most likely to end the study of math, either by not taking a math course or by dropping out of school altogether.

Considering the thresholds for English, shown in Figures 6.3C and D, it is apparent that most students enroll in college preparatory English. Still, for both Grade 11 and Grade 12, black females are more likely than other students to enroll in college prep English.

Figure 6.3 A–D demonstrates the importance of estimating different thresholds for different race/ethnicity and gender groups. Future research on the prospects of attaining different positions must be sensitive to the complexities indicated by this figure.

Figure 6.3 Eleventh- and Twelfth-Grade Mathematics and English Destinations by Race, Ethnicity, and Sex

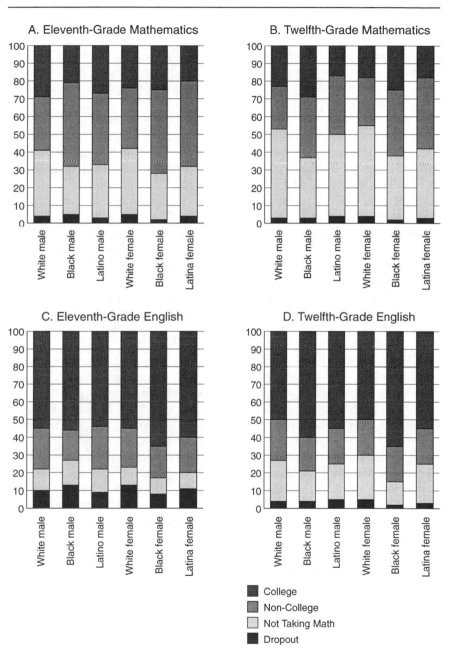

A. Eleventh-Grade Mathematics

B. Twelfth-Grade Mathematics

C. Eleventh-Grade English

D. Twelfth-Grade English

■ College
▨ Non-College
▢ Not Taking Math
■ Dropout

SUMMARY AND CONCLUSIONS

Like any study, the study of the process of obtaining high positions has embedded within it unstated commitments concerning what is important and what is not. Contrasting Hallinan's 1996 analysis of track mobility with other studies of track mobility revealed that Hallinan asked a subtly different question, and by doing so reached a dramatically different conclusion.

Unlike other analysts who found an association between origins and destinations, Hallinan investigated whether the direction of movement was associated with origins. However, pursuing this question will lead an analyst into all sorts of vexing statistical problems, because this question requires one to analyze what is in essence a mobility score. A mobility score necessarily includes information on the origin as well as the destination, and thus builds in a negative association between origins and outcomes.

The problem with using mobility scores as a dependent variable has long been known; over 30 years ago Blau and Duncan (1967, pp. 152–153, 194–199) provided a demonstration for the case of interval-level variables and noted that the problem is fundamentally the same in the categorical data case. However, in my search of the literature, I could not find a demonstration for the categorical data case, and therefore I addressed the question directly. The illustration of the differences between asking whether origins are associated with destinations and asking whether upward mobility is associated with origins revealed that the latter question is problematic for empirical investigation.

When secondary school track mobility in the United States is investigated by asking whether origins are associated with destinations, it appears that higher curricular origins are associated with higher curricular destinations. This finding appears to hold across all demographic groups analyzed, across both combinations of secondary school academic years studied, and regardless of what other explanatory variables are considered.

This finding should not be surprising. There are very good reasons to suspect that the Matthew Effect operates among students in schools just as it appears to operate in scientific fields (Long & McGinnis, 1981; Merton, 1968), and few reasons to expect the opposite. Despite the relatively lower number of upward mobility destinations for the well-placed student, students in higher curricular locations are likely to have not only more *real* opportunities to move up, but also more information about the requirements necessary for upward mobility, than their curricularly disadvantaged peers. Given the propensity to stop taking courses once requirements are fulfilled, one might theorize that if high track students satisfy graduation requirements earlier than others, they would tend to have higher chances of downward mobility. Yet, graduation requirements rarely focus on reaching a particular level of competence and, instead, call on students to spend a certain number of years studying (at any level) the subject. In such a system students that are high in the stratified curriculum and students that are low in the stratified curriculum tend to satisfy graduation requirements at about the same time; thus, graduation requirements do not provide a reason for expecting highly placed students to have greater chances of downward mobility than their less advantaged peers. Moreover, to the extent that earlier courses serve as prerequisites for later study, students who are lower in the hierarchy are more likely than are others to be unable to pursue advanced instruction on the basis of having failed to satisfy prerequisites. Thus, prerequisites may make upward mobility across some barriers exceedingly difficult.

Still, these differences in likelihood do not completely determine the destinations of students whose curricular origins might advantage them. Early analyses were consistent with an important role for requirements in maintaining student involvement in the core curriculum. As requirements are fulfilled, students, no matter how advantaged, may opt out of the sequence of academic courses. Much of the downward mobility from elite college math, shown in Chapter 5, may be explained by this process.

Moreover, social class, missing from the analysis of mobility patterns presented in Chapter 5, clearly plays an important role in students' attainments. Given that central social-psychological and cognitive covariates of social class—college aspirations and measured achievement—are controlled, the impact of social class most likely reflects the effects of greater parental knowledge, financial advantages, and explicit intervention. Thus, despite the revolution in school practice, wider societal inequality continues to advantage those of more means.

In addition, I found important racial, ethnic, and gender differences in the prospects for entering college preparatory courses, for staying in school, and for not taking academic courses. Many of these findings are consistent with other research that has shown a net black advantage in high school graduation (McNeal, 1995; Upchurch & McCarthy, 1990). Another way to convey this finding is to note that whites tend to need higher scores than do blacks on the latent destination variable in order to remain in school. Yet, prospects for entering high-level classes vary, sometimes advantaging whites, sometimes advantaging blacks.

Finally, when it comes to merit, the effects of individual-level factors on within-subject mobility are equivocal. Although placement is related to prior placement and achievement in the domain, social class still matters. The equivocal nature of the findings is not unanticipated. However, the pattern of findings can help us understand the desire of some critics to generalize their critique of broad-based tracking, common prior to 1975, into a larger critique of subject-specific curriculum differentiation. For the findings above imply that students' prospects under subject-specific curriculum differentiation resemble, in some important ways, their prospects under the old regime with its overarching programs.

However, once one considers the paradoxes of the decline of overarching programs, detailed in earlier chapters, the basis of some of the critics of de-tracking also becomes comprehensible. For the associations shown in this chapter provide insufficient evidence to abandon subject-specific curriculum differentiation; abandonment of the differentiated curriculum must be considered in light of the alternative that would take its place. Earlier chapters strongly suggest that the decline of overarching programs has not ushered in an egalitarian era of in-school stratification. Given that relatively little attention has been given to the likelihood of complex unintended and potentially negative consequences of de-tracking, skepticism as to the wisdom of de-tracking certainly is also a defensible posture.

To this point I have investigated both scope and mobility. I have found some important changes in the structure of scope and mobility, but some enduring features as well. Despite the change in school practice, those of modest means are disadvantaged in placements. Achievement in arguably less relevant domains still seems to matter. Track structures appear more rigid in schools with greater socioeconomic diversity. The incidence of mobility has increased, but the vast majority of mobility is downward. Yet, enough upward mobility occurs to support rejection of the tournament mobility metaphor. Even so, those who occupy the top of the curricular hierarchy early on are far more likely to remain there than others are to either join them or supplant them.

At this juncture this mix of apparent change and stability is intriguing. It is intriguing because one motivation for investigating scope and mobility was to determine whether differential socialization is as easy after the unremarked revolution as it appeared to be before. Although I have speculated throughout that these changes may matter for socialization, I have yet to provide a single bit of empirical evidence bearing on this point. In Chapter 7 I bring evidence to light to address this set of issues, a set of issues that has formed the unanalyzed backdrop to the entire study so far.

CHAPTER 7

Selected Effects of Curricular Location

So far I have proceeded under the assumption that the *structure* of the stratification system, coupled with persons' *location* in the stratification system, matters for their individual development and opportunities. Heretofore the analysis has focused on the structure of the system of stratification and the factors affecting persons' placement within it. The analysis of course taking has shown that the in-school system of stratification is more complex than prior to 1975, by which time a major change in school practice had occurred. Although I have speculated as to the implications the new structure may have for students' experience of school, I have not presented any evidence bearing on this point. This chapter provides just this kind of evidence. To close the investigation, I consider whether students' location in the complex stratified structure is associated with three important outcomes—interest in school, cognitive achievement, and college entry.

This analysis is essential to the investigation. The system of in-school stratification that existed prior to 1965 had been self-consciously theorized to socialize students for different futures (Finney, 1928). It is that system of curricular locations that analysts often have in mind when they observe that tracking facilitates differential socialization.

However, the changes in school practice appear to have altered the prior system of in-school stratification in a fashion that can only be called dramatic. Despite this striking change in course assignment practices, it is quite possible that differential socialization occurs just as some of the designers of tracking intended. I may find that the complex stratification structure has an impact on students' interest in school that looks very much like what the originators of previous in-school stratification systems planned. Or, as I anticipate, differential socialization may have become a neglected by-product of in-school stratification, perhaps so neglected that location in the in-school stratification system is no longer associated with socialization outcomes. The inertia of school organization may maintain quite different social relations at different levels of instruction, but because individual students move across the levels throughout the school day and throughout their school careers, this socialization may not be systematic.

These musings refer to some logical possibilities that may follow from apparent changes in the stratification system of the school. The existing literature on attitudes toward school provides a base for assessing whether the prior organization furthered or did not further differential socialization. For, although the organization for differential socialization was deliberate, its success was not ensured thereby. After considering this literature, it will be useful to assess the implications of the new in-school stratification system for socialization and, by extension, the stability of social systems.

IN-SCHOOL STRATIFICATION AND IN-SCHOOL SOCIALIZATION

Enduring Low-Track and High-Track Class Differences

Widespread evidence suggests that low-track classes have unsupportive climates, while high-track classes tend to have supportive climates (Page, 1990). Page's analysis of 1982–83 high school students documents, for the era under study here, the enduring difference between low-track and regular-track classes.

Page's analysis is revealing because she studied an award-winning, upper-middle-class school in a medium-sized midwestern city. Approximately 90% of students at pseudonymously named Southmoor High School are white. Page reports that the school "abolished" tracking in the 1960s, but immediately thereafter instituted advanced placement and special needs classes to serve top and handicapped students, respectively. Still, teachers, who virtually run the school, argued that some students were unable to keep up with the regular curriculum. To serve these students, an informal "additional needs" program was constructed. This program serves as the lower track at Southmoor.

Page documents several aspects that differentiate low-track classes from high-track classes. The repetitive nature of drill in Southmoor's low-track classes contrasts with the spontaneity and encouraged creativity in Southmoor's regular-track classes (Page, 1990). Also, Page points to and interprets the texts given students in low-track classes, which, even at Southmoor, are simplified versions of the texts used in regular-track classes (Page, 1990). Texts used in low-track classes provide lists that students are to memorize, rather than data that high-track students are to sift, synthesize, contrast, and/ or reject. Further, teachers encourage high-track students to question and probe and challenge both teacher and text; students in low-track classes who question the same teacher are viewed and treated by the teacher as insubordinate (Page, 1989).

These and many other differences between low-track and high-track classes cumulate to produce distinctly different experiences of school. Such differences may lead those in high-track classes to become committed to the institution, while leading those in low-track classes to become alienated from the institution.

Thus, Page (1989, 1990) documents the potentially alienating curriculum in Southmoor's lower track. Despite the resources that apparently are available, in the form of teachers with great and broad experience, students who are relatively better prepared than the average lower-track student, and more, Southmoor replicates, in its own idiosyncratic way, the underproduction of knowledge in lower-track classes.

Although different analysts offer different explanations for and evaluations of the differences between low-track and high-track classes, the differences that Page documents are similar to differences found at other times and in other places (Oakes, 1985; Willis, 1977).

Effects of Differences in Class Environments

Given these differences between classes in different tracks, some analysts have theorized that track location causes students to adopt proschool or antischool attitudes (Schafer & Olexa, 1971). Researchers have found that students in high tracks exhibit more interest in school, while low-track students are less interested (Kelly, 1976; Metz, 1978; Schwartz, 1981).

Wiatrowski, Hansell, Massey, and Wilson (1982) noted that early investigations of tracking and socialization, while suggestive, did not control for initial attitudes. Thus, early research was unable to determine whether students were placed in low tracks because of their antischool attitudes, or whether they developed antischool attitudes after track placement. Using longitudinal data that followed 1966 tenth graders for several years, Wiatrowski and colleagues were unable to show any effect of track placement on students' attachment to school in Grade 12.

One limitation of Wiatrowski and colleagues' analysis is that it did not control for dropping out. Students that drop out of school may have had strong antischool attitudes and may be more likely to come from the lower tracks. Thus, if dropouts are omitted from the analysis, one may understate the gap in interest in school between students in the different tracks. Berends (1994) investigated whether students' self-reports of their track location were associated with their attitudes toward school. He found that attitudes were more positive for students who perceived themselves to be in higher tracks, once propensity to drop out is controlled. Yet, the association was small.

If the studies above actually pertain to the old regime, the differences in findings leave some doubt as to whether tracking worked to socialize students differently prior to the decline of overarching programs. However, whether all the studies apply to the old regime is not clear. Schaefer and Olexa studied a cohort who entered tenth grade in 1961, presumably prior to the decline of formal programs. Yet, because the vast change in school practice occurred during a 10-year period (1965–1975) at different rates in different locales, it is unclear whether other studies captured students exposed to the old regime or the more recent one. For example, Metz studied one ninth-grade school in 1967 and two seventh–eighth-grade schools in 1967–68; Kelly studied 1973 juniors and seniors; and the timing of Schwartz's study is unclear. Thus, one possible explanation for the varying findings across studies is that some of the studies may reflect the experience of students exposed to the regime characterized by overarching programs, while others may reflect the experience of students in schools without formal programs.

Hence, because much of the existing research on the role of tracking in creating proschool and antischool attitudes pertains to students embedded in track systems whose characteristics are unknown, and because the findings from the research on earlier cohorts is contradictory, the role of tracking in differentially socializing students prior to the decline of formal programs remains equivocal. However, research on cohorts who entered secondary school *after* the change in school practice, illustrated by Berends, has shown that an indicator of tracking is associated with socialization outcomes.

Berends uses the same data set used here. Thus, one can wonder, why address the question anew? One reason to address the question is that the questions are different. Berends considered the proximal factor that should be related to students' school attitudes, namely, their understanding of the program they are following. Students' attitudes about their courses of study are important. Yet, many discussants in the debate about the socializing role of tracking viewed track location as a set of structural positions. Given this perhaps implicit interest in structural positions, it is important to consider whether the structural positions are systematically related to students' socialization. Prior to considering this question, a brief discussion of social-psychological and structural dimensions of track location is in order.

Social-Psychological and Structural Placement in the Curriculum

As I make the transition from studying tracking as a structure to studying tracking as a determinant of other outcomes, it is important to recall the distinction, briefly mentioned in Chapter 1, between social-psychological and structural track location. Throughout the analysis, I have endeavored to investigate students' structural location in the curriculum, not their social-psychological track identification. The distinction between social-psychological placement and structural placement in the school is analogous to the distinction between social class identification and social class location in the world of adults. Jackman and Jackman (1983) argue that social class identification is an important dimension of class in America. This dimension is related to material factors such as occupational location and capital ownership, but cannot be reduced to material factors alone. As Jackman and Jackman write:

> While socioeconomic distinctions provide the basis for class identification, it is also clear that class incorporates more than this. When asked what factors define class membership, most people name cultural factors, such as life-style and beliefs and feelings, as well as socioeconomic factors. When they assemble these various criteria to define their class, people do not always assign the same weights to each one, and those weights provide the implicit guidelines they employ in formulating their own class identification. (p. 217)

Jackman and Jackman investigated the makeup of social class identity and demonstrated the importance of identity. Considering social class identity adds to analysts' understanding not only of many outcomes, such as propensity to vote and party preference, but also of the process by which these outcomes come to be. However, as the final sentence in the quotation above suggests, social class identity is not reducible to material factors alone, and material resources also matter. In the same vein, and returning to the distinction between social-psychological and structural track location, one may view students' structural position in the educational hierarchy as one important dimension, and students' understandings of their place in the hierarchy as another important dimension. These dimensions are related but neither is reducible to the other.

One can find this distinction in the tracking literature, as many analysts have begun to interpret the self-report of track location as a measure of social-psychological track location (Gamoran, 1987; Rosenbaum, 1980). As I noted in Chapter 1, using the self-report in this way is to take seriously the Thomas and Thomas (1928) dictum that "if persons define situations as real they are real in their consequences" (p. 572).

Yet, relatively few have claimed that analysts should confine research attention to persons' definitions of their situations alone. By analogy, just as one would not limit oneself to the study of social class identity if one wanted to understand social class in America, one also need not confine oneself to the study of social-psychological track location. Instead, as I remarked in Chapter 1, it is important to follow through on an important corollary to the Thomases' maxim: Only misunderstanding can result when what is real in its consequences is taken to be real as such.

Social-psychological curricular location—captured in many research efforts by students' self-report of their programs—reflects students' attitudes about whatever courses of study they are engaged in. Surely this is important. The important corollary implies, however, that analysts can never develop a full understanding of the effects of courses of study if analysts limit research attention to student attitudes about their courses of study, just as one cannot develop a full understanding of inequality in America if one is forced to consider either the subjective or the material dimension of social class but not both.

Moreover, given the complexity of in-school stratification that the foregoing chapters have shown, and given specifically that the college/non-college distinction does not best characterize the structure of students' course taking, it is just as much a mistake to attempt to adjudicate students' claims to college track placement by using their course taking as a criterion as it is to attempt to adjudicate adults' claims to middle-class status by using their occupational positions as a criterion. One can be certain that there is slippage across the structural and social-psychological dimensions, and one can be certain that much of this slippage is not "error." Analysts need accept both structural and social-psychological dimensions as potentially important.

A major part of the debate about socialization concerned the way in which students react to explicit in-school stratification. Yet, the positions are no longer explicit. Berends (1994) has already shown that despite the decline of formal overarching programs, students' understandings of their programs matter, albeit to a small degree. The question I take up here is whether the complex *structural* positions are associated with students' interest in school, now that overarching programs have been largely dismantled.

Socialization and the Transformed Structure of Tracking

Many theorists expect student attitudes to flow from the disparate environments students in different programs encounter. And, indeed, investigation of low-track and high-track classes has shown differences between the environments in these classes, although, as Oakes (1985) suggests, the climate differences often are overstated. To the extent differences exist, and to the extent that track structure is as originally designed, the expectation that students will be socialized differently is plausible.

However, previous chapters have suggested that tracking has changed. This change has profound implications for the process of socialization in schools. Analysts have documented, and continue to document, important differences in instructional strategies, teacher attitudes, and student experience in low-track and high-track *classes*. What the present analysis has shown, however, is that a student in a low-track class in one subject may be in a high-track class in another subject; indeed, Chapter 2 showed that the majority of students take discrepant levels of math and English. Also, Chapter 5 showed a high incidence of mobility over academic years. Thus, while sitting in a low-track class, a student likely experiences the environment researchers have shown to exist in low-level classes. Yet, while sitting in a high-track class, during what easily could be the very next class period, the student is just as likely to experience the environment researchers have shown to exist in high-level classes. And, as the previous chapters have shown, most students will experience a mix of low-track and high-track classes.

Thus, even if low-level and high-level classes differ markedly and systematically, as researchers have documented, the change in school practice has problematized the comparison of low-track and high-track classes. If one hopes to compare these polar opposites in order to document the possible range of students' experience, then the comparison is valid. But if one hopes to compare low- and high-track classes to describe the disparate experience of two dominant types of students, the strategy fails. The strategy fails at this task because, if the latter is the aim, the comparison requires a consistency of exposure to one socialization "treatment," which the evidence does not bear out. If every student were in equivalent locations across subjects, then the climate in the low-level and high-level classes would reflect the distinctly different climates that two dominant groups of students experienced. Or, if mobility were nonexistent, then consideration of students' locations at one point in time would completely summarize their socialization experience. Yet, the results show that neither is true—students are in discrepant locations at one point in time, and many experience (most often downward) mobility over time. As a majority of students experience divergent locations, one cannot infer student experience from the characterization of the climate in low-level or high-level classrooms.

The high incidence of discrepant course taking is a profound structural change with potentially significant implications. When persons occupy structural locations that expose them to discrepant and perhaps even contradictory socialization, it is quite likely that the socialization that does occur will not vary systematically with the structural locations they occupy. Thus, the change in the structure of tracking, ushered in by the decline of formal programs, makes it quite possible that I will find that track location has no systematic association with interest in school.

If I find no association between track location and interest in school, then it is fair to say that tracking no longer serves to systematically differentially socialize students. Given the changes in structure documented in the previous chapters, I anticipate that track location will *not* have a major bearing on students' interest in school.

THEORETICAL PLACE OF INTEREST IN SCHOOL

This analysis requires a measure of student socialization. I use whether the student is interested in school as a proxy for whether students have been socialized differently. Ideally, I would use direct measures of socialization and alienation. Unfortunately, there is no consensus as to what measure to use for this research area. Kelly (1976) used several measures, including students' grade point average, college plans, extracurricular activities, job aspirations, and attitude toward school (measured by the question, "Do you like school?"). Wiatrowski and colleagues (1982) used an attachment to school scale composed of three dimensions: (1) positive attitudes toward school; (2) negative attitudes toward school; and (3) academic achievement. Each of these three dimensions is measured by several questions. The positive attitude index comprises 15 items, including four that ask students whether they enjoy school for various reasons. The negative attitude index is composed of eight questions, including two asking whether students are bored by school and whether they feel school is a waste of time (Bachman, 1975).

Berends (1994) also constructed factors to tap students' attitudes toward school. His factors measure college expectations, absenteeism, disciplinary problems, and engagement. The two items in Berends's engagement scale are "interest in school" and the amount of homework the student reported doing.

As these examples suggest, there is no consensus on how to measure students' attitudes toward school. However, interest in school is a useful outcome for several reasons. First, interest in school is theoretically interesting in and of itself. Any of the graphic comparisons between low-track and high-track classes provides good reason to suspect that students in a low-track class might be less likely to be interested in school than their counterparts in a high-track class. If some structural positions are more likely to lead to a withdrawal of interest, this is by itself an important fact to learn.

Moreover, interest in school is related to any measure of alienation one might devise, and many theories argue that school alienates those students who occupy disadvantageous positions in the institution (Bowles & Gintis, 1976). The different ways in which instruction is organized in the different levels of courses limit the opportunity of those at the bottom to experience the sheer pleasure of work, and increase the chance for those at the top to do so. Courses at the bottom are characterized, much as Finney (1928) suggested, by rote learning and memorization of disconnected facts (Oakes, 1985). Courses at the top of the hierarchy delve into the why of matters and are far more likely to provide space for individuals' creativity and to reward creative initiative. For those in the lower-level classes, the expectation that work can be an intrinsically rewarding activity is likely to fall; for those in the higher-level classes, the expectation that work can be intrinsically rewarding is likely to rise. Reasoning that persons who are alienated from an activity should report less interest in the particular activity, I expect that students who are alienated from the institution will report that they are not interested in school. If so, interest in school can serve as an indicator of whether or not a student has become alienated from the school.

Finally, interest in school is a dependent variable, or part of a dependent variable, in many analyses of students' attachment to school. Thus, using interest in school as a dependent variable is to link this study, at the conceptual level, to existing research on attitudes toward school.

For these reasons I use interest in school as a dependent variable. If tracking socializes students systematically and differently, then one would expect students in lower tracks to be disinterested in school, and students in the higher tracks to be interested in school.

IN-SCHOOL STRATIFICATION, COGNITIVE ACHIEVEMENT, AND COLLEGE ENTRY

Differential socialization was only one of the self-conscious goals of the previous tracking regime. Two other goals were cognitive achievement and the rationing of college access.

Interest in effects of track location on cognitive achievement increased after publication of the Coleman Report. Coleman's finding, that school differences explained little of the variance in achievement, sparked renewed interest in the stratification system inside schools, which resulted in the agenda of track effects research.

Two consistent findings from this line of research are that track location is positively associated with achievement (Gamoran, 1987; Gamoran & Mare, 1989; Jencks & Brown, 1975; Kerckhoff, 1986; Lucas & Gamoran, 1991) and with college entry (Hauser, Sewell, & Alwin, 1976). With respect to achievement, tracking, and courses, Gamoran's 1987 investigation is particularly illuminating. He used both students' self-report of track location and measures of their course taking. He reported that the effects of the self-report were reduced when courses were included in the model. Moreover, the association between courses and achievement was statistically significant.

Given Gamoran's finding, it is very likely that the complex track structure is associated with cognitive achievement, and as courses affect cognitive achievement, so too may courses have at least indirect effects on college entry. Indeed, no theory suggests that course taking will be irrelevant to measured achievement. Because overarching tracks may have systematically prevented students who were poor in one subject but adept in the other from obtaining instruction in the subject in which they excelled, overarching tracks may have heightened the distinction between students at the top and those at the bottom. But even in the absence of overarching tracks, one would expect measured achievement to be associated with students' placements. As achievement is consistently related to college entry, it is likely that track location matters for college entry as well.

Why, then, present findings here on achievement and college entry? One reason is that tracking *has* changed. While the reasoning above is plausible, the only way to confirm it is to inspect the findings. Second, I anticipate that there will be no systematic effect of track location on socialization. One way to explain a "no-effect" finding is to note that track location has become more complex and therefore students are exposed to discrepant and potentially contradictory locations. An alternative explanation for a "no-effect" finding is that track location was poorly measured. However, if track location *is* poorly measured, then the effect of track location on other outcomes *also* should be greatly reduced, perhaps even to zero. Thus, the analysis of cognitive achievement and college entry serves to check both the reasoning—that courses matter for some outcomes in and of themselves even without the existence of formal programs—and the analysis of differential socialization.

METHOD OF INVESTIGATION

To determine whether the more complex curriculum structure is associated with students' interest in school, cognitive achievement, and college entry, I regress these dependent variables on different sets of explanatory variables. Both interest in school and college entry are dichotomous variables, so I use logistic regression techniques; I use ordinary least squares (OLS) regression for the two measures of cognitive achievement, twelfth-grade math achievement and twelfth-grade English achievement.

For each outcome, I estimate a simple baseline model that does not include track location. The baseline model for interest in school is essentially the model Berends (1994) uses. The only difference is that I include a control for prior interest in school but omit controls for other attitudinal variables. However, if their omission has any effect, it is likely to bias results in favor of finding systematic effects of track location. The baseline for the other outcomes contains many factors that analysts have found to be important for achievement and college entry. (See Appendix C for the covariates in the baseline models.)

After estimating the baseline model, I estimate models that include different variants of track location. Given that students' track locations are now quite complex, it is unclear just what the most relevant distinction is for any given outcome. Thus, I estimate five different models, each using a different variant of track location. This approach increases the chance that I will find an effect of track location if one does exist. Appendix C contains exact descriptions for the variants of track location used, but the major point here is that if any one of the track location models fits better than the baseline model, then track effects play a role in the outcome of interest.

Thus, after estimating the baseline and track location models, I compare the models using the BIC* statistic. If the BIC* statistic is better for the baseline model, then I infer that the various versions of track location do not add much to the explanation of the dependent variable. (The BIC* statistic, unlike R^2 but like the sequential F-test for multiple regression, is appropriate for comparing models in this way.)

This analysis focuses on the overall fit of the model rather than the specific coefficients from the model. This focus follows from two factors. First, many analysts have argued that tracking regimes socialize students in a profound way, and have erected a critique of tracking on this basis. If these analysts are correct, one should find that track location is essential to any understanding of students' interest in school. One direct way to discern whether this is so is to consider whether the fit of the model improves with the inclusion of track location.

Second, formerly analysts often compared low-track and high-track students to determine whether they differed in their level of interest in school. However, the very reason for conducting this analysis is that one cannot compare low-track and high-track students, because a simple dichotomy no longer accurately describes students' course taking. Instead, the particular places in the curriculum are more complex than they were in the past. Yet, there is no theory that posits how systematic differences in socialization would be arranged across such a complex set of places. Thus, it is problematic to focus on coefficients that compare the students who occupy the different places, because one might be unable to differentiate between a pattern of results that supported the thesis of differential socialization and one that did not. Instead, one can discern whether tracking seems to be associated with outcomes by determining whether the model improves, or does not improve, once track location is included.

The central analysis of this chapter is the investigation of the determinants of interest in school. I also investigate measured achievement in twelfth grade as well as college entry. This will allow determination of whether a failure to explain interest in school is based on some problem with the measures of track location, as well as whether structural track location is associated with these important outcomes. Thus, the analysis begins with investigation of measured achievement and college entry.

RESULTS: CORRELATES OF INTEREST

It is quite likely that outcomes such as achievement and college entry are associated with structural track location. Table 7.1 contains the BIC* statistics for models explaining senior-year achievement in math and senior-year achievement in English.

For each area of achievement, all but one of the variants of track location produces a better explanation than does the baseline model. However, the best model for mathematics achievement is a model of track placement, whereas the best model for English achievement is the model that contrasts students in consistent locations for math and English with students in inconsistent locations for math and English. This implies that in the new environment investigation of the role of track location in producing achievement must be sensitive to the domain in which achievement occurs; the distinctions that matter most for math achievement are not the same as the distinctions that matter most for English achievement.

For English achievement, students who occupy consistent locations for math and English score higher than students in discrepant positions. For math achievement, students enrolled in college preparatory math score much higher than students enrolled in non-college prep mathematics, and the latter

Table 7.1. Fit Statistics for Ordinary Least Squares Regression of Twelfth-Grade Measured Achievement

Model	MATHEMATICS			ENGLISH		
	R^2	p_k	BIC	R^2	p_k	BIC
Tracking Ignored	0.631	11	−3651.05	0.646	11	−3787.13
Track Placement	0.689	28	−4152.91	0.666	28	−3864.45
Consistent Locations	0.672	17	−4043.71	0.661	17	−3899.44
Consistent vs. Inconsistent	0.649	13	−3822.28	0.681	13	−4159.41
Degree of Discrepancy	0.644	21	−3703.35	0.681	21	−4093.60
Track Mobility	0.693	100	−3608.91	0.681	100	−3443.81
Effective *n*		3753			3734	

also appear to score somewhat higher than students who do not take math (see Appendix C for the model results). Taken together, these results indicate that track location matters for measured achievement. This finding is not unanticipated.

Table 7.2 contains the BIC* statistics for models of college entry. Three of the five specifications of track location provide a better explanation of college entry than does the model without track location. The best model of college entry highlights consistent locations. It appears that students who enroll in college prep courses for both math and English in either Grade 11 or Grade 12 are more likely to enter college than students who follow a discrepant course-taking pattern. Students who take neither math nor English in Grade 12 have lower chances of college entry than students taking discrepant course patterns. But students who take non-college prep math and non-college prep English are no more or less likely to enter college than students who take discrepant courses in math and English (see Appendix C, Table C.3).

Thus, in all three cases—mathematics achievement, English achievement, and college entry—the addition of track location improves the explanation. Thus, even though the in-school stratification system has become more complex, students' location in the complex structure is still associated with important cognitive and stratification outcomes.

Turning to interest in school, my expectation is that systematic socialization for different futures does not occur in the new environment. I posit that students are not led to like or dislike school on the basis of track location, because students occupy discrepant and potentially contradictory course locations in the in-school stratification system. Thus, students are not exposed to consistent socialization. If this reasoning is true, adding track location will not improve the fit of the model of interest in school.

Table 7.2. Fit Statistics for Logit Models of Four-Year College Entry (effective $n = 3,014$)

Model	L^2	p_k	BIC*
Tracking Ignored	−1474.72	13	−811.71
Track Placement	−1383.74	29	−865.48
Consistent Locations	−1391.19	19	−930.68
Consistent vs. Inconsistent	−1440.91	15	−863.29
Degree of Discrepancy	−1463.52	23	−753.98
Track Mobility	−1385.22	93	−349.81

Table 7.3 presents the summary statistics from six models predicting whether students are interested in school. None of the models has a negative BIC* statistic, as even the baseline model has a positive BIC* statistic. Thus, by the BIC* criterion, even the baseline model does not appear to provide a good explanation for interest in school. Notably, the poor explanatory power of the baseline model is evident even though interest in school in Grade 10 is included as an explanatory variable.

When important variables are omitted from a baseline model, that leaves more room for any added variables to improve the fit of the model. Thus, the poor fit of the baseline model for interest in school increases the opportunity for track location to improve the fit of the model. However, track location does not improve the fit of the model, as the model without track location has the lowest BIC* statistic. This means that if one ignores track location, variously specified, one will have a better model than if one does not ignore it. Substantively, the result suggests that the structure of places in the curriculum is so complex, and students' movements through those places are so varied, that systematic differential socialization does not seem to be occurring. Thus, whether students are or are not interested in school—which serves as a proxy for whether students are or are not alienated from the school—does not appear to be systematically related to their locations in the curriculum.

CONCLUSION

Students in different structural locations still exhibit differences in cognitive achievement and college entry. These differences are important, in several ways. The effect of track location on college entry means that track location

Table 7.3. Fit Statistics for Logit Models of Interest in School in Twelfth-Grade (effective $n = 3,014$)

Model	L^2	p_k	BIC*
Tracking Ignored	−522.86	13	9.87
Track Placement	−509.38	29	110.94
Consistent Locations	−514.06	19	40.32
Consistent vs. Inconsistent	−519.31	15	18.78
Degree of Discrepancy	−518.96	23	82.18
Track Mobility	−502.36	93	609.75

likely continues to have effects on educational attainment. Thus, this analysis echoes others' work in finding direct effects of track location on college entry even when achievement is controlled; hence, one can be confident that in-school stratification matters beyond the high school years.

Track location also has effects on cognitive achievement. Cognitive achievement has a direct impact on individual students' lives, determining their personal resources in a deep and abiding way. Any factor that affects achievement must be important.

But track differences in measured achievement have other important implications. Achievement is an important direct determinant of matriculation to college. If track location determines achievement, then in addition to the direct effect on college entry, track location also has indirect effects on college entry.

Equally important are the indirect effects of achievement. Success in school is likely to raise a student's standing in the eyes of teachers. As teachers have important gate-keeping functions, especially for movement to elite postsecondary institutions (e.g., writing recommendation letters, advising), impressing teachers is an important part of students' educational careers. Tracking affects the opportunities students have to make positive impressions.

Differences in achievement associated with track location have still another and, one may surmise, more important implication. One of the surest ways of confirming the legitimacy of a system that, although hidden, continues to stratify students is for teachers, other school personnel, and well-connected parents to see students in different locations in the curriculum go on to achieve at different levels. Thus, the achievement differences that are themselves the *result* of differential placement may serve to maintain the system of in-school stratification, just as a self-fulfilling prophecy can, in some cases, authenticate the wisdom and knowledge of the one who pronounces it.

Even as I find effects of track location on achievement and college entry, socialization does not seem to be closely tied to students' structural locations, broadly considered. I hasten to add that I am *not* claiming that discrepant course locations do not matter. Even though students are in discrepant course locations, an association between placement and achievement is apparent. However, I find no systematic effects of track location on interest in school, a socialization outcome.

Of course, it must be noted that owing to a lack of consensus on how to measure socialization outcomes, this finding is suggestive. It is based on students' answers to one (albeit important) survey question. Thus, my conclusion must remain provisional at this point.

However, while taking the provisionality of my finding to heart, one can still identify mechanisms that would make the socialization effects of course locations weak. For one, with the decline of formal programs, students are much freer to design their own programs than before (although still not free enough to overturn persistent socioeconomic- and achievement-related inequities). Thus, if a student cannot tolerate a particular level of course, she or he is freer to change levels. For some that eventually may mean not taking math or English. This process of sorting means that if students do not like some aspect of their place in the stratification system, they can change it (within limits). In this environment, one should not be surprised to find no systematic effects of socialization. However, this is not to say that discrepant course locations do not matter. Quite the contrary, it is exactly because course locations are discrepant, and because processes of course assignment do not completely check the discrepancy-creating forces, that I obtain the result that I do. Thus, discrepant course taking matters very much when it comes to understanding how tracking does not work to socialize students differentially in the current regime.

The implications of this apparently new situation for the maintenance or transformation of the larger stratification order are potentially profound. But assessing those implications in detail calls for analysis of another important institution in the lives of Americans—the economy. As analysis of the economy is beyond the scope of this research, this investigation has reached its end.

At this point the thrust of the implications of the unremarked revolution may be summarized briefly. The unprecedented change in school practice subtly but profoundly altered the structures within which students experience school, and in this way also may have transformed the sum total of their school experiences. Given the character of these structural changes and socialization outcomes, the unremarked revolution has major ramifications for how to understand and investigate the nexus between education and other institutions of society.

CHAPTER 8

After the Unremarked Revolution: Summary and Conclusions

Between 1965 and 1975 the vast majority of American secondary schools dismantled the procedures for assigning students to overarching curricular programs that determined students' courses for the duration of their high school years. On its face this change appears revolutionary. It ushered in an era in which students could enroll in discrepant levels of courses for different subjects. It made mobility possible. It allowed students to transcend low achievement in one domain by seeking demanding instruction in other subjects.

Despite the plethora of opportunities created by these changes, the change in school practice I have called the unremarked revolution appears to have failed. That is not to say that the previous regime is in some sense preferable. It is to say, however, that students now encounter a more hidden in-school stratification system. The implications of that system for students are profound.

KEY FINDINGS

Egalitarian and Meritocratic Placement

For one, the potential for students to pursue study based on their achievements in the domain of the subject appears dashed, as mathematics achievement is more important for English placements than is English achievement. This is true even when other factors, such as aspirations and graduation requirements, are controlled.

Moreover, social class effects continue. Students from advantaged family backgrounds reap advantages in placement, even after many of the widely accepted mechanisms through which social class might convey advantage (e.g., aspirations, prior achievement) and many of the widely unaccepted but clearly associated factors (e.g., race, ethnicity) are controlled. One may, of course, propose additional statistical explanations for this pattern of effects, including the classic explanation of omitted variable bias. There is no ironclad defense against this criticism because it is *always* possible to note that something has been left out of the model or explanation. Still, the most plausible explanation for the pattern of results is the proactive behavior of middle-class parents.

This interpretation squares with ethnographic research showing that middle-class parents intervene to obtain advantageous positions for their children, even against the advice of school personnel. This interpretation is also consistent with the research here showing that schools with greater socioeconomic diversity have more pronounced tracking regimes, an outcome compatible with Oakes's claim that middle-class parents are the protectors of the existing in-school stratification system. It is quite unlikely that middle-class parents would work to maintain a stratification regime for all students, yet sit on their hands while their own child was placed at a low level in that stratification system.

The likely activity of middle-class parents gives meaning to the claim that knowledge is power, for it is knowledge (or information) that makes their activity both strategic and effective. Ironically, the dismantling of formal programs has probably *increased* the information gap between the haves and have-nots. Research shows that middle-class parents are more likely to have access to the networks necessary to obtain information relevant to the placement of their child, such as evaluations of teachers and courses. Moreover, setting aside networks, middle-class parents have a key individual resource that lower-class parents tend to lack—college experience. Those of lower social class are less likely to have attended college, and even if they did attend college, are less likely to have attended 4-year college, and even if they did attend 4-year college, are less likely to have attended an elite institution. Thus, their understanding of what is required for college entry is likely to be either nonexistent or woefully inadequate in comparison to the information to which children of advantage have access. True, the decline of overarching programs increased the nominal access to classes for all students. Yet, the dismantling of overarching programs removed clear markers through the curriculum, markers that the middle class did not need the school to supply for they have their own sources to tell them what courses are necessary and useful. Socioeconomically disadvantaged students tend not to have this information. Hence, disproportionate access to information seems to have played a major role in transforming a potentially egalitarian reform into an inegalitarian one. When it comes to class advantage, the major outlines of placement after the unremarked revolution lend truth to the claim that *plus ça change, plus c'est la même chose.*

Structure of In-School Stratification

Profound changes did, however, occur in the structure of tracking. These changes appear consequential. After the unremarked revolution, students were more likely to take discrepant courses than before. Indeed, the vast majority of students are in discrepant courses. Moreover, the patterns of mobility indicate that students will occupy different levels over time.

The increased tendency for students to take discrepant courses at one point in time and over time greatly complicates socialization. Indeed, the findings suggest that track location is not systematically associated with a socialization outcome. Yet, evidence indicates that track location, variously defined, is still an important determinant of cognitive achievement. How, then, may one understand the lack of socialization effects?

One undeniable possibility is that the measure of socialization used is a poor one. Given the available data and the lack of consensus on how to measure socialization in school, the analysis can only be suggestive at this juncture. Clearly, more research along these lines is to be encouraged.

However, if one accepts the finding as provisionally sound at this point, another more substantive way to understand the lack of socialization effects is to start from the premise that different levels of courses likely will utilize different methods of instruction, be imbued with different social relations, and have different implications for cognitive achievement. Ethnographic evidence supports the veracity of this claim. In this environment the prevalent pattern of mobility means that many students in lower-level classes will be exposed to the social relations within higher-level classes and the social relations within lower-level classes in the same subject, while the prevalence of discrepant course taking means that at one point in time the student may occupy discordant courses in different subjects. The simultaneous placement in different levels will work against *any* level socializing students for different places in the adult system of stratification. Thus, systematic differential socialization will not occur even though instructional strategies and socialization aims vary systematically by course level. Accordingly, the change in school practice may have greatly diminished the ability of tracking to systematically socialize students differently, even as *de facto* tracking continues.

IN-SCHOOL STRATIFICATION AND SOCIOLOGICAL THEORY

The stratification order is at the heart of much sociological theory, and an understanding of the role of educational systems in maintaining the stratification order is indispensable for any theory of social stratification. The findings noted above suggest that major transformations have occurred in the way in which tracking works. Therefore, these transformations, together with the enduring aspects of in-school stratification, have potentially important implications both for an understanding of schools and for an understanding of the maintenance of society.

Conduits for Track Effects

Analysts have identified three possible mechanisms—instructional, social, and institutional—through which track effects might be produced. Theoretically, instructional effects occur because higher tracks cover more content than lower tracks (Gamoran, 1989). Social effects are thought to occur because tracks provide a social context within which students develop an understanding of themselves and their capabilities; because tracks offer systematically different instruction, tracking serves to socialize students in systematically different ways. Institutional effects are thought to occur because tracking is a persistent organizational school form and placements are stable (at least in secondary schools) and public (at least in elementary schools) (Pallas, Entwistle, Alexander, & Stluka, 1994).

These theories of how tracking might produce its effects depend in large part on a particular understanding of how tracking was arranged in schools. Prior to 1965, schools followed procedures that divided students into explicit mutually exclusive groups. After 1975, this practice was far less common. This change has implications for the conduits through which track effects come to be.

It is likely that instructional effects continue even though formal programs have been dismantled. Calculus still offers a systematically different type of instruction than does arithmetic; the same may be said for advanced placement English in comparison to a course called spelling (Page, 1990). Consistent with this claim, I find an effect of placement on measured achievement.

The presence of social effects remains unclear at this point. Still, I find no systematic association between students' structural location in the school and their interest in school. The research on track effects on student attitudes has yet to settle the issue; the finding here does not settle it either, but it does suggest that perhaps the answer is to be found in the joint consideration of social-psychological and structural track location. Further research on that possibility is to be encouraged.

While the implications of the findings for the existence of social effects of tracking are equivocal, institutional effects of *de facto* tracking appear less likely given changes in the tracking system. The evidence reported here suggests that of the three factors that facilitated institutional effects of tracking, not one still describes the track system of secondary schools (although they may still apply to middle and elementary schools). First, *formal* programs have been dismantled, and therefore the organizational form no longer persists at the secondary level. Second, placements in the differentiated curriculum are not stable, as approximately 50% of students move from year to year. And third, as formal programs have been dismantled, placements are neither necessarily public nor easily assessed to the extent that they are public. Thus, the likelihood of finding institutional effects of track location among secondary school students would seem to be low.

Differential Socialization and Consciousness

These changes in how schools work may mean several additional things. First, they may mean that *differential* socialization is not key to the maintenance of inequality, but *common* socialization is. Common socialization could mute social protest by, for example, teaching all students that high-stakes competition is the appropriate way to allocate rewards. In this account, rather than serving to socialize students differently, tracking becomes one of the arenas within which high-stakes rewards are offered.

While common socialization may be important for legitimating the status quo, and while aspects of the school may accomplish this aim, this particular role for in-school stratification is unlikely. In order for track location to serve this role, tracking would need to be a salient conceptual category for students. That is, students would need to consistently organize their thinking about school in terms of track location. The evidence presented here, particularly the evidence showing that the college/non-college dichotomy does not make sense of student placements, is inconsistent with the claim that track location serves as an organizing principle in students' minds. Instead, students seem to organize their course taking around the only information to which they all have access—graduation requirements. Given this fact, it is unlikely that tracking serves to provide common socialization to students.

So, outside of allocating students to more instruction, what does the structure of *de facto* tracking do? A digression into analytic Marxism is illuminating here. A continuing problem in Marxist sociology concerns how to define class. Post-World War II economic transformations provided even more reason to doubt the veracity of Marx's division of persons into two dominant warring classes of capitalist and proletariat. Some analysts maintain that the burgeoning division of labor simply masked deep cleavages that map identifiable groups directly onto Marx's dichotomy (Freedman, 1975). These analysts attempt to suppress the problem posed by the growth of structural places by denying that the structural places are different in any important respect from the places in the dichotomous typology.

Wright (1985), however, proposed that more than two structural positions existed and, moreover, that the persons occupying the positions actually were situated in contradictory locations within class relations. The contradictoriness of positions arises because classical capitalists have authority over both workers and capital. However, managers, who are employees, have authority over workers but lack large accumulations of capital. And owners of very small shops have capital but no workers and thus lack relations of authority over personnel. Therefore, self-employed persons who supervise no one, and employee managers both occupy contradictory positions. Managers have authority but not (necessarily) capital ownership; self-employed persons have capital ownership but not (necessarily) authority. Reflecting on the development of the concept of contradictory locations in class relations, Wright (1985) remarks:

> In the first presentations of the research we referred to such . . . positions as having an "ambiguous" class character, neither fish nor fowl. In a seminar discussion of the conceptual framework, the suggestion was made that this was not quite precise: such positions were really *both* fish and fowl, and therefore they should be seen as internally contradictory rather than ambiguous.
>   That shift in labels—from ambiguous locations to contradictory locations—was the crucial step in the development of the new concept. "Ambiguity" suggests that the problem is taxonomic: some people don't fit the slots properly; "contradictoriness," on the other hand, suggests that the slots themselves have a complex character that can be identified as internally contradictory and given a positive theoretical status. (pp. 44–45; emphasis in original)

The development of the concept of contradictory class locations allowed Wright to address another continuing challenge for Marxist thought, namely, the relatively low level of class consciousness in many nation-states, most notably the United States. Wright's use of the concept of contradictory class locations to study the correlates of class consciousness can be interpreted as a way to demonstrate that class in itself (i.e., class defined as objective relations to production) exists in America, while allowing analysts to understand the social dynamics that may check the rise of class consciousness and thereby prevent the formation of class for itself (i.e., class defined as organized self-interested entities) at a particular place and time. The important point here, however, is that persons who occupy contradictory class locations greatly complicate any easy expectation of the formation of class consciousness and the realization of the inherently political nature of economic relations.

My finding of discrepant course taking is structurally similar to some aspects of Wright's claim. It should be noted that the finding also has affinities with Lenski's (1954) concept of status crystallization, in that I focus on those in discrepant positions. Wright and Lenski differ in their understanding of the implications of occupying discrepant locations. Lenski posited that those in discordant positions may experience stress owing to the contradiction and that this stress might make persons in discordant positions more likely to support social change. Wright makes no such prediction concerning the attitude of those who occupy discordant positions, for the attitude and strategy that those in discordant positions adopt are contingent on the options available, the perceived options, and the wider political environment.

Thus, where Lenski implies that those who occupy discordant positions will be more sensitized to the possibly oppressive hierarchies in which they are embedded, Wright's perspective is consistent with the view that discordant positions actually may check the development of consciousness of the hierarchy under certain conditions.

Surely, which of these two possibilities occurs, or whether some other possibility occurs, may turn on what dimensions the contradiction concerns. Yet, for the substantive area under consideration here, the findings suggest that discrepant positions seem to occur in concert with noneffects of track location on socialization. Thus, it appears that tracking has more in common with Wright's contradictory class locations than with Lenski's concept of status crystallization. The prevalence of discrepant course taking gives rise to the possibility that the in-school stratification system may be characterized by the educational equivalent of contradictory class locations, or, in other words, contradictory course locations.

The emergence of contradictory course locations and their rise to prominence provide one way to understand how systematic socialization through tracking of the old stripe may not be occurring, even as institutional inertia ensures that low-level and high-level classes continue to follow disparate instructional strategies. It should be noted, however, that given the change in track structure, some entirely new kind of socialization may be occurring. If so, further research and additional theorizing will be needed to find it.

Stratification Theory

The paradigmatic theories of the production and maintenance of social stratification gave schools a prominent place. In-school stratification, while somewhat transformed, remains an important feature of American education. What does the new arrangement of in-school stratification imply for research traditions in social stratification?

Many of the findings are consistent with what one would expect on the basis of human capital theory. Human capital theory emphasizes productivity gains related to cognitive growth as the motivation for investing in education. The analysis has shown that track location continues to be associated with cognitive achievement. Thus, human capital theory can accept the transformations in school practice without adjustment, for the relation between its focal factor—cognitive achievement—and track location remains.

Similarly, the social-psychological theory of educational and occupational attainment (often dubbed the Wisconsin model) also need not change very much. Under this perspective, curricular placement is seen as partially determined by social background and prior achievement, and as partly determining aspirations, significant others' appraisals, and educational attainment. Much in the analysis supports this overall theory. I find course taking to be associated with cognitive achievement and college entry, an educational attainment outcome. However, whether structural track location is associated with significant others' influence, once social-psychological track location is controlled, remains an open question, because structural track location is less obvious to many potentially significant others than it might have been in the past. In addition, although I do not find socialization effects of track location, I did not directly investigate the same kinds of attitudinal factors investigated in the social-psychological model. Further research may be needed to investigate this issue in more detail as well.

Research on cognitive complexity and personality (Kohn, 1977; Kohn & Schooler, 1986) is faced with a slightly more serious anomaly. Researchers in this line of inquiry contend that the actual cognitive complexity of coursework matters for students' attitudes in the same way that the cognitive complexity of occupational tasks matters for workers' attitudes. Yet, I find no systematic effects of curriculum placement on student attitudes toward school. The implication of this finding can be questioned, however, because (owing to data limitations) the particular personality trait discussed in the literature on cognitive complexity, educational self-direction, was not considered here. Although it is very likely that interest in school is related to educational self-direction, further research will be needed to establish this link and assess the implications for educational self-direction of students' placement in the complex structure.

Two theories more deeply affected by the findings are reproduction theory and resistance theory. Bowles and Gintis's correspondence theory, a Marxist theory of schooling, is structurally related to the research on personality and cognitive complexity. Bowles and Gintis make additional claims, however, arguing that schools legitimate the social order through differential socialization. Bowles and Gintis assert that the structural locations students occupy in school correspond with places in the economy.

Bowles and Gintis were very quickly criticized for treating students as passive receptacles of bureaucratically determined treatments (Willis, 1977). Thus, many Marxist-leaning researchers turned away from reproduction theory and toward theories of resistance that focused on class, and later to theories that included many additional bases of resistance (e.g., race, ethnicity).

However, reproduction theory can be reconsidered in light of the finding of discrepant course taking. One of the limitations of the reproduction framework is that, to many, it suggested there were only two structural positions in both schools and the economy. As research on the complexity of places in the economy (Wright, 1979) and fluidity of social mobility (Hauser, 1978) called this duality into question, the idea of correspondance fell out of favor on empirical grounds, even as the concept of reproduction was being attacked on theoretical grounds for having an overly passive view of students in school. Yet, once one juxtaposes the finding of discrepant course taking to Wright's concept of contradictory class locations, it is apparent that neither the school nor the economy is captured adequately by a simple dualistic perspective. Given this new finding concerning the in-school stratification system, reproduction theory—and even some variant of the correspondence claim—may be salvageable as a way to understand the link between schools and the economy.

Davies (1995) has argued that resistance theorists, in search of an agent of historical change, formerly regarded every untoward act of lower-class students as a sign of resistance per se. However, Davies contends, frustration that students did not seem to be radicalizing has led many, including some post-Marxists, to turn elsewhere in search of an agent of social change. The finding of discrepant course taking and the associated concept of contradictory course locations may be germane to resistance theorists and post-Marxists, not because it can identify some agent of change, but instead because it provides one mechanism by which they might explain students' attitudes toward school and how those attitudes fail to coalesce into a thoroughgoing critique of hierarchical structures. Because their experiences are so varied, students are likely to regard differences in classes as idiosyncrasies of the teacher or subject. If systematic differences in treatment are (inadvertently) masked as idiosyncratic, it is unlikely that students will develop an awareness of the deeper social relations of the school.

I hasten to add that only subsequent research can show whether this claim will find sustained empirical support. Yet, the findings suggest that it is still too early to dismiss some of the claims of late-1970s Marxists and more recent resistance theorists.

Theory, Substance, and the Emergent School/Economy Relation

The analysis has focused on describing the in-school stratification system, and one motivation for doing so was to understand the school/economy relation. This motivation was based on the idea that much of the thinking about this important nexus had proceeded without consideration of potentially important changes in the operation of *schools.* Although I have referenced some contending paradigmatic descriptions of the economy, I have not subjected the economy itself to formal analysis. Thus, at this juncture there is insufficient evidence for me to state a preference for a particular explanation of the school/economy relation. For this reason, I resist the temptation to select one preferred description. Nevertheless, some comment concerning what may be an emerging school/economy relation is warranted.

It cannot go without notice that the apparent ebbing away of mechanisms that were designed to further systematic differential socialization has occurred very close in time to the ebbing away of a blue-collar middle class. That is, the decline of high-paying blue-collar jobs, the decline in union rates, and the hastening bifurcation of the labor force all describe the labor market that students entered immediately after completing high school in 1982. There may be value in considering what factors might be broadly associated with these kinds of structural changes. Despite this observation, it would be a colossal mistake to posit some kind of conscious organized effort to oppress students by removing systematic differential socialization from the in-school tracking regime. Indeed, if one looks to the evidence, one will find that the primary actors in favor of the change in school practice were civil rights activists, and their aim was to end what they claimed to be unfair school practices that disadvantaged minority youngsters. Similarly, it would be erroneous to posit an invisible hand that forced the school and the economy into corresponding relations because that was "necessary." Quite the contrary, one could argue that in a world without high-paying blue-collar jobs, differential socialization is even *more* necessary for maintaining social stability than before. Thus, noting that the economy and the school seem to have changed, should be interpreted not as identifying a transparent process but, instead, as a call for more research on this relation and its dynamics over time.

This seems necessary because the findings suggest that tracking does not seem to provide systematic differential socialization, and this finding emerges at the very time that many analysts and commentators are suggesting that transformations in the economy seem to be making large sections of the populace economically superfluous (Aronowitz & DiFazio, 1994; Darity, 1993; Rifkin, 1995). Such massive changes in the structure of the economy cannot help but have major implications for other institutions. While it would be a major error to see the in-school changes as caused by either an invisible hand or a malicious cabal, it also would be a mistake to ignore the ways in which both institutions—the economy and the school—likely have some articulation with each other. Given recent history, it probably would be useful to investigate, with various types of analyses, how the transformations in both institutions may or may not be jointly understood.

What all this means for the stability of the stratification order in general depends even more on how one theorizes the economy and on what aspects one views as legitimated by schools. Still, it is apparent that a particular facet of the old view, that *differential* socialization in school tied to rigid and unchanging tracks legitimated the structure of the economy and the process by which those places were allocated, is no longer an accurate description of how schools legitimate economic arrangements in America. If schools do legitimate the American stratification order, they must do so with some other mechanism, or they must do so in some other way.

FUTURE TRACKS FOR TRACK RESEARCH

Schools' wholesale retreat from overarching programs has been well documented. Oakes (1981), Moore and Davenport (1988), and Carey, Farris, and Carpenter (1994) all suggest that explicit forms of tracking have ceased to exist in the large majority of American schools. Garet and DeLany (1988) showed that the college/non-college dichotomy did not provide an accurate account of track structure. These research efforts provide a justification for turning to courses as the key to understanding in-school stratification in America.

If researchers turn their focus to courses, a wealth of questions awaits analysis. Many of these questions, such as those raised by the theoretical concerns detailed above, will require investigation of how tracking works in other times and places. Thus, fully investigating the implications noted above as well as others will require tracking research to break out of the ever-present here and the eternal now and begin to engage in comparative empirical research.

Certainly one option for track researchers is to develop a cross-national program to study the structure, mobility, and effects of tracking, or, less parochially, a cross-national program to study curricular stratification. By this I mean the active development of comparable data collection efforts and the coordination of analyses by an international cast of researchers.

An ongoing cross-national effort to describe and assess curricular stratification is not out of the question and would likely pay large dividends in terms of substantive understanding, theoretical development, and methodological advance. Many existing institutionalized research efforts (e.g., International Sociological Association Research Committee Number 28) provide models that would, if adapted to the study of in-school stratification, enhance the prospects for cross-national investigation.

Clearly, there is an existing program of cross-national comparative research on education systems (Meyer, Ramirez, Rubinson, & Boli-Bennett, 1977; Meyer, Ramirez, & Soysal, 1992). Although this research is illuminating, analysts have yet to link the descriptions of educational structures and analyses of their expansion and development to studies of persons' placement and movement within the structures cross-nationally. The existing detailed analyses of the forces behind the development of educational systems provide an extremely useful resource that researchers would do well to unite with equally detailed analyses of persons' movement through the systems that have been and are being constructed constantly. To do so will require data on students' locations in the hierarchical curricula of several nations.

This cross-national research program will proceed most effectively if a course-based approach, rather than the opportunity to learn concept, is adopted. The history of the OTL concept makes it unwieldy, imprecise, and problematic for research (see Chapter 1). In contrast, at present courses have a much more precise referent. Of course, the cross-national research program may need to bring in factors that are linked to the OTL concept, such as the physical plant to which students have access and the physical safety of the teachers and students in school. Still, in order to study placement in and movement through structural locations, it is important to use a concept that makes the structural locations comparable, even if all that surrounds them is not. Only in this way can analysts investigate the likely importance of environmental factors in determining the prospects for students to attain certain placements and move to better ones over time. The most likely way to construct comparable indicators of structural location is to use a course-based approach as the foundational means of studying in-school stratification.

A second area of development for tracking research concerns cross-time comparisons. All of the analyses presented in Chapters 2 through 7 pertain to *one* cohort in the United States. However representative of that cohort the data are, ongoing social change makes necessary continued investigation of track structure, mobility, and effects. True, there is much more to learn from this cohort. Indeed, to facilitate ongoing research using these data, I have placed several of the cross-classifications analyzed on the world wide web (see Appendix C for more details). And to enable research that requires unit record data, I have placed the CBI codes (Lucas, 1990) linked to HS&B student identification numbers in the Inter-University Consortium for Political and Social Research (ICPSR) depository. Still, plumbing the depths of these data will never substitute for cross-time comparative research, and thus cross-time analyses must be encouraged.

A third direction in which tracking research might profitably move would be to investigate more thoroughly the nexus between social-psychological and structural track location. A series of interesting questions concern how social-psychological track can constrain students' placement by determining what placements students see as possible and/or desirable. Although my focus here has been on structural locations, clearly analysts must collectively treat both social structural and social-psychological aspects in order for a truly encompassing understanding of how tracking works to emerge.

Finally, in the American case at least, pursuing this agenda depends on the systematic and consistent collection of transcript data. Student reports of their courses cannot substitute for the information provided in transcripts and catalogs. To coders experienced in categorizing courses, the catalogs provide a wealth of information; without the coders' effort none of the analyses conducted here would have been possible, and none of the future research suggested above will be possible.

REFLECTIONS ON SCHOOLS AND THE ENDURING CHARACTER OF AMERICAN SOCIETY

Every scholarly and folk theory of the production and maintenance of social stratification has to come to terms with the school. And the school, set inside American society, bears the marks of an American ethos. Consistent with this ethos, and in contrast to some nations, the United States makes little effort to reduce the fungibility of various resources. Therefore, as in the American economy, where capital amassed in one undertaking can be used to gain leverage in other unrelated endeavors, so too in students' assignments to courses in schools, where achievement in unrelated domains appears to provide access to high-level classes.

Similarly, some nations equalize access to information or reduce the effect of disparate information. For instance, until recently Japanese managers could not own stock in their own company (Fischer et al., 1996). Thus, managers in Japan, who are likely to have inside information, were prohibited from directly profiting from that information. But in the American economy, inside information can create a fortune; similarly, in the American school, those who depended on the public information provided by the overarching programs now appear to suffer the consequences of their parents' lack of knowledge of the school.

Thus, for all that the unremarked revolution may have changed about schools—students' experience of schools, students' prospects for mobility, indeed, the very "tracks" students may follow—it did not change some essentially nonmeritocratic features of schools. The enduring features may have as much to do with the general set of assumptions Americans bring to any enterprise as they do about schools in particular.

America, the land of abundance, has contradictions in abundance as well. The search for advantage, the attempt to pass advantages on to one's children, and the stated commitment to equal opportunity all come together in an always uneasy truce. No wonder, then, that the only institution whose *raison d'être* is the production and transmission of knowledge and skill contains many of those same contradictions.

The decline of formal programs occurred in this environment, and thus the change bears the stamp of contradiction as well. The dismantling of overarching programs allowed students to combine courses much more freely. Yet, advantaged places continue to be allocated in nonmeritocratic ways. Mobility is now more possible than before. Yet, over time most (but not all) students are moving downward. And the likelihood of reaching advantaged positions still is greater for those who bring advantages to the school or who already have advantaged positions in the academic system.

These changes foreshadow potentially stark changes in socialization. Downwardly mobile students either will encounter climates less supportive of learning or will move out of coursework for the subject altogether. Those who remain in higher locations will have experiences that are more and more isolated from the experience of other students, even as their own prospects for elite postschool placements increase. Owing to the complexities of the curriculum, many students who were in higher levels of coursework at one time, but have fallen into lower levels of coursework, will be unlikely to learn, until years later, that there is indeed a system of stratification in schools. Finally, students from lower socioeconomic backgrounds apparently must navigate the curriculum with little help from the institution and with often inadequate assistance from parents.

Once we consider all of these ramifications together, the ostensibly egalitarian change seems a cruel and callous ruse. Given the actual way in which the allegedly egalitarian change worked in the American context, there is good reason to question whether any structural change in schools alone can bring about equal opportunity for disadvantaged students.

This picture of in-school stratification after the unremarked revolution may be disheartening, but if so it is *not* because one should mourn the passing of rigid placements and efforts at lock-step socialization. No, if it is disheartening, it is because in many ways the new system seems little better than the previous one. For even after the unremarked revolution, the in-school stratification system still seems to unfairly consign many to disadvantageous positions. The major difference is that the system of stratification, formerly an overt and obvious set of channels students needed to negotiate, now is submerged beneath currents that drive many students, often unknowingly, to the same disadvantageous destinations.

EPILOGUE

The foregoing has offered a particular vision of in-school stratification and suggested some of the implications of that perspective for schools' ability to differentially socialize students and for the school/economy relation. Certainly more research is needed, and I have suggested some directions in which tracking research might move. Of course, these suggestions do not exhaust the possible set of additional steps that may need to be taken. Still, what has been learned so far is of immediate policy relevance.

At present there is an ongoing debate about the value and inequity inherent in tracking. Some scholars and policy makers call for the wholesale abandonment of tracking (Oakes, 1994a, 1994b; Wheelock, 1992), while others call for adjusting tracking to reduce its inegalitarian aspect (Hallinan, 1994a, 1994b). Certainly, well-meaning, conscientious persons can disagree about this policy issue. Many of the findings presented above bear on these two positions, and it is hoped that, where relevant, the findings can be applied to assess the value of specific proposals for reform in specific instances. However, the findings also have direct implications for how we think about, talk about, and evaluate policy options around tracking. At this juncture I want to reflect on these meta-political implications of the research, using the de-tracking debate as a vehicle for doing so.

First, a major implication of this analysis is that any reform will occur within the larger context of American society. Thus, for any reform to accomplish its aims, it must be sensitive to this context. Any reform that is not sensitive to the wider American context is likely to either fail to win the day, or fail if it does win the day. Failure is extremely likely because reforms that do not attend to the wider American context are likely to be undone by unforeseen and unintended consequences.

This observation is based on the foregoing analysis. It is germane in that, at present, insufficient attention has been paid to the possibly unintended and negative consequences that may accompany widespread de-tracking. Certainly some research is ongoing in this connection (Wells & Oakes, 1996; Wells & Serna, 1996), and this research must continue to unearth the possible contradictions that will, if unanticipated, undo any apparent de-tracking success. This research is extremely important, for a rush to adopt de-tracking approaches can easily do more harm than good.

For just as contemporary advocates claim that de-tracking will bring about equal opportunity, earlier advocates claimed that the dismantling of overarching programs would be an egalitarian change. Yet, the dismantling of formal programs simply submerged a stubborn stratification system, and thus lowered the chance that students of disadvantaged backgrounds would learn of the implications of the courses they took. This occurred because the reform succeeded in dismantling programs, but in doing so it forced the removal of the signposts that lower-class students sorely needed in order to realize the implications of present choices on their future options.

Many of the same features of the wider American context that rendered the unremarked revolution impotent continue to exist at the present time. It is this wider context that makes widespread de-tracking so frightening to many who truly care about the children of America. De-tracking is frightening because it is far easier to remove a set of labels than it is to maintain vigilant and effective oversight over a perpetual process of curriculum allocation and student instruction. If de-tracking advocates are successful, what will stop teachers from re-tracking inside their classrooms once students are no longer divided by course assignments? If teachers re-track inside classrooms in this manner, what kind of education will be available to students who occupy the new bottom positions in the class? And if teachers re-track in this manner, what means will exist to document this occurrence? Additionally, what will stop parents and/or teachers from coordinating to re-track informally, so that first-period English becomes the formerly elite college prep (because all of the students who were in that level last year just happened to be assigned to first-period English in the subsequent year)? Barring these responses, what will stop middle-class parents from moving their children into private schools and voting into place voucher plans that further de-fund public schools and privatize education? All of these possible responses are likely if teachers are not convinced that de-tracking is both logistically manageable and pedagogically sound. Until de-tracking advocates can successfully address these and similar questions, de-tracking is a gamble I am wary of taking.

These questions need to be part of the de-tracking debate. Unfortunately, this is not the only presently unsatisfying aspect of the public debate over tracking. Indeed, much of the public debate about tracking is miscast, because the terms of the debate allow well-meaning persons to talk past one another. A crucial foundational commitment of this work concerns the distinction between curriculum differentiation and tracking, a distinction I draw from the work of Barr and Dreeben (1983). I have already (several times) suggested what this meant for research strategy and for particular findings, particularly differential socialization. But another important implication of this commitment is that tracking and curriculum differentiation are not the same. Curriculum differentiation concerns the division of students into groups for instruction. This can be most helpful to students and teachers if students studying similar matters at similar levels are grouped together. Thus, it is common to divide students into algebra, geometry, calculus, and arithmetic classes, and taken together these classes provide an illustration of curriculum differentiation.

Tracking, in contrast, concerns the extent to which the group assignment in one differentiated curriculum is associated with the group assignment in another differentiated curriculum. Tracking, then, concerns whether the students who take algebra are placed in the same English class, and whether the students who take arithmetic are placed together in a different

English class. Or, tracking concerns whether the students who take arithmetic will never be able to take algebra.

The language of the debate obscures this distinction between curriculum differentiation and tracking. Many (but not all) de-tracking advocates stand against curriculum differentiation; that is, many de-tracking advocates want high school mathematics teachers to teach heterogenous classes in which some set of students are studying algebra, another set are studying calculus, and another set are studying arithmetic. Using the term *de-tracking* obscures this stand against curriculum differentiation. It is quite possible that some political advantage is gained by referring to the movement as a "de-tracking" movement, for tracking has become a difficult-to-defend practice for many school officials. But the label is a misnomer, for in actuality most schools have de-tracked *already*, at least formally. What remains is a differentiated curriculum, and it is the differentiated curriculum that is under attack. While this attack may be deserved and might indeed be pedagogically sound, ideally the public debate would center around the *content* of the proposed policy, and not be misleading because of the *label* of the proposed policy.

Most research does show that assignment practices are often unfair in many locales. But given that the potential unintended consequences of de-tracking have not been thoroughly aired, Hallinan's response, to note the problems in assignment and call for their correction, is at this juncture preferable to insisting upon yet *another* change that may issue in all sorts of unintended and negative consequences for students.

These observations flow from the realization that one may distinguish between tracking and curriculum differentiation, and that doing so means *it is possible to have a differentiated curriculum and not have tracking*. Regardless of what critics and proponents of "tracking" state, this fact remains analytically true.

Those of us who teach on college campuses know this to be true experientially as well. We do not constrain access to, for example, French classes by considering students' performance in, say, physics. Nor do we labor to form heterogenous groups for instruction, ensuring that each major is represented in each class. We neither require everyone to study the same exact material at the same level (as a completely undifferentiated curriculum would) nor assume that anyone who earns an A in one subject will be equally adept, motivated, or successful at other unrelated subjects (as some systems of tracking do). Thus, we neither hold back students who are ready to go on, forcing them to wait for their peers to catch up, nor push students into courses for which they are unprepared, simply because they succeeded elsewhere. Instead, we allow interest, a modicum of breadth requirements, patterns of success, and requirements in specific courses and majors to dictate what students study. On college campuses, we accept (even celebrate) the diversity of expertise and the likelihood that everyone is successful (and unsuccessful, by the standards of professional accomplishment) at something.

This same approach can be adopted in high schools. Students can be allocated to classes on the basis of prior preparation and (especially once requirements are satisfied) interest. Students who do *A* work in one subject need not by virtue of that performance be placed into equally demanding classes in other subjects. Similarly, students who have difficulties in one subject need not have those difficulties hold them back from reaching heights of excellence in other subjects.

It may be time for high schools to look to colleges for something other than the number of units students need in particular subjects. Instead, high schools might adopt the ethos of collegiate institutions. On their best day colleges are collections of fully human scholars seeking knowledge at various levels in a variety of important domains; high schools can be the same.

This vision of high schools sets aside the de-tracking debate to focus on an important pedagogical and public policy question, namely, how can we teach children to reach their fullest potential, whatever that is, in whatever domain of inquiry? It is hard to imagine a scenario in which this question is answered efficaciously without the maintenance, indeed, the elaboration of curriculum differentiation. To call for the elaboration of curriculum differentiation is not to defend tracking, that is, is not to defend a particular degree and kind of association between the level of students' work in two different subjects. Instead, calling for the elaboration of curriculum differentiation is to propose that schools take seriously the contours of students' achievements and assign students to classes in ways that build on their achievements in various specific domains. In short, I call for schools to hold out the possibility of nearly individualized instruction to every student attending school.

The means of doing so are not mysterious. Counselors need time with every student, not just the students that are having visible and potentially disruptive problems. Counselors need an opportunity to consult with teachers about students' performance. Teachers and counselors need to be given greater authority in allocating students to courses, and they need the backing of the administration when parents attempt to apply pressure. Of course, some means of appeal should be in place, but the burden of proof for such appeals should be on the plaintiff, and the criteria for successful appeal need to be the student's performance and potential as measured by a variety of means. Finally, this kind of change would be consistent with viewing teachers as the professionals they are; we need only give them tools and support and step back and let them teach. These changes likely would be supported by teachers because they would maintain homogenous classes, which teachers routinely regard as essential. (As a teacher I must agree with this assessment of the value of homogenous classes.) And these changes also might increase the likelihood that more classes would be composed of motivated students. Finally, if teachers did support these changes, such changes would not be so easily circumvented by the exit option, as teacher recommendations often are needed for private school admission.

If these simple changes seem to call for a radical shift in how schools work, and an impossibly large increase in the funding going to secondary school education, that they do speaks more about the lack of political will to make schools work fairly for all students than it does about the ineffectiveness of the policy prescriptions. But I submit that if the amount of effort going into de-tracking were shifted into supporting this kind of change, both students and teachers would fare far better.

These policy prescriptions are not under discussion. This is unfortunate, for ongoing transformations in the organization of work make this a potentially propitious moment for advocating nearly individualized instruction in secondary schools. Who knows how long this opportunity will be available, or if it has already passed?

However, barring these kinds of changes, students need to be given explicit information about the opportunities attached to different choices. Thus, more information, not less, needs to be given to parents and students. What this means, however, is that de-tracking advocates are proposing a policy that moves in exactly the opposite direction. For if the titles of courses no longer describe their place in the curricular hierarchy, the in-school stratification system, hidden to some degree by the decline of overarching programs, will become even more submerged.

This is so because in all likelihood curriculum differentiation in some form, as a formal institutional arrangement or as a *de facto* set of practices, is here to stay. That is not a tragic outcome, however, if access to the full variety of classes is based purely on achievement and, given sufficient achievement, interest. We would want nothing less in the college classrooms in which we teach; we should want nothing less for the high school classes in which teachers and all our children join together to teach and to learn. Indeed, if we implement this kind of collegiate organization in high schools, then students might learn a far more important lesson as well: We all have something to teach, and we all have something to learn from each other.

APPENDIX A

Measuring Track Location: Assumptions and Implications

How should track location be measured in the United States? At least since Rosenbaum (1980), analysts have been aware of problems that attend the measurement of students' track location in secondary school. Three different responses to the measurement challenge have been developed: (1) use students' self-reports of their track location; (2) use school personnel reports of students' track location; or (3) use information on courses to construct a measure of track location, a measure that may be termed a *course-based indicator* (CBI) of track location.

These different measurement strategies are based on different assumptions and have different strengths and weaknesses. In the first part of this appendix I discuss some of the thinking behind these strategies and suggest some of the advantages and disadvantages of each. After detailing some of the important works that have used the CBI approach, I describe the theory upon which I constructed this *particular* CBI using High School and Beyond (HS&B) transcript data. I then describe the coding process, including the criteria used for categorizing courses and the procedures used for assigning students to tracks. I close with reflections on the course-based approach in general, this particular CBI, and its utility for future research on tracking.

SELF-REPORT STRATEGY

The self-report strategy is simple and direct—ask students to which program they belong. Indeed, national surveys commonly ask students, "Which of the following best describes your present high school program?" (National Center for Education Statistics, 1981). In many national studies students are given three categories in which they may place themselves—general, college preparatory, or vocational. In the HS&B version of the question, the vocational category is broken down into seven additional specific vocational areas (e.g., agricultural, office).

This was the first question asked of 1980 sophomores in the High School and Beyond survey, and the same question was asked of high school seniors. A similar question was asked of eighth graders in the National Educational Longitudinal Study of 1988 (NELS:88), as well as seniors in the National Longitudinal Study of the High School Class of 1972 (NLS–72). Follow-ups to the former two studies in 1982, 1990, and 1992 asked similar questions.

A major advantage of the self-report is cost. If one is administering a questionnaire to students, the cost of obtaining the self-report is the cost of asking one more question.

The question requires students to summarize their programs and several assumptions are embedded in that requirement. One assumption is that students are *sufficiently* adept at the summarization task; a second assumption is that students are *equally* adept at the summarization task. I know of no published evidence bearing on either assumption. A third assumption is that programs are sufficiently distinct that students will be able to classify themselves easily as one or the other. Depending on whether and how the question is recoded by analysts, fuzzy lines between programs may cause problems.

For example, a student who is, say, equally pursuing two different vocational programs may encounter difficulty stating which of the seven vocational programs best matches his or her program. Yet, if students identify any one of the vocational programs as their own, this decision will have little impact on research, because usually the many categories of vocational programs are collapsed into one vocational category. Often even more information is ignored, as it is common to collapse the general and vocational programs into one non-college category, and to study the college/non-college program dichotomy. Thus, for much research the only way that indeterminance about a student's program can matter is if the student has difficulty identifying his or her course of study as general, vocational, or college preparatory.

Collapsing the data may offer little protection against problems, however. Ethnographic, historical, and survey research evidence suggests that the way students register for courses makes indeterminance possible. National Center for Education Statistics reports show that no more than 15% of American high schools assign students to tracks that determine their courses (Carey, Farris, & Carpenter, 1994). Thus, the vast majority of students are now enrolled in schools whose structure makes indeterminance possible.

Studies using students' self-reports of group membership abound. However, these studies have widely differing interpretations of what the self-report actually measures. For example, Gamoran (1987) uses HS&B sophomore cohort data to assess between- and within-school differences in the distribution of opportunity. Gamoran argues that self-reported track location is actually a measure of students' *beliefs* about their programs. He contends that these beliefs are useful for at least two reasons. First, students' beliefs may affect outcomes of interest and therefore are worthy of consideration. Second, because students play a role in the determination of their program (Powell, Farrar, & Cohen, 1985), students' beliefs about their programs are important measures of track position.

In contrast, much research that uses the self-report assumes (implicitly if not explicitly) that the self-report is an accurate indicator of structural location. For example, Hallinan and Williams (1989) use students' self-reports of their program to investigate students' selection of cross-race or same-race friends. The authors' interest is not in the effect of track per se, but in the prevalence of same-track or different-track friendships. They reason that because tracking divides students for instruction, it may determine students' prospective peers. Given this interest, Hallinan and Williams's use of the self-report requires that they assume it captures students' actual structural locations.

These studies highlight the different ways in which the self-report has been treated. Students' self-reports have been treated as a measure affected by students' attitudes toward school but useful despite (or because of) this relation, and self-reports have been treated as a statement of the grouping of students so concrete that their peers are identifiable on its basis. The question of which is the *correct* way to view the measure is not directly at issue at this point; it is simply a fact that researchers treat the measure in different ways.

A consequence of the interpretational disagreement is doubt as to the meaning of some statistical findings. For example, Velez (1989) uses data from the HS&B sophomore cohort to determine whether certain factors heighten the probability of dropping out for Hispanic and non-Hispanic white students. Velez, who uses a dichotomized version of the sophomore year self-report, finds that for white, Cuban, and Puerto Rican students, a college prep program serves as a defense against dropping out.

Velez cites the selectivity of the academic track as possibly leading to the isolation of a population less likely to drop out in general, but also contends that because the advantage of academic-track enrollment remains even once grades are controlled, the preferential treatment given to academic-track students by school officials is a factor in the higher school retention of academic-track students. Velez noted also that Chicano students in academic programs were more likely to drop out than were Chicanos in nonacademic programs. Velez speculates on two possibilities for this result: Chicano students may enter the academic track with less preparation than other students, or they may experience more discrimination than Chicano students in nonacademic tracks.

These speculations about track selectivity, preferential treatment of college-track students, and greater discrimination against Chicanos in the college as opposed to the noncollege track are useful if the self-report identifies different structural locations. Yet, if the self-report is interpreted as an indicator of students' beliefs about their programs, different explanations for Velez's findings—highlighting, perhaps, potential patterns of self-attribution and ethnic differences in those patterns—suggest themselves.

These different interpretations, then, boil down to thinking about the self-report as an indicator of *social-psychological* track location—where a student *believes* he or she is in the curricular structure—versus thinking about the self-report as an indicator of *structural* track location—where a student *is* in the curricular structure. Clearly, both structural and social-psychological dimensions may have effects. Still, one may question what exactly the self-report reflects, and how one may interpret results of analyses based only on the self-report of track location.

The two different interpretations are accompanied by different assumptions as to the accuracy of self-reports. If the concept one aims to tap is social-psychological, the student reports appear accurate. Who better to ask about students' beliefs than the students, and what better way to ask about a student's beliefs concerning track location than to ask the student to report his or her track location?

If the concept one aims to tap is structural, then in order to use students' self-reports one must assume the self-report is a highly accurate indicator of concrete phenomena. Yet, the accuracy of students' reports of their location in the school structure is open to question.

While the decline of overarching programs detailed earlier may affect the accuracy of student reports, at least one other factor may conspire to reduce students' accuracy in reporting their track location—the timing of data collection. This effect is potentially quite serious. Senior-year data collection efforts that span the late winter to late spring season may be very sensitive to the timing of survey administration because it is during this time that college admissions offices are mailing out their admissions decisions. If high school seniors use their status with respect to college admission to assist them in answering the question about their high school program, and the researcher-identified groups include a college preparatory one, then the timing of the data collection effort may have different effects on the self-report of students of different subpopulations of interest. The effects are most likely nonrandom because different types of colleges may have different application deadlines, notification of acceptance dates, and financial award notification procedures. In addition, the college selection process is not random. Thus, different types of students with different types of college options may behave differently with respect to the high school program question; the problem is exacerbated in that the differential behavior is not constant but instead will vary over the field period. Indeed, the field period for the in-school, senior-year HS&B study was February to June, precisely the time interval during which the self-report of high school program may be most sensitive to the date of survey administration.

Thus, answers to research questions may vary simply depending on when the data are collected. For example, regarding the question of track mobility, questionnaires administered in the sophomore year may elicit comparatively low incidence of college-track reports because students do not have a college admission status to which they may refer in answering the question. Questionnaires administered late in the spring of senior year may elicit comparatively high incidence of college-track reports, given that colleges vary in their admissions requirements and many colleges do not require college preparatory work in high school (hence the existence of remedial programs in colleges). If the measure is sensitive to the timing of data collection in this manner, one cannot be sure whether apparent track mobility is real mobility or simply an artifact of the timing of the data collection, regardless of the pattern observed. This timing effect is, in the language of experimental design, an effect of history, and as such it threatens the internal validity of the study (Campbell & Stanley, 1963).

If from this vantage point one decides to reject the structural interpretation of the self-report in favor of the social-psychological interpretation, one need not reject all previous research. Some kinds of studies, such as Velez (1989), can be retained with a simple switch in interpretation, because the research operations remain the same. Other research, however, will need to be redone entirely, because the rejected assumption is embedded so deeply inside the research that one cannot simply accept the parameter estimates and adjust their interpretation.

A good example of how assumptions about the properties of a measure can be deeply embedded in a study is provided by Kilgore's (1991) analysis of variation in track structure across different school environments. Kilgore raises theoretically and substantively important questions about whether and how track structure is related to teachers' understandings of their role, their power in the institution, and other factors. Because Kilgore's questions concern the structure of tracking, it is apparent that she requires structural indicators, not social-psychological ones.

However, structural indicators were not available. Thus, Kilgore made the best of a problematic situation by constructing structural indicators. To do so it was necessary to: (1) dichotomize students' reports of their track location as college/non-college; (2) estimate a model predicting in which track each student was "enrolled"; (3) calculate the probability of "enrollment" in the college track for each student; (4) subtract the estimated probability of college-track "enrollment" from each student's "actual" track location (using the self-report as an indicator of actual track); and (5) calculate the percentage of students in each school who were (a) above and (b) below their predicted track. These percentages were used to measure track structure in each school, and Kilgore then investigated the association between teacher and school characteristics on the one hand and the measure of track structure on the other.

At least two difficulties attend this approach. First, the dichotomy of track location assumes that the most salient dimension of track structure is the college/non-college divide. Yet, research suggests this is not so (e.g., Garet & DeLany, 1988). Second, to calculate the percentages of students "above" and "below" their expected track location requires one to assume that students' reports actually reflect students' structural location in the curriculum. But there is good reason to doubt that this is so.

The problems in this approach are made plain once the five operations listed above are described using a social-psychological interpretation of the self-report. Interpreting the self-report as a social-psychological rather than a structural measure means that in these operations the researcher has: (1) dichotomized students' beliefs about their programs as college/non-college; (2) estimated a model predicting whether students regard their programs as college prep or not; (3) calculated the probability that students will believe that they are following a college preparatory program; (4) subtracted the estimated probability of students' believing that they are following a college preparatory program from their indicated belief that they are or are not following a college preparatory program; and (5) calculated the percentage of students in each school who are (a) more likely to believe they are following a college preparatory program than one would predict on the basis of their characteristics, and (b) less likely to believe they are following a college preparatory program than one would predict based on their characteristics. Given this description of the operations, which is based on interpreting the self-report as an indicator of social-psychological track location, it is quite likely that rejecting the structural interpretation of the self-report means that those mathematical transformations of the self-report do not produce an indicator of the structure of tracking in the school.

The foregoing discussion of the self-report suggests the conditions under which it is an appropriate measurement strategy. If the researcher is interested in capturing the social-psychological dimension of tracking, the self-report is a good strategy. Even with the social-psychological interpretation, one must acknowledge the possibility of history effects when comparing the reports of seniors, if the survey administrations occurred over more than a few weeks. But history would seem to have little impact on comparisons across students prior to the second semester of senior year.

In contrast, if the analyst is interested in students' structural location, using the self-report strategy requires one to assume a high degree of student accuracy. Changes in school practice, long field periods, and variation in knowledge across students all make this assumption questionable.

SCHOOL PERSONNEL REPORT STRATEGY

Given the distinction between *social-psychological* and *structural* track location, it might seem that school personnel would be good sources of information on students' structural track location. To follow the school personnel strategy one must ask school personnel, such as guidance counselors, teachers, or principals, to report on the program of study students are following. This may require the respondent to locate the records of each student before answering the question. The logistical challenge may make asking school personnel more expensive than asking students. School personnel may need to be induced to perform the task with an honorarium.

For NLS–72 both the self-report and a school personnel report were obtained. Although the school personnel were asked virtually the same question that students were asked, namely, which of three programs best describes each student's program of study, this question immediately followed a relatively detailed query concerning students' course taking. In this detailed question, school personnel can report on each student's course taking in four areas: (1) science or math courses, (2) English or language courses, (3) social studies courses, and (4) vocational-technical or job-training courses. For each area and for each student, school personnel were to report whether the student took a course in the subject area the previous year, whether this subject area was tracked at the school, the number of tracks in the subject area in the school, and the student's location in the school tracking structure. Immediately following this question school personnel are asked to summarize the student's high school program (Levinson, Riccobono, & Moore, 1975).

This approach appears to first request reports of students' specific placements and then asks for a summary of students' placements. The value of this approach is weakened by two factors. First, the four parts of the introductory question have already forced some degree of summarization. Most notably, it is not possible to distinguish between placement in science and placement in mathematics. The question forces only one answer to what can, in principle, be two questions. One is not sure how school personnel will answer for students in different places in the two subjects—use the higher placement, the lower placement, the mean placement, the math placement, the science placement, or somehow construct a weighted mean. Also, every counselor is free to follow his or her own decision rule. Thus, whether or not the answers are comparable across schools is unknown. In addition, the term "English or language courses" is ambiguous because language may or may not refer to foreign language courses.

While these issues are important, by far the greater impediment to this approach is evident in the local reference of the question. The introductory question asks for a report of the students' group position relative to the other groups in the school, which makes the frame of reference for the question the curriculum of the school. If one school has only two groups, and another school has four groups, analysts cannot determine which groups follow commensurate curricula. Even if two schools have the same number of groups, one cannot necessarily assume that the groups are commensurable.

Some studies of tracking that have used the reports of school personnel have used the summary indicator provided in the follow-up question to signify students' location in a cross-school curricular hierarchy (Gelb, 1979).

The assumption embedded in the use of school personnel reports is that the reports are commensurate across schools. As asked in NLS–72, the summary reports may be commensurate, but they may not be. The appearance of the question directly after a detailed subject-specific, site-specific question (presumably a strategic decision to increase the accuracy of the summary) increases the likelihood that the question will be answered primarily with a local reference. The local reference is not necessarily destructive, given that schools are very similar in their structure. However, the problem is that there is no way to assess how the summary was produced.

One might contend that tracking occurs *inside* schools, so persons' location in the local school hierarchy is all that one wants. This argument is akin to saying that occupations are held *inside* companies, so persons' location in the company hierarchy is all that one wants. Clearly, studying individual company hierarchies and individual school hierarchies is important. Still, it remains true that there is a translocal reality within which the local context is embedded. Thus, despite the site-specific occurrence of tracking, and the site-specific occurrence of labor, often analysts also want to know where the student or employee stands in the national structure of tracking and the national structure of occupations.

This "national structure of tracking" is not merely a researcher construct. Indeed, analysts such as Meyer (1977) have pointed to the translocal character of school-specific factors as allowing, for example, students who change communities in the middle of the school year to be placed in their new school. This translocal character is also evident in that when students attempt to make the transition to college (or the labor market), they compete against students who were not in their school but who did have a (perhaps different) place in the national structure of tracking. Indeed, different colleges may draw from different locations in the national structure of tracking.

Thus, while students are dispersed throughout the nation, individuals' fates are affected by a translocal structure. Just like the labor market, which has both local variation (e.g., the mix of industries in different regions, local differences in tax policy) and broad nationwide aspects (e.g., the state of technology in the nation, the national law with respect to corporate taxes), the national structure of tracking likely has local perturbations as well as broad nationwide aspects. Therefore, the parameters of the national structure of tracking, like the parameters of the national labor market, are useful to know because they are relevant to ultimate attainments. These parameters cannot be estimated using indicators that are incommensurate from place to place.

To illustrate the incommensurability of reports based on a local reference, all one need do is consider the meaning of class rank. Being the 120th ranked student at, say, Exeter, may have one implication for one's rank in the national graduating class of a given year; being the 120th ranked student at an average public high school may have quite another implication for one's rank in the national graduating class; and being the 120th ranked student at a demanding public school may have yet a third implication for one's rank in the national graduating class. But once researchers combine those rankings across schools, they implicitly are assuming that the number signifies the same place in the *national* queue. This is unlikely to be correct. And if this is an incorrect way to treat class rankings, it is also an incorrect way to treat school personnel reports of track location as collected in NLS–72.

The foregoing discussion of the school personnel report suggests the conditions under which the school personnel report is an ideal measurement strategy. Incommensurability presents little difficulty if the researcher is not interested in generalizing beyond the particular school in which the research is conducted. But the larger the geographic and institutional framework to which the researcher seeks to generalize, the more problematic the school personnel reports become. The local reference creates a violation of unknown degree in the assumption of commensurability, and it is this assumption that allows researchers to treat students in the same nominal track as being in the same actual structural location in the curriculum. Because of the problems discussed above, this assumption appears untenable.

USING THE SELF-REPORT AND SCHOOL REPORT TOGETHER

One important question to raise is whether the problematic aspects of the self-report and school personnel report can be resolved if both reports are used together. First, the features that may create problems with the school personnel report are conceptual, not statistical. While statistical adjustments may be useful, one cannot completely and surely correct for the conceptions embedded in the way the question was asked and the missing information on how the question was answered, at least in the NLS–72 survey.

Second, whether using the two reports together is appropriate still depends on one's conception of what each is measuring. The exchange between Rosenbaum and Fennessey is instructive here. After comparing student and school personnel reports of students' high school programs, Rosenbaum (1980) argued that students' misperceptions of their high school program serve to limit their opportunities for postsecondary education. Fennessey, Alexander, Riordan, and Salganik (1981) contend that Rosenbaum overstates the discrepancy. In the exchange, *both* treat the self-report as a (perhaps flawed) measure of students' structural location in the tracking system, and both treat the school personnel report as the correct structural measure. However, the above discussion suggests the school personnel report is not a knowably good structural measure. Moreover, even if the school personnel report is taken as the indicator of structural position, if the self-report is viewed as a social-psychological variable, one might interpret student/ school personnel disagreement as student resilience or even defiance in the face of school personnel classifications, rather than as student "misperception." Using a social-psychological interpretation of the self-report, one might view estimates of the effect of students' self-reported track location on college matriculation as a measure of the contribution of students' beliefs in their futures, net of school support of those beliefs. Thus, although Rosenbaum (1980, 1981) and Fennessey and colleagues used the *language* of track perception, neither adopted a social-psychological interpretation of the self report—both viewed the self-report as a more or less useful way to identify or try to identify students' actual programs. And both uncritically accepted the report of school personnel, even though those reports are as abstracted as those of students.

This example shows that substantive interpretations of parameter estimates hinge on one's view of the variables as structural or social-psychological. By considering the substantive interpretations a researcher draws, one can infer whether the measure was viewed as structural, social-psychological, or in some other manner. There is no use in combining the indicators unless one is confident that the indicators work together to tap a broader construct or to correct errors in variables that tap the same construct. As it is unclear to what the school report refers, using both the self-report and the school report may not solve the problems one seeks to solve.

A BRIEF HISTORY OF COURSE-BASED INDICATORS

The two previous strategies—the self-report and the school personnel report—have different strengths and weaknesses. The strength of the self-report is that it taps the social-psychological dimension of placement. The strength of the school personnel report is that it may more easily tap the local curricular structure. If one is interested in the social-psychological dimension of tracking, or in a particular locale, the course-based strategy may offer little.

But for some questions, the strengths of the self-report and the school personnel report are weaknesses. If one is interested in the structural dimension of tracking, the self-report is not the best indicator. The course-based approach is better given a focus on structural issues or effects. Also, if one is interested in a translocal curricular stratification system, the school personnel report is not necessarily the best indicator. Instead, an approach that focusses on courses would be better.

There are several noteworthy uses of the course-based approach. For example, Hauser, Sewell, and Alwin (1976) used the admissions requirements of one selective collegiate institution to develop an indicator of track location from students' reports of courses taken. Using the Wisconsin Longitudinal Study (WLS), a sample of one-third of the Wisconsin high school graduates of 1957, Hauser, Sewell, and Alwin divided students into those whose course taking satisfied the entry requirements for the University of Wisconsin–Madison and those whose course taking did not.

However, the Hauser, Sewell, and Alwin strategy of looking to the flagship institution in the state educational system cannot work in the national case because there is no flagship of a national university system. Hence, it is impossible for researchers using national data sets to directly emulate the Hauser–Sewell–Alwin strategy. Moreover, 1957 high school graduates' college entry predated a dramatic upsurge in the diversity of collegiate institutions (Karabel, 1972). Thus, in 1957 it may have been more tenable to speak of a single college track than is presently the case. In constructing the CBIs, therefore, it will be useful to distinguish among types of college tracks as well as between college and non-college tracks.

Another alternative is provided by Hotchkiss and Dorsten (1987), who use two measures termed curricular variables. One variable is defined as an index linked to the sum of credits taken in particular courses. Courses are chosen for reference to reflect what Hotchkiss and Dorsten term the status hierarchy of high school courses. This variable is based on earlier work by Hotchkiss (1986). A second curriculum variable reflects degree of student participation in a vocational curriculum (Campbell, Orth, & Seitz, 1981). Using these two variables with HS&B data, Hotchkiss and Dorsten find strong curriculum effects on several post–high school outcomes.

The Hotchkiss and Dorsten approach is also suggestive of many possibilities. By scaling courses, they allow one to consider distances along one or two dimensions. However, because my interest is in preserving the cate-

gorical character of courses prior to the analysis, I use (in this study) categorical indicators of curricular program. Also in contrast to Hotchkiss and
Dorsten, I use subject-specific measures (which I elsewhere have turned into
summary measures; see Lucas, 1990), whereas Hotchkiss and Dorsten seem
to devise summary measures only.

Instead of following in the exact footsteps of these analysts, I follow
the spirit of their example. The Hauser–Sewell–Alwin strategy is based on
a theory of institutional linkages; focusing on the link between high school
and college, they devised a measure of track location. Hotchkiss and Dorsten
explicitly link their categorization to the hierarchy of subjects. In a similar
way, I classified courses into categories based on a theory of the organization of instruction in schools.

A THEORETICAL BASIS FOR COURSE-BASED INDICATORS

If good measures are based on a theory of the phenomena to be measured,
then a good measure of structural track location may be based on a theory
of school organization. Defining organizational differentiation as the "division of a school's student body into sub-groups of a permanent character,"
Sørenson (1970, p. 355) contends that organizational differentiation—the
division of students into grades, classes, sections, and ability groups—is a
pervasive and definitive feature of formal education. Sørenson argues that
groups are constructed either to (1) reduce the variation in characteristics
regarded as relevant for learning, or (2) reduce the variation in the skills or
knowledge educators attempt to transmit to students during a certain period
of time. Grouping for the first reason is termed vertical differentiation; the
second is termed horizontal differentiation.

Sørenson distinguishes vertical and horizontal differentiation analytically, but in real schools the value of vertical differentiation for instruction
requires a horizontally differentiated curriculum. For vertical differentiation
to mean anything in cognitive terms, it must match a horizontally differentiated system to students. In other words, if students are grouped on the basis
of test scores or some other criteria showing their readiness for new material,
but all groups are taught the same material at the same pace, then grouping
makes no sense. Because vertical differentiation—grouping based on reducing variation in students' characteristics—requires a horizontal curriculum,
that is, a curriculum organized so as to differentially distribute knowledge,
researchers may attend to the horizontal curriculum in devising measures of
students' locations in the vertical differentiation.

To illustrate the co-occurrence of vertical and horizontal differentiation,
I consider foreign language study. Students may choose relatively freely

between French and German, yet they are unable to choose freely between French I and French II. We may view the differentiation of French and German instruction as pure horizontal differentiation. But the distinction between French I and French II is not pure vertical differentiation because it involves a division both in the characteristics relevant for learning (i.e., how much French a student knows) and in the amount and type of skills and knowledge taught in the two different courses.

Dividing students on the basis of skills (vertical differentiation) without division in the curriculum (horizontal differentiation) would mean segregating students on the basis of skills but teaching them exactly the same material at the same pace and in the same way. As this is unlikely, researchers may capitalize on curricular distinctions to construct measures of vertical differentiation.

Sørenson argued that research was weakened by a tenuous link between theory and measurement. The measurement strategy of course-based indicators, grounded in a view of the organization of instruction in schools, is one way to address Sørenson's criticism.

Although the CBI meets the need for a structural measure, it does have its own blind spots. To the extent that one is interested in students' own appraisals of their location in the curricular stratification system, and the implications of that appraisal for achievement, the CBI is of limited utility. Students' understandings of their place are probably extremely important, given that secondary schools usually have mechanisms of course selection that require student input into the design of their schedules. The CBI is unable to capture the important social-psychological dimension of tracking, but it can reflect the structural location that may be both a cause and a consequence of social-psychological track location.

PRODUCING THE PARTICULAR CBI USED IN THE ANALYSIS

The measure of structural track location used here, constructed from students' courses, is a CBI of track location. High School and Beyond was the first nationally representative data set to obtain students' high school transcripts. In earlier work, I recoded the transcript-based reports into tracks; the details of that project are available (Lucas, 1990). Here I briefly describe the major elements of that coding effort. These preliminaries describe the basic data around which all the analyses presented here revolve.

The Raw Data

Although coding decisions were discussed with several colleagues, I was the sole coder of HS&B transcript data. (The primary discussant for the

codings was Adam Gamoran.) I *recoded* course codes; I did not *code* the
original transcripts. Actual transcripts were coded in 1982 by project staff
according to the *Classification of Secondary School Courses* (Evaluation
Technologies Incorporated, 1982). Thus, to the extent that one can ensure
comparability across schools in their courses, much of that work was done
before the data became publicly available.

One result of having project staff first code transcripts is that different
course titles often are assigned the same course code number in the data
file. This means that specially trained project staff, with a nationally representative set of curricula on the table in front of them, regarded the disparate
course titles as referencing the same content coverage and degree of depth.

HS&B transcript data contain information on all courses taken by students during their 4 years of high school. I restricted my attention to mathematics, English, science, social studies, and foreign language courses. In
devising their measures, Meyer and Muraskin (1988) used all of the courses
students took. Their interest was in stratifying the vocational tracks, and in
this sense they were consistent with the work of Gelb (1979). I am most
interested in stratifying academic subjects. Perhaps at some point it might
be possible to conduct comparative analyses of the two approaches to devising course-based indicators; whether one loses too much by using only the
five subject areas I selected is an empirical question. It is true that in much
research, achievement is measured with particular reference to mathematics
and language skills, which would seem to suggest that at least some researchers are primarily interested only in those types of academic courses.
Still, one must note that Meyer and Muraskin's attention to the full range
of courses is consistent with both the theoretical foundation of my coding
effort and general research practice. Some researchers might be interested
in combining the two approaches; both can be used with HS&B data.

HS&B data contains information for each course taken by a student,
including the course title, number of credits, grade received, and term in
which the course was taken. In addition to this information, I used the book
of course descriptions (Evaluation Technologies Incorporated, 1982) that
matched the codings in the datafile to more extended descriptions of the
content, aims, and/or methods of the courses.

Using the course titles and course descriptions, I classified courses into
five groups: remedial; business or vocational; lower college; regular college;
and elite college. When insufficient information was available to classify
the course, the course was coded as missing.

I gave each course one code for each academic year. Often I assigned
the same codes for all academic years, but in many cases the code I assigned
varied across years. The reasoning is that if two students take the same
course at different times in their high school careers, they are on different
trajectories. Compared with students who take an advanced course late in

their high school careers, students who take an advanced course early in their high school careers have an opportunity to build upon that course with additional advanced courses. Another general principle I used flows from Bernstein's (1977) observation that in a differentiated curriculum, demanding courses will introduce students to knowledge as a work in progress, while less demanding courses will present knowledge as a *fait accompli*. The examples listed below may clarify how these general principles were invoked.

After classifying courses, I assigned students to categories based on the courses they had taken. When doing so I assigned the code of zero to students who had not taken a course in the subject during the year. Also, although many students took courses for the full year, schools also divide the academic year into semesters, trimesters, and quarters. Some students took more than one course in a given term in a given subject, while some students took two, three, or four courses in a given subject during the course of the year. A number of courses taken sequentially in the same subject in the same academic year may or may not be coded in the same track. I took account of the temporal nature of schooling in assigning students to tracks in such situations. I reasoned that the later courses in a given year would be better indications of a student's track location. One might justify the assumption by arguing that over the year school personnel become familiar with students, so that the courses in which students are placed/enroll near the end of the academic year are of more interest to researchers. However, one could argue that the emphasis on later terms is problematic. When students categorized on the basis of full-year courses are compared with students categorized on the basis of fourth-quarter courses, problems may ensue. This is a research question that one could address using the course-based indicators.

I also reasoned that tracks should reflect as much of the year as possible, so I categorized students using the course taken in the longer of the two terms, if the terms ended simultaneously. These decision rules take care of multiple courses in the same subject across terms. Some students, however, took more than one course in the same subject during the same term. Occasionally these courses would assign the student to different tracks. In such situations the course with the highest number of credits was used to classify students.

It was important to develop decision rules for all of these situations, but most classifications were not covered by those decision rules. For mathematics, 88% of the ninth graders were classified on the basis of a full-year course or did not take a course for the entire year, 84% of the tenth graders, 81% of the eleventh graders, and 82% of the twelfth graders. The percentages of students are universally lower for English, as we would expect given the different organization of English instruction. Still, 84%, 76%, 68%, and 68% of ninth-, tenth-, eleventh-, and twelfth-grade students, respectively, were classified into tracks in English on the basis of full-year courses or as not taking a course for the entire year.

Below I provide more detail relevant to the particular subjects of math and English.

Mathematics

According to the system used to classify courses for HS&B data, the prefix 27 designates mathematics courses; I used all courses with the classification prefix 27. In addition, I treated some courses with the prefix 07 (business and office courses) as mathematics courses. In all, I coded 68 course groupings representing 131 mathematics course titles. Codes are at the level of the course grouping. I classified six of the course groupings (seven of the titles) as missing; the remainder of the courses were given valid codes.

The sequential relation of mathematics courses greatly aided the classification effort. Thus, I was able to classify most courses by considering which courses were prerequisites for it, as well as for which courses it served as a prerequisite.

Table A.1, which contains information that was used to code seven mathematics courses, as well as the CBI codes I assigned, illustrates the coding process. First, note the detail available in the course descriptions. Not every course had such detail, but the common presence of such detail makes it incorrect to say that the CBI is a coding of course *titles*. Note also that each course grouping has one code number in the datafile, which is the only link to students, but some course groupings have more titles than others. These seven course groupings reflect 29 separate course titles (i.e., about one-fifth of the course titles for mathematics); thus, comparability in coverage of material has already been arranged to some degree.

Even though course numbers 27.0408 and 27.0409 cover the same substantive material, they are recorded as completely different courses in the HS&B datafile because they cover that material with different degrees of depth. This allows the CBI to reflect differences in the level of rigor with which the subject is treated. The difference in rigor could be inferred from the titles, and the descriptive information lends even more weight to the inference. Notice also that the higher course identification number (27.0409) actually refers to a course that conveys less depth.

Table A.1 is meant to illustrate the coding process, not to imply that, for example, it is impossible to find a math course that is elite college track in senior year. There are courses that were coded as elite college track if taken at any time during high school, such as linear algebra and calculus.

Table A.1. Selected Mathematics Course Codes, Titles, Descriptions, and CBI
Codings for Grades 9, 10, 11, and 12

	Information Available to Code Courses		CBI Codings by Grade[a]			
Code	Title(s)	Description	9	10	11	12
27.0103	Mathematics 8	arithmetic; metric system; real numbers; negative numbers; ratio and proportion; exponents	1	1	1	1
27.0105	Mathematics, Basic; Arithmetic Review; Mathematics, Remedial; Mathematics, Essentials; Mathematics Lab; Competency Mathematics	terminal course; computational skills; remedial work; simplified approach; decimals; percents; competency test	1	1	1	1
27.0110	Mathematics, Vocational; Shop Mathematics; Mathematics for Trade and Industry	practical shop problems; applied arithmetic; applied geometry; metrics; skill development	2	2	2	2
27.0401	Pre-Algebra; Algebra Skills; Algebra Principles; Algebra Introduction; Algebra, Basic; Algebra Practical	exploratory algebra; practical applications; graphing; exponents; negative integers; simple equations	3	3	3	3
27.0408	Geometry	plane and solid geometry; theorems; construction problems; lines; volume; unified geometry	5	4	4	4
27.0409	Geometry, Informal; Geometry Physical; Geometry Intuitive; Geometry, Practical; Geometric Design; Geometry, Occupational	simplified geometry; de-emphasized proof; practical applications	2	2	2	2
27.0416	Analysis, Introductory; Mathematical Analysis; Pre-Calculus; Elementary Functions; Limits and Functions; Analysis; Elementary	pre-calculus course; analytic geometry; limits; derivatives; quadratic functions	5	5	4	4

[a] CBI codings are 1 = Remedial, 2 = Business and Vocational, 3 = Lower College or General, 4 = Regular College, and 5 = Elite College.

English

To create the English track variables, I identified 217 courses as English. According to *Classification of Secondary School Courses* (Evaluation Technologies Incorporated, 1982), the prefix 23 designates English courses; I used all courses with the classification prefix 23 as well as some courses with the prefix 07 (business and office courses). The 217 course titles were reflected in the datafile by 109 course groupings. I classified four of the course groupings (four titles) as missing; the remainder of the course groupings were given valid codes.

With English, I did not take into account the attributes of individuals presumed to be served by the course and the association between those attributes and measures of achievement, because doing so would be to turn the codes into a self-fulfilling prophecy. For example, black literature is one of the course titles. Black students may constitute a plurality of the students taking black literature, and black students have, on average, lower measured verbal achievement than white students. But black literature is a literature course, and the literature that students study in the course is as rich and powerful as the literature that students study in American literature. Therefore, I code the black literature course and the American literature course the same. Obviously, one problem with my approach is that it ignores the value society may place on mastering American literature rather than black literature. Although the differential value society may place on certain types of knowledge may be an interesting subject, I chose to avoid using presumed societal hierarchies of knowledge to determine the value of the course for learning.

I used clear appellations, such as honors, advanced placement, basic, and remedial, to aid in the classification. Moore and Davenport (1988) suggest that when schools dismantled the formal overarching programs, they often assigned the titles of the programs as level designations of the courses. The course titles for English provide ample evidence of this practice, and this greatly facilitated the coding of courses. In addition, I gave courses higher classifications if they used literature from other countries (without ranking certain national literatures above others). If courses taught skills such as how to apply for a job, how to fill out a tax form, and the like, I classified the course as business/vocational.

Table A.2 contains examples of the English codings. There are eight course groupings that cover 26 course titles. Note that the descriptions are integral to successfully coding many English courses. For example, both course 23.0153 and course 23.0521 have the word "independent" in the title. Yet, the description of the first course informs us that basic reading skill development constitutes the work of the course, while the description of the

Table A.2. Selected English Course Codes, Titles, Descriptions, and CBI Codings for Grades 9, 10, 11, and 12

Information Available to Code Courses			CBI Codings by Grade[a]			
Code	Title(s)	Description	9	10	11	12
23.0110	English 2; English 10, Average	on grade level English; reading, writing, listening, speaking skills; mechanics; usage, genres	5	4	3	2
23.0111	English 2, Honors; English 10, Honors	above grade level English; language origins; genres; in-depth study of reading, writing, listening, speaking skills	5	5	4	3
23.0146	Youth and Literature; Adolescent Fiction; Books and the Teenage Reader	authors focusing on youth	3	3	3	3
23.0153	Reading, Independent Study; Reading Laboratory; Reading and Conference; Literature, Individualized; Reading, Individualized; Best Sellers; Effective Reading; Reading for Pleasure	reading under contract; basic reading skill development	1	1	1	1
23.0401	Composition, Expository; Writing Practice; Contemporary Composition; Expository Writing	basic composition structure; models; skill improvement	4	4	4	4
23.0405	Spelling	study of spelling words; assigned lists; self-identified lists	1	1	1	1
23.0521	Creative Writing, Independent Study	Short story; plays, poetry; independent writing projects	5	5	5	5
23.0731	American Dream in Literature; American Heroes; American Dilemma; American Cultural Patterns; American Philosophy in Literature	study of Puritanism; Transcendentalism; Naturalism; Pragmatism; Existentialism; American dream representations	4	4	4	4

[a]CBI codings are 1 = Remedial, 2 = Business and Vocational, 3 = Lower College or General, 4 = Regular College, and 5 = Elite College.

second course notes that students engage in independent writing projects. Thus, the description makes it possible to differentiate courses that demand a high level of independent work, such as 23.0521, from courses that separate the student from grade-level work for remedial instruction, such as 23.0153.

This comparison suggests how I applied Bernstein's observation that courses that treat knowledge as a given are less demanding than courses that treat knowledge as a work in progress. However, using this principle meant more than simply coding every course with the word "independent" in the title as an elite college preparatory course. Successful application of this principle required fuller descriptions than were available in course titles; for this reason, transcript data that are linked to course descriptions are much more useful for drawing these kinds of distinctions than students' reports of courses they have taken, because students' reports probably will be confined to the course titles alone.

Course titles were useful by themselves in some cases, as evidenced by courses 23.0110 and 23.0111. These kind of straightforward level designations and notions of grade-appropriate courses greatly facilitated the coding. Yet, there is no denying that English is a subject with courses, such as American dream in literature, that challenge the coding effort. However, the challenge is not very different from the challenge one faces in trying to classify some rare set of duties and tasks into an occupation in occupational coding. The difficulty with doing so and the inescapable role of judgment do not invalidate the effort, nor do they invalidate the results of the effort, whose value or lack of value can be shown only through use in research.

CONCLUSION

The foregoing has compared three strategies for measuring track location and described a specific instance of the third approach. As a general strategy, the CBI does indeed augment the strengths of other measurement strategies. If one is interested in assessing the social-psychological dimension of tracking—its effects, its causes, its univariate structure—then the self-report is the strategy of choice. If one is interested in a particular local situation, then the school personnel report is the best strategy. But if one is interested in students' placement in a translocal curricular structure, and how their location in that structure creates or constrains their opportunities, the course-based indicator approach is a viable strategy. Because the latter are the questions of this work, the course-based approach is the strategy used to measure track location.

However, using this CBI means that every finding in my analysis is conditional on my coding of courses being correct within some degree of error. Yet, it is easy to overstate both the degree to which errors are fatal to the analysis and the threat of error.

Does the conditional nature of findings based on this CBI render the findings useless? If so, then there is no point to conducting *any* empirical research, because *every* research finding is conditional on the measures used being correct within some degree of error. No amount of tradition and no amount of believing in the chimera of objectivity can dissolve the conditional aspect of empirical research. Perhaps the only response to this dilemma is triangulation. Triangulation can allow one to find and perhaps adjust for the blind spots in different research approaches. This strategy works best when the scientific community collectively implements triangulation through a series of separate studies by different researchers. Thus, the conditional nature of the findings in this case is no more troubling than the conditional nature of *any* research findings; the counsel in both cases is more and different research that subjects the embedded assumptions to continued and rigorous testing.

However, consider how one easily may overstate the threat to correct codings. First, one may argue that whatever courses are listed in the catalog, the CBI cannot capture what is actually taught inside the classes. That criticism, however, seems to confuse the instructional and structural aspects of tracking. The CBI does not measure instructional differences across tracks, but, instead, taps the structural locations within which instruction occurs. No matter what the measure of structure, instructional information can always be useful in evaluating how the effects of structural location are generated. Thus, to the extent this criticism is aimed solely at the CBI, it seems unwarranted.

Second, one may argue that schools may title courses in any way they want, and there is no overarching national curriculum within which courses must be placed. Thus, course titles need not reflect comparable subject matter across schools.

However, project staff used catalogs to code courses before I used course information to assign students to tracks. Thus, the issue of comparability has already been addressed to some extent. Moreover, while there is no overarching national curriculum, there are other mechanisms that render the information in the catalogs an important indicator of the curriculum. For example, colleges use students' transcripts in making admissions decisions. If one doubts that comparability across high schools is possible, then to be consistent one also must doubt the efficacy of many elements used in the college admissions process (e.g., grades, teacher recommendations). By this reasoning, possibly the only elements one can use in admissions decisions are standardized tests, because they were *designed* to allow cross-institutional comparisons. Yet, rather than throw away grades and recommendations, a better approach probably is to accept that many mechanisms make the comparability of courses possible although not perfect.

Still, I have not claimed that either the course-based approach in general, or this CBI in particular, provides perfect indicators of track location. Indeed, I submit that this CBI is *not* perfect. Like any measure, this CBI has advantages and disadvantages. If we are fortunate, it illuminates parts of the social world that other measures do not, and its blind spots correspond to the strengths of other indicators. Only continued research and its dissemination can reveal whether we have been so fortunate.

APPENDIX B

A Primer on Log-Linear Models

Education researchers from a variety of disciplines have used analysis of variance (ANOVA) and ordinary least squares (OLS) regression. Using these techniques of analysis, researchers have deepened our understanding of how social factors are implicated in the process of education. Both ANOVA and OLS regression require an interval-level dependent variable (such as yearly earnings). One may, of course, use a dependent variable such as scores on a test or years of education, if that variable takes on several values in a data set. If the variable does take on several values, then one can act as if the interval-level assumption, required for classical OLS regression and ANOVA, is met.

Analogous statistical models, such as logit models and structural equation models, relax some of the assumptions of OLS regression and ANOVA. But these techniques remain essentially ways of investigating one or a few dependent variables.

Sometimes, however, none of the variables of interest is truly a dependent variable. In such cases one is often interested in both the *strength* and the *pattern* of the association between the variables. When those variables are categorical—either nominal or ordinal—one may turn to models for categorical data to explore their association. The most commonly used method for exploring relations between categorical variables is the log-linear model and models related to the log-linear model. Such models figure prominently in Chapters 2, 4, and 5. This appendix serves as a basic introduction to these models.

This introduction presumes familiarity with either OLS regression or ANOVA. Interested readers may find good introductions to OLS regression and/or ANOVA in Neter, Wasserman, and Kuttner (1989), and in Wonnacott and Wonnacott (1990).

In this primer I first list some of the options log-linear and log-multiplicative models provide. I then introduce the log-linear model for a cross-tabulation of two categorical variables, that is, the two-way table, and then describe the general issues involved in selecting a subset of preferable models out of the set of possible models. Next I extend this model to investigation of cross-tabulations of three or more variables. Afterwards I introduce association models, and then log-multiplicative models, the latter of which are not log-linear models but do have some affinities with log-linear models. I then return to some basic issues in log-linear and log-multiplicative models, basic issues that impart a particular advantage to log-linear modeling as a way to assess the association between variables. Finally, I close by detailing some common challenges log-linear modelers face.

LOG-LINEAR AND LOG-MULTIPLICATIVE MODELS: FLEXIBLE AND ROBUST

Essentially, log-linear models allow analysts to describe the association between two or more categorical variables. To fix ideas, consider the cross-tabulation table of students' math and English courses in ninth grade (see Table 2.1). The numbers in the cross-tabulation table detail how the two variables are associated. In the cross-tabulation in Table 2.1, it is apparent that 327 students took neither English nor math in ninth grade; another 147 took remedial courses in both subjects, and so on.

Simply stating the number of persons in each combination is not enlightening. To apprehend the pattern in the data, analysts seek to determine whether the two variables are associated, and to do so it will help to obtain a parsimonious summary of the association between the two subjects. However, common approaches to summarization, such as the Pearson correlation, fail in the categorical data case because the variables do not satisfy the Pearson correlation assumption that both variables are interval-level. Moreover, even the correlation measures that are appropriate, such as the polyserial correlation, allow us to estimate the linear association but will not allow assessment of curvilinear relations.

In contrast, the log-linear model is a very flexible apparatus for discerning the association between categorical variables. There are several classes of log-linear models—hierarchical log-linear models, topological or levels log-linear models, association models—and some related models, such as log-multiplicative models. Taken together, these models can describe the pattern and strength of association between two or more categorical variables. An appealing feature of log-linear and log-multiplicative models is that they are useful even if the categories have no obvious order (e.g., when one of the variables is religion, region, race/ethnicity, nation-state, or similar nominal-level variables) and/or if the distances between the categories are not known (e.g., when the categories of a variable are, for example, strongly agree, somewhat agree, somewhat disagree, and strongly disagree, or never, rarely, sometimes, and often). Yet, the log-linear and log-multiplicative models are flexible enough to use information on the order and distance between categories when that information is available. In addition, log-linear and log-multiplicative models do not require one to specify one of the variables as a dependent variable. Moreover, these models allow one to easily test a virtually unlimited set of possible patterns of association. Even so, the log-linear model is not unduly complicated. It is, simply, a regression model in which the dependent variable is (basically) the *count* of people in each cell in a cross-tabulation table. The unit of analysis for this model is the cell of a cross-tabulation table, not the individual person.

TOPOLOGICAL LOG-LINEAR MODEL FOR
TWO-WAY CROSS-TABULATIONS

I begin with the levels log-linear model (Hauser, 1978, 1979), also called the topological log-linear model (Hout, 1983). This is a good class with which to begin for a number of reasons: (1) it can be used to great effect in describing the association between two nominal-level variables, (2) it allows one to explore a variety of possible patterns of association, (3) it requires very few assumptions, and (4) it can be used to convey the building blocks for log-linear and log-multiplicative models that provide more information but also require more stringent assumptions. I also convey in this section some of the basics of log-linear models.

The outcome variable of a log-linear model is the frequency (f) in a cell of a cross-tabulation table. Typically, the row variable is said to have I rows, and the column variable is said to have J columns. In the table of ninth-grade math and English placements, there are rows 1, 2, 3, 4, 5, and 6, and columns 1, 2, 3, 4, 5, and 6. Thus, the outcome variable for a log-linear model for this table is f_{ij}, the frequency of cases in row i, column j.

However, because the process generating the frequency of a given combination of row and column placements does not satisfy the assumptions required for OLS regression (especially the assumption of normally distributed errors), the dependent variable for a log-linear model is the natural log of the frequency in a cell, $\ln(f_{ij})$, rather than the untransformed count in the cell. For that same reason, the error term for the log-linear model is not normally distributed; it follows, instead, the Poisson distribution. However, the outcome variable is directly analogous to Y_i in an ordinary least squares regression model, for it stands on the left-hand side of the equation and is the quantity to be predicted by the regressors in the model. This value, $\ln(f_{ij})$, is conventionally written as $\log(f_{ij})$; I adopt that convention as well. Finally, in relating models, one either refers to the expected value [e.g., $E(f_{ij})$] and omits the error term, or one may include the error term. Below I will always be focused on the expected value; I define $E(f_{ij})$ to equal (F_{ij}). Given these conventions, the topological log-linear model is of the form

1) $$\log(F_{ij}) = \alpha + \beta_{1i} \text{ Row}i + \beta_{2j} \text{ Column}j + \beta_3 \text{ X};$$

which is very similar to the ANOVA model with the form

2) $$\mu_{ij} = \alpha + \beta_{1i} \text{ Row}i + \beta_{2j} \text{ Column}j$$

Equation 2 is the two-way ANOVA model. In it, α reflects the grand mean, and the βs reflect the effect of being in a particular row or column. Note that β_3 is missing from equation 2, but one could add an interaction term to the two-way ANOVA model and β_3 would capture the interaction effect.

Equation 1 is also similar in form to the linear multiple regression model

3) $$Y_i = \alpha + \beta_1 X_{1i} + \beta_2 X_{2i}$$

Yet, the set of usable explanatory variables for Y_i is as large as the number of variables in the data set. What, one may ask, are the possible explanatory variables for f_{ij}, given that f_{ij} is just the count in a cell of a cross-tabulation table? A reconsideration of the concept of association will make plain the vast set of possible explanatory variables available for topological log-linear models for even the apparently stark case of two-way tables.

When analysts say that two variables are associated, they are saying that some combinations of values on variables *A* and *B* are more common than other combinations of values on variables *A* and *B*. Interval-level variables are by definition ordered. Thus, in the interval-level situation the order of the variables can allow analysts to ignore the details of the combinations of the variables. In such situations analysts simply may summarize their expectation by saying that persons who have high scores on variable *A* are likely to have high scores on variable *B*. Although our theories might be more illuminating if they described exactly what values or range of values on *A* are likely to be paired with what values or range of values on *B*, it is not necessary to provide such detailed descriptions in order to estimate models for interval-level data.

But when analysts move to the topological log-linear model, they are forced to flesh out their ideas of what they mean when they say that two variables are associated. They must state which sets of combinations of variables *A* and *B* they expect to be equally likely.

This process begins with two unequivocal facts about each cell of the cross-tabulation table. One knows the row in which the cell is located and the column in which the cell is located. These two pieces of information allow one to estimate a first log-linear model, the independence model.

Writ large, and with explicit reference to the data in Table 2.1, the equation for the independence model is

4) $\log(F_{ij}) = \alpha + \beta_{11}$ Row1 $+ \beta_{12}$ Row2 $+ \beta_{13}$ Row3 $+ \beta_{14}$ Row4 $+ \beta_{15}$
     Row5 $+ \beta_{16}$ Row6 $+ \beta_{21}$ Column1 $+ \beta_{22}$ Column2 $+ \beta_{23}$ Column3 $+$
     β_{24} Column4 $+ \beta_{25}$ Column5 $+ \beta_{26}$ Column6

where α stands for the grand mean, and each β stands for the "effect" of the cell being in a particular row or column. This long equation may be rewritten in a more general way as

5) $\log(F_{ij}) = \alpha + \beta_{1i}$ Rowi $+ \beta_{2j}$ Columnj

where, again, α stands for the grand mean, β_{1i} stands for the "effect" of the cell being in row i, and β_{2j} stands for the "effect" of the cell being in column j. Note that in equation 5 the apparent variables Rowi and Columnj are not single variables. Instead, in equation 5 "Rowi" signifies *I* dummy variables, one for each row. Similarly, "Columnj" signifies *J* dummy variables, one for each column. To enable estimation of the β coefficients, either one of the Rowi and Columnj dummy variables are dropped, or one must constrain $\Sigma \beta_{1i} = \Sigma \beta_{2j} = 0$.

Thus, this model bears some resemblance to two-way ANOVA; each row has its effect, each column has its effect, and there is a grand mean. In other words, there is a certain amount of heaping or piling up of cases in cell ij because the cell is located in Row i, a certain amount of heaping in cell ij because the cell is located in Column j, and a certain amount of heaping that is attributable to the "table," that is, the grand mean. If the densities in the cells can be explained with this model, then just knowing the frequency distributions of the two variables will tell one the relative densities in the cells. If this is true, then there is no association in the table.

If this is not true, then one can infer that the variables are associated in some manner. The task then becomes developing a model that describes the data. To do so one needs to turn to theory to develop an expectation about which cells might have common levels of concentration or, in other words, which combinations of values on variables *A* and *B* might be equally likely.

For the table of ninth-grade course taking (Table 2.1), one might guess that students are more likely to enroll in the same level of class than they are to enroll in different levels of classes. The dependent variable is f_{ij}, the frequency in the cell of the cross-tabulation table. Thus, the unit of analysis is the cell of the cross-tabulation table. The sets of variables already used—row and column—are variables measured on the unit of analysis, which is the cell. Acting on the hunch that students are more likely to enroll in the same level of course than to enroll in different levels of courses, one can construct another variable, D, that equals one if the cell contains students who are taking the same level of course in both subjects, and zero otherwise. Looking at the cross-tabulation table of ninth-grade math and English, one can note that these cells are all on the diagonal that runs from the upper left-hand corner to the lower right-hand corner of the table. In a table such as this, where the rows and columns have the same names, this diagonal is termed the main diagonal (and such a table is termed a square table). Returning to the model, however, one can easily note that the variable D is a dummy variable (that may be called Diag) that is one when the cell is on the main diagonal and zero otherwise. The equation for this model is

6) $$\log(F_{ij}) = \alpha + \beta_{1i}\ \text{Rowi} + \beta_{2j}\ \text{Columnj} + \beta_3\ \text{Diag}$$

Estimating this model is to fit a first "advanced" topological log-linear model. In a regular regression model, researchers obtain the estimated coefficients and peruse them to see whether the net association is in the hypothesized direction. One may do the same for a log-linear model. I posited this model based on a theory that the diagonal cells would have greater densities. However, the parameter estimates can reveal whether the diagonal cells have greater densities (if $\beta_3 > 0$) or lesser densities (if $\beta_3 < 0$), or whether there is no statistically significant difference in the densities of diagonal and nondiagonal cells (if $\beta_3 \approx 0$).

The model in equation 6 can be represented also by a design matrix (see Figure B.1). In the body of the text, I used design matrices to convey

Figure B.1. Design Matrix for Model in Equation 6

M\E	NT	RM	BV	LC	RC	EC
NT	b	a	a	a	a	a
RM	a	b	a	a	a	a
BV	a	a	b	a	a	a
LC	a	a	a	b	a	a
RC	a	a	a	a	b	a
EC	a	a	a	a	a	b

Key: M = mathematics, E = English, NT = Not taking, RM = Remedial,
BV = Business/Vocational, LC = Lower College, RC = Regular College, EC = Elite College

the models. In Appendix C, I use equations. The representations are equivalent, but equations are often more compact. Thus, in this primer I will continue to use equations to convey the models. However, every equation can be restated as one or a series of design matrices.

At this point one can note that the number of possible explanatory variables is, if not infinite, extremely large. Analysts can create many different combinations of cells. For example, one can specify a model in which each diagonal cell has its own density, and all other cells are equally (un)likely. An equation for this model is

7) $\log(F_{ij}) = \alpha + \beta_{1i} \text{ Rowi} + \beta_{2j} \text{ Columnj} + \beta_{3d} \text{ Diagd}$

where d = 1, 2, 3, 4, 5, or 6, and Diagd is a set of *D* dummy variables. There is no need to limit attention to the main diagonal. If one believes that students are likely to take a math course more advanced than their English course, but less likely to take an English course more advanced than or equal to their math course, one can specify such a model

8) $\log(F_{ij}) = \alpha + \beta_{1i} \text{ Rowi} + \beta_{2j} \text{ Columnj} + \beta_{3} \text{ MathOverEnglish}$

where the variable "Math Over English" equals one if i > j and zero otherwise.

In the table with 6 rows and 6 columns (a 6×6 table) there are over 34 billion possible combinations of cells. Some of these combinations upon closer inspection might reduce to re-parameterizations of each other. Still, it should be clear that even when used to excavate the hidden association between only two variables, the topological log-linear model opens the door to a set of possible models that, to be accurate, must be regarded as immense. Given the vast set of possibilities, one is encouraged to focus attention only on theoretically important combinations.

So far I have intimated that the log-linear model in general, and the topological model in particular, offers a virtually limitless array of possibilities for analysis. There is a final topological log-linear model one may fit that will detail aptly the limits of the log-linear model. If one believes that each combination of courses is unique, one may construct a variable for each cell. A model with a variable for each cell would predict perfectly the count in each cell. This occurs because there are as many parameters as there are cells; thus, one has not summarized the association, but simply has restated every single distinction between the individual cells. This model is called, therefore, the saturated model; every bit of information has been used in the description so that there is no more information available. However, this model is rarely illuminating, because it produces results little different from the result one would obtain from simply perusing the table. The saturated model states that every cell is different, but stating this is also to say that one should read off the numbers cell by cell. Usually commentators desire a *summary* of the association, which leads analysts to value parsimony when comparing otherwise equal models.

Given the vast set of estimable models, it is necessary to attend to only a subset of them. Procedures of model selection are, therefore, extremely important. Analysts use the classic troika of scientific investigation—elegance, simplicity (or parsimony), and symmetry—in evaluating models. Of these, parsimony is exceedingly important; thus, analysts tend to prefer models that account for the association with as few terms as possible, in as theoretically meaningful a way as possible, all else being equal. Given the importance of model selection in log-linear modeling, it is essential to note a few issues relevant to model selection before turning to other classes of models.

MODEL FIT AND MODEL SELECTION

When one estimates a log-linear model, one is positing that the model may provide an adequate summary of the association in the table. But an analyst cannot be sure. Once the model is estimated, one will obtain several summary statistics. These summary statistics can show whether the model does indeed provide an adequate summary of the association in the table.

There are many indices one may use. Some of the indices currently in use are the Pearson chi-square test, the likelihood-ratio chi-square test, the Bayesian Inference Criterion (BIC), and the Akaike Information Criterion (AIC). The likelihood-ratio chi-square test formerly was the most common. One difficulty is that sometimes the likelihood-ratio chi-square test is indeterminant. This may occur if two models fit the data but neither model is nested in the other. To directly compare two models using the likelihood-ratio chi-square test requires that the two models be nested. That is, in order to compare models A and B directly, it must be possible to specify one of the models by starting from the other and either adding or subtracting variables. If one needs to both add and subtract variables to move between models, then the models are not nested, and no comparison may be possible with the likelihood-ratio test.

However, the likelihood-ratio test began to lose favor among sociologists when they came to appreciate that the test is sensitive to sample size (e.g., Grusky & Hauser, 1984; Raftery, 1986). In a log-linear model with 1,000 cases, the model might be accepted, but with 15,000 cases, the same model, with the same parameter estimates and the same pattern of cases, might be rejected. As survey research has become more sophisticated and survey data have accumulated over time, it is not uncommon to have data sets of 15,000 cases, and it is becoming common to have data sets with hundreds of thousands of cases. In such a situation tests that do not adjust for sample size present serious problems.

One index that addresses this problem is BIC, which I have used in this text. BIC and AIC are similar in that both are based on Bayesian statistics. Currently statisticians are debating the relative merits of these two indices. However, sociologists have come to use BIC more and more, in the context of event history models, structural equation models, and more, and through this use its characteristics are becoming familiar. BIC has several desirable properties. One feature is that BIC allows one to compare nonnested models. In addition, BIC is not sensitive to sample size. Finally, BIC or an approximation to BIC is relatively easy to compute from standard statistical output, and it is easy to interpret.

If BIC is positive, the model is less effective than the saturated model at capturing the association. In other words, one would do better to *not* summarize than to use the posited summary. If BIC is zero, the saturated model and the posited model are equally appropriate. If BIC is negative, the posited model provides a better summary of the data than does the saturated model. The more negative BIC is, the better the model is at summarizing the association. However, the more parameters a model fits, the more difficult it is for BIC to be negative, if all else is equal.

At this point it should be noted that there is no guarantee that any two indices of model fit will agree. Thus, the selection of an index is an important step in the research process. Considering two or more indices can be useful for highlighting different features and providing a guide to additional model development. However, whatever index or set of indices one uses, one may determine whether the model fits the data. If a model fits the data, then it is useful to consider the coefficients, but if the estimated model does not fit the data, then some potentially important aspect of the association between two variables has not been captured. Thus, rather than interpret the parameter estimates, one is encouraged to continue the search for a preferred model.

HIERARCHICAL LOG-LINEAR MODELS

So far I have been considering the simplest of tables, the square table. Often, however, analysts are concerned with the relation of more than two categorical variables. At such times they may continue to use topological log-linear models. Indeed, I did as much in Chapter 5; I investigated track mobility

over 3 years using topological log-linear models. Yet when researchers have three or more categorical variables, they have another analytic alternative as well, and that is to turn to the hierarchical log-linear models. These are not to be confused with multilevel models or hierarchical linear models. Hierarchical log-linear models allow one to investigate whether interactions between categorical variables can account for the association (e.g., Bishop, Fienberg, & Holland, 1975).

Consider again the independence model for the two-way table

9) $$\log(F_{ij}) = \alpha + \beta_{1i} \text{ Rowi} + \beta_{2j} \text{ Columnj}$$

And consider the next (and only other) model one can estimate for square tables in the hierarchical log-linear framework

10) $$\log(F_{ij}) = \alpha + \beta_{1i} \text{ Rowi} + \beta_{2j} \text{ Columnj} + \beta_{3ij} \text{ (Rowi, Columnj)}$$

In this model each i,j combination has a parameter (β_{3ij}) associated with it. This is the saturated model. Thus, there are only two models one can estimate for the two-way table within the framework of hierarchical log-linear models: (1) the independence model, and (2) the saturated model. Considering these two models can convey the meaning behind "hierarchical" in the phrase hierarchical log-linear model. Equation 10 contains terms for the interaction between row and column. It also contains terms for the "main effects" of all variables in the interaction. In hierarchical log-linear models one may fit what are called higher-order terms—interactions between variables—but one cannot fit a higher-order term without also fitting the lower-order terms that contain the individual variables. This can be illustrated most easily with the three-variable case. If I were to cross-tabulate ninth-grade math by ninth-grade English by race/ethnicity, I would obtain four 2-way cross-tabulations—one for whites, one for blacks, one for Latinos, and one for other students.

In addition to having a row variable (X) with I rows, and a column variable (Y) with J columns, this new cross-tabulation also would have a *Layer* variable (Z) with K layers. This table would be a three-way table. The table is composed of rows (the X variable), columns (the Y variable), and layers (the Z variable). Equation 11 shows the saturated model for the three-way table.

11) $$\log(F_{ijk}) = \alpha + \beta_{1i} \text{ Rowi} + \beta_{2j} \text{ Columnj} + \beta_{3k} \text{ Layerk} +$$
$$\beta_{4ij} \text{ (Rowi, Columnj)} + \beta_{5jk} \text{ (Columnj, Layerk)} + \beta_{6ik} \text{ (Rowi, Layerk)} +$$
$$\beta_{7ijk} \text{ (Rowi, Columnj, Layerk)}$$

The outcome variable is the natural log of the expected frequency in a cell of a three-way table [$\log(F_{ijk})$]. The first row of this equation contains the main effects of row, column, and layer. The second row contains the effects of interactions between row and column, column and layer, and row and layer. The third row contains the three-factor interaction. In hierarchical log-linear models for the three-way table, one must fit the first row, one may fit any set of terms in the second row, but one may fit the third row only if all terms in the second row also are included in the model. It is in this sense that the model is hierarchical. The number of steps in the hierarchy is dependent on the number of variables under investigation; four- and five-variable hierarchical log-linear models are not unknown.

If one fits such models, one also will obtain indices of fit, which can be used to select between models. Because of the hierarchy, however, hierarchical log-linear models often are nested within each other. Thus, the likelihood-ratio test may be useful. However, one may start with a null model and add terms, or one may start with a saturated model and remove terms. Just as stepwise least squares regression can lead to different results depending on the starting point of the process, in hierarchical log-linear modeling, the order of estimation can lead to selection of different models as best fitting. This may provide a reason, even in the case of hierarchical log-linear models, to prefer a method that allows nonnested models to be compared.

If a check of model fit shows that an interaction needs to be retained, then one may infer that to account for the association in the table, those relationships are important. To determine the pattern of the association one may consider the parameter estimates from the model.

ASSOCIATION MODELS

Association models are another class of log-linear models. Association models offer a way to take advantage of an *a priori* ordering of the categories of the variables. In the specific example I have been using, the cross-tabulation of math and English course taking in ninth grade, one might be willing to state *a priori* that students not taking math are below students taking remedial math, who are themselves below students taking business and vocational math, who fall below students taking lower college math, who fall below students taking regular college math, who are second only to students taking elite college math. One also might be willing to state the same ordering for English courses. If one is willing to make these assumptions or at least some assumption about the order of the categories, and if one allows the categories to be equally spaced, then one may specify the uniform association model (Duncan, 1979).

12) $\log(F_{ij}) = \alpha + \beta_{1i} \, \text{Rowi} + \beta_{2j} \, \text{Columnj} + \beta_3 \, (Xi \times Xj)$

Until this point Rowi has signified a set of dummy variables, and Columnj also has signified a set of dummy variables. Rowi and Columnj continue to signify two sets of dummy variables. However, Xi is one variable that takes on six values, one value for each row. Xj is similar, taking on the values 1, 2, 3, 4, 5, and 6 to denote the column in which the cell is located.

In equation 12 the variable $(Xi \times Xj)$, the product of *a priori* row and column scores, is entered as a variable in the model. β_3, the coefficient for this product, provides an estimate of the association between math and English, and can be interpreted in a manner similar to a regression coefficient.

The association model assumes that the scaling distances—the distances between the categories—and the order of the categories can be asserted. This assertion can be erroneous and may lead to poor fit for the uniform association model. Two additional models—the row effects model and the column effects model—are in the same class as uniform association and may result in a better fit to the data. However, development of the uniform association model and similar models led to the development of another model that promises to resolve several difficulties with log-linear modeling. To that model I now turn.

LOG-MULTIPLICATIVE MODELS

A final model for consideration is the log-multiplicative model; this model is used in Chapter 4. With this model one may estimate the order of the categories of the variables and the distances between the categories, and obtain a measure of the association between the row and column variables. Note that one may obtain a parsimonious estimate of the association *without positing an order to the categories*. Technically, this model is not a log-linear one. It is discussed here because it addresses a limitation of the topological log-linear model for comparative analyses. In effect, the log-multiplicative model estimates the values of the row and column scores, and replaces Xi and Xj from equation 12 with the newly estimated scores.

Often one wishes to compare the association between two variables, given a third variable. A classic case is the desire to compare the association between parents' occupation (origins) and child's occupation (destinations) in different countries. This comparison is both theoretically important and substantively illuminating. However, it can be difficult to make the kinds of comparisons one might want to make using the topological log-linear model, because the best-fitting model may have many different parameters, all of which are required to capture the association. Some of the parameter esti-

mates may suggest, for example, that country *A* is more open to mobility, while other parameter estimates may suggest that country *B* is more open to mobility. In contrast, the log-multiplicative model concentrates all differences into one parameter, thereby easing comparison. Yet, if this concentration results in poor model fit, one may introduce additional (theoretically interesting) terms to improve model fit and still obtain a more parsimonious indication of the association between two variables in different countries.

To begin to convey the log-multiplicative model, recall the saturated model for the three-way table

13) $\log(F_{ijk}) = \alpha + \beta_{1i}$ Rowi $+ \beta_{2j}$ Columnj $+ \beta_{3k}$ Layerk $+$
β_{4ij} (Rowi, Columnj) $+ \beta_{5jk}$ (Columnj, Layerk) $+ \beta_{6ik}$ (Rowi, Layerk) $+$
β_{7ijk} (Rowi, Columnj, Layerk)

As before, the saturated model fits the data perfectly, but provides no more information about the association than a perusal of the table. Thus, what one wants to do is remove terms to make the model more parsimonious than the saturated model, but still useful as a description of the table.

In the log-multiplicative model, one removes two terms, β_{4ij} and β_{7ijk}. In their place the researcher substitutes $e^{\phi_k \mu_i \nu_j}$. This produces the model below.

14) $\log(F_{ijk}) = \alpha + \beta_{1i}$ Rowi $+ \beta_{2j}$ Columnj $+ \beta_{3k}$ Layerk $+$
β_{5jk} (Columnj, Layerk) $+ \beta_{6ik}$ (Rowi, Layerk) $+$
$e^{\phi_k \mu_i \nu_j}$

The key term in equation 14 is $e^{\phi_k \mu_i \nu_j}$. This term is composed of two types of elements. First, μ_i and ν_j are scores for the row and column categories *that are estimated from the data*. These take the place of the *a priori* row and column scores used in the uniform association model of equation 12. Also, regardless of the way in which the data are entered, one will obtain the same μ_i and ν_j scores. Thus, one need not posit an order to use this model; one may estimate the model and one will obtain an order.

Second, the ϕ_k terms reflect the strength of association between row and column variables. One may use the ϕ_k for each layer (k) to compare the strength of association.

This model is extremely flexible. It is possible to constrain μ_i and ν_j scores to be the same across layers or allow them to vary. The ϕ_k also can be allowed to vary without constraint, or constrained to follow particular patterns. For example, if the layer variable (Z) is year, one may specify a time-series type pattern to the ϕ_k. Yet, if the layer variable (Z) is nations or regions of a country or schools, one may estimate the ϕ_k without constraint.

Finally, all these different specifications may be evaluated by the standard indices of model fit.

Clearly, this model is a powerful analysis instrument. Yet it does make more stringent assumptions than the topological log-linear model. For this reason, both the log-multiplicative and the topological models, as well as association models and hierarchical log-linear models, have a place in the categorical data analysts' toolkit.

AN AS YET UNSTATED BUT IMPORTANT PROPERTY OF LOG-LINEAR AND LOG-MULTIPLICATIVE MODELS

Each model for two-way tables that I have discussed has included variables that "pull out" the effect of the row and column, that is, the marginals. Also, the models for three-way tables pull out the effect of row, column, and layer marginals. Inclusion of terms for the marginals in log-linear modeling is very similar to inclusion of the intercept term in OLS regression. The latter is necessary to turn R^2 into an interpretable measure, whereas the former is required to make the estimates of association in the log-linear model margin-free or margin-invariant. Margin-free estimates of association are desirable.

To detail the advantage of margin-free measures of association, consider the Pearson correlation coefficient. As is commonly known, the logical range of this measure is -1 to 1, with the maximum and minimum signifying perfect positive and perfect negative linear association, respectively. However, in any real data set the true maximum is likely very much lower than 1 and the true minimum is likely very much higher than -1.

This might occur if, for example, two cases in the data set have the same value on X but different values on Y. Table B.1, which contains two frequency distributions, illustrates this possibility. One frequency distribu-

Table B.1. Frequency Distributions of Scores on Hypothetical Tests A and B

Test Score	Test A	Test B
20	1	1
40	1	2
60	1	0
80	1	1
100	1	1
Total	5	5

tion pertains to the scores on hypothetical Test A for five students, no two of whom obtained the same score.

The second frequency distribution pertains to the same five students' scores on Test B, on which two students obtained the exact same score. If we could assign the students' scores on both Tests A and B, no matter how we made such assignments, it would be impossible to achieve a correlation of 1.0 or −1.0. The reason this is impossible is that the marginal distributions of the two variables are such that there is no way the two variables could be perfectly correlated. Indeed, the maximum correlation for these two variables is .963. (This example is meant to be illustrative only. The matter can be made more complex by, for example, introducing the distinction between samples and populations. But these additions do not alter the main point of the illustration, and to treat them would require more statistical preparation than this primer assumes.)

Clearly, the marginal distribution is not the only factor that determines the Pearson correlation coefficient; it matters which students obtain which scores. While the maximum correlation for Tests A and B is .963, reassigning the scores yield correlations including .770, .289, and .096. Thus, the *joint* distribution also plays a role in determining the correlation between two variables. This is as it should be; measures of association aim to tap the joint distribution between variables.

However, in evaluating whether two variables are associated, analysts often presume that the maximum value of the correlation coefficient is 1.0. This is the absolute maximum, but the real maximum value depends on the marginal distribution of the variables. This means that in any given analysis the real maximum value for the Pearson correlation coefficient easily may be lower than 1.0 if there are two or more cases with the same exact scores on one of the variables. The only way that the maximum value of the correlation could be 1.0 would be for the cases that share a value on X to also share one (appropriate) value on Y.

In other words, the marginals affect the Pearson correlation, and thus the Pearson correlation is not a margin-free measure of association. The marginal distributions of the variables limit the range of the Pearson correlation coefficient. This observation has important implications for analysts. First, for example, when researchers report that two variables are correlated at, say, .2, often an implicit comparison is made with the logically possible maximum correlation of 1.0, which would signal perfect linear association. However, the marginal distributions might have lowered the maximum attainable correlation so far that a correlation of .2 actually might reflect that the variables are as correlated as possible given their marginal distributions. If so, from one point of view a .2 correlation could be an indication of very high association. Consequently, and despite the well-known truism that the logical range of the correlation coefficient is −1 to 1, the margin-bound nature of the Pearson correlation coefficient means that there is no standard by which to judge whether the association is as strong as it might be in a given circumstance.

Second, the margin-bound nature of the Pearson correlation coefficient provides one explanation for common ambiguity in what is a large amount of explained variance in multiple regression. For example, in multiple regression each independent variable may have a modest number of cases with the same exact values, but when taken together, the incidence of cases with the same exact values may overwhelm the dependent variable and result in low R^2. Yet, researchers cannot be sure the R^2 is low, for it may be as high as possible given the marginal distributions of the independent variables.

The reason I have discussed the margin-bound nature of the correlation coefficient is to provide a contrast with the measures of association upon which the log-linear model is based, for these measures of association are margin-free or margin-invariant. This means that log-linear models do not conflate the effect of the association between variables with the effects of individual marginal distributions. Clearly, a measure of association should tap the association between variables and nothing else. Thus, margin-invariance is an advantageous property for measures of association to have. The measures of association on which the log-linear models are based have this advantageous property.

However, to obtain this property in log-linear modeling, researchers first must remove any effects owing to marginals by fitting the marginal effects. Then, they may add parameters to the model. Because the marginal effects have been removed, additional parameters can be said to capture the association in the table.

This necessity has important implications for substantive research. If a researcher believes that the driving force behind the joint distribution of two variables is their marginal distributions, a few log-linear models and a few related models, such as the model of marginal homogeneity (Hout, 1983), are available for use. This is not an uncommon analytic interest; for example, when social analysts claim that the economic structure has changed over time such that there are fewer blue-collar jobs, and because of this change the prospects of intergenerational upward mobility have increased, this claim is about the effect of the marginal distributions of occupations at two different points in time on the life chances of individuals. Similarly, when an analyst claims that more recent cohorts of students are more likely than older cohorts to attend college, and because of this the occupational distribution is being upgraded, this too is a claim about the marginal distributions. Despite the vast interest in these kinds of claims, as of yet the detailed analysis of the effect of marginal distributions is rare, and the tools for such an endeavor are under development. Discussion and debate of those tools is beyond the scope of this primer, but see Logan (1996) for an introduction to these new models.

The important point to make is that the tools for assessing the role of marginal distributions on the pattern are limited. And, in order to draw appropriate inferences about the association between variables from log-linear models, one must fit the marginal effects.

SPARSE TABLES AND RESULTING ZERO CELLS

To this point I have outlined the logic of log-linear modeling. However, it is important to note some specific challenges the log-linear modeler faces. One difficulty is that parameter estimates may be wrong and inferences of model fit and model selection may be erroneous if the table contains cells with zeros. This often occurs when the table has few cases and many cells and thus is a *sparse* table. Recall that the outcome variable is not (f_{ij}), but $\log(f_{ij})$. If (f_{ij}) = 0, then $\log(f_{ij})$ is undefined. Indeed, Table 2.1, the table of ninth-grade math and English course taking, has a zero cell.

However, for purposes of estimation (and theoretical reflection), all zero cells are not the same. Some cells may be zero because the combination of values on the variables is impossible. For example, in a cross-tabulation of sex (male, female) and reason for hospital admission, one will find several impossible combinations. The total number of males admitted to hospitals to give birth will be zero; the total number of females admitted to hospitals for prostate surgery also will be zero. At present these are impossible combinations of the variables sex and hospital admission. Impossible combinations are regarded as *structural* zeros and do not present a problem for the analysis. These cells simply may be deleted from the analysis.

However, some cells are zero because the combination is rare but in principle possible. In that case, a sufficiently large sample would record at least one case in the cell. In such situations the zero is regarded as a *sampling* zero. Sampling zeros can cause serious problems for the analysis.

One fix for sampling zeros calls for the analyst to add a small constant to each cell of the table. This will make a zero cell have a defined value when the log is taken. The problem is that this procedure biases results toward the independence model.

One also might resolve the sampling zero problem by combining categories. So, in the example I have been using (see Table 2.1), one might combine the remedial and business/vocational categories to obtain a table without zero cells. Combining categories in this way is problematic for several reasons, but essentially these problems imply that combining categories in order to avoid cells with zeros can distort the association between variables. Goodman (1981) proposed tests one might conduct to determine whether combining cells distorts analyses.

A final alternative is to analyze the data as they are and to make no change or adjustment in the analysis. Depending on sample size and the number of rows and columns in the table, one may still obtain appropriate indices of model fit and encounter little difficulty in obtaining model estimates for relatively parsimonious models (Agresti, 1990). Indeed, because my sample size is large relative to the number of cells, this is the strategy I followed in the text.

CONCLUDING COMMENT

Education researchers have much to gain by the use of log-linear and log-multiplicative models, and much to contribute to their development. For although many of the variables that concern educators are amenable to OLS regression (e.g., test scores), many are not (e.g., college quality). And although many earlier limitations of the log-linear model (e.g., the neglect of order) have been addressed, it is likely that education researchers have distinctive substantive problems whose solution will require further development of the log-linear model. Surely, models for categorical data can be applied in illuminating ways to the field of education, and their application holds promise for both educators and researchers interested in extending the flexibility of the log-linear model. This primer should be sufficient as a brief introduction to those models and as preparation for reading many sections of Appendix C as well.

APPENDIX C

Strategies of Analysis

In this appendix I describe in greater detail the specific operations followed in conducting the analyses. The sophomore cohort of High School and Beyond (HS&B), the data used in this study, was drawn on the basis of a multistage, stratified, sample design rather than a simple random sample design. Therefore, this sample should not be analyzed as if it were a simple random sample because complex sample designs tend to produce less efficient parameter estimates than do simple random samples. One may use a design effect, which expresses the relative efficiency of a simple random sample compared with a complex sample of the same size, to adjust the fit statistics and standard errors. All results presented, therefore, reflect adjustments on the basis of a design effect of 3.18 (Jones, Knight, Butz, Crawford, & Stephenson, 1983). In the text I refer to the design-effect adjusted sample size as the "effective N."

Moreover, several weights are available for adjusting for nonresponse and differential selection. I use the transcripts weight for all analyses. The use of weights in most of the analyses is straightforward, but their use in log-linear and log-multiplicative models is not. Clogg and Eliason (1987) show that an appropriate way to use weights for log-linear analyses is to fit cell counts divided by the inverse of the cell weights, because simply using weighted cell frequencies or unweighted counts leads to inefficient parameter estimates. I use their procedure for log-linear models, and reasoning by analogy I use the same procedure for the log-multiplicative models.

All log-linear and log-multiplicative models were estimated using GLIM 4.0 on a Dec Alpha. All other models were estimated using Limdep 6.0. To facilitate continued work on the issues addressed in this work, I have placed unit record data in ICPSR. Moreover, I have placed raw counts and the weighting factors used in the national analyses on the world wide web. They can be found at http://socrates.berkeley.edu/~slucas.

CHAPTER 2

This section provides more details on the analysis of Chapter 2. There are several classes of log-linear models (for a discussion of different classes, see Agresti, 1990; Hout, 1983). The class of models I begin with are levels models (Hauser, 1978, 1979). Given the state of knowledge about how students' courses are associated, and given that levels models are extremely flexible because many forms of association can be tested, it seemed prudent to begin the analysis with the levels models. Levels models provide a good starting point because they do not, in general, require or imply assumptions of order or distance between categories.

Specification

I estimated 11 levels models. I presented detailed results of the main seven in the text and mentioned only briefly the results of the other four. In the text I gave models suggestive names, but some models are drawn directly from research on social mobility. Design matrices for the main models appeared in Chapter 2; four additional models were briefly discussed there, but design matrices were not provided. Figure C.1 lists the name of the model, the equation for the model, and the constraints on coefficients for the four additional models. For all equations, F_{ij} is the expected count in cell (i,j), α is a parameter for the mean count in each cell, β_{1i} controls for the

Figure C.1. Additional Log-Linear Models Estimated for Chapter 2

Text Name	Equation[a]	Constraints[b]
No Math	$+ \lambda_1+\lambda_2+\lambda_3+\lambda_4+\lambda_5+\lambda_6$	if j=1, λ_1=1 if i=1 and zero otherwise, λ_2=1 if i=2 and zero otherwise, λ_3=1 if i=3 and zero otherwise, and so on, through λ_6, and for j≠1 λ_i=0
No English	$+ \lambda_1+\lambda_2+\lambda_3+\lambda_4+\lambda_5+\lambda_6$	if i=1, λ_1=1 if j=1 and zero otherwise, λ_2=1 if j=2 and zero otherwise, λ_3=1 if j=3 and zero otherwise, and so on, through λ_6, and for i≠1 λ_i=0
No Math/No English I	$+ \lambda_1+\lambda_2+\lambda_3+\lambda_4+\lambda_5+\lambda_6$ $+\lambda_7+\lambda_8+\lambda_9+\lambda_{10}+\lambda_{11}+\lambda_{12}$	λ_1=1 if i=1 and zero otherwise, λ_2=1 if i=2 and zero otherwise, λ_3=1 if i=3 and zero otherwise, and so on, through λ_6, and λ_7=1 if j=1 and zero otherwise, λ_8=1 if j=2 and zero otherwise, λ_9=1 if j=3 and zero otherwise, and so on, through λ_{12}
No Math/No English II	$+ \lambda_1$	λ_1=1 if i=1 or j=1 and zero otherwise

[a] All equations include the terms for the independence model

[b] All constraints include those for the independence model

row marginals, β_{2j} controls for the column marginals, $i = (1, \ldots, 6)$, $j = (1, \ldots, 6)$, and $\beta_{11} = \beta_{21} = 0$.

Commentary

Slot Supply. All of the models remove the effect of the marginal distribution; thus, each focuses on the association remaining after any disparity in gross enrollment numbers is controlled. If these effects are not removed, one will confound the marginal effects and the association in the table. If one believes that slot supply in the two courses—the number of desks in the classrooms in which the courses are (or can be) taught—is a key part of track structure, one has no option at this juncture, for information as to the number of desks in the classrooms is lacking. Whatever the theoretical claims, the frequencies cannot serve as an indicator of slot supply, and thus there is no way to adjust for slot supply. Given this state of affairs, to avoid confounding marginal effects and the association, analysts control for marginals and confine their attention to the association remaining in the table.

It is true that in some studies of intergenerational occupational mobility, analysts have attempted to distinguish between structural mobility—the amount of mobility forced by differences in the marginals for origin and destinations—and circulation mobility. Researchers have debated which, if any, parameterizations can separate structural and circulation mobility (Hope, 1981; McClendon, 1980; Sobel, 1983). In the present case, one may apply this same distinction, but the concepts would need to be altered slightly. One would no longer be able to refer to structural mobility; one would, instead, need to refer to mismatched curricular differentiation. Using the parameterization of Sobel, Hout, and Duncan (1985), and if the quasi-symmetry model fits the data, one would be able to estimate the extent to which the densities in the table are driven by mismatches in the different curricular structures.

However, I stress that it is *possible* to obtain such estimates. What those estimates mean, however, is another matter. It is my view that such estimates indicate whether and to what extent there is a mismatch, but they fail to reveal whether the mismatch is owing to *slot* supply. Appropriately parameterized models reveal whether the *filled* slots force a particular set of densities in the table. Yet, if there are unfilled slots, and classrooms often contain (at least momentarily) empty desks, then one cannot use the parameters of the model to explore whether imbalance in the number of slots creates curriculum differentiation mismatch. Thus, I have not presented the Sobel–Hout–Duncan model of exchange and structural mobility (or, in my terms, a model of curricular differentiation mismatch).

Parallel Placement. Two models were estimated to determine whether students were in parallel placements. Parallel placement I corresponds to quasi-independence (QI); parallel placement II corresponds to quasi-perfect mobility–constrained (QPM–C). QI fits a parameter for each diagonal cell, while QPM–C fits one parameter for the entire diagonal. Estimating both models is necessary because QI could fail to fit because degrees of freedom are wasted by fitting trivial distinctions between the diagonal cells, while QPM–C could fail to fit because its implicit assumption that there are no important differences between the diagonal cells is incorrect. As the point of estimating QI is to determine whether off-diagonal cells can be ignored, it is important that lack of fit on the diagonal not be the basis on which the model is rejected. Estimating both QI and QPM–C offers some protection against this eventuality.

CHAPTER 3

Chapter 3 uses the multinomial logit model, which is analogous to the binary logit model. The equation for the multinomial logit model is

$$P(y_i = j) = \frac{e^{(\beta'_j x_i)}}{1 + \sum_{j=1}^{J} e^{(\beta'_j x_i)}}$$

where $j = (0, 1, \ldots, J)$ unordered outcomes, and where to norm the equation, $\beta_0 = 0$. This model is often difficult to interpret, and there are other modeling strategies one might adopt. Therefore, the reasoning behind my selection of the multinomial logit model is detailed below. First, however, the data are described.

Data

The dependent variable in this analysis is students' joint placement in math and English. Using the full 6×6 tables would make the analysis extremely complicated. Thus, to reduce the complications, I sought to collapse the table prior to analysis. To do so I turned to theories about school, empirical results presented earlier, and criteria for combining categories. All three justify collapsing each six-category variable into a three-category variable, with categories for not taking a course in the subject, taking a non-college preparatory course in the subject (remedial, business and vocational, and lower college), and taking a college preparatory course in the subject (regular college, elite college). Thus, the 6×6 table is collapsed into a 3×3 table. The dependent variable for the analyses in Chapter 3 is students' location in the 3×3 math by English table for Grades 11 and 12.

Theory and previous research suggest that a key distinction in the curriculum is that between college and non-college preparation. Thus, I preserve this distinction. In addition, Chapter 2 showed that for studies of curriculum structure, the binary distinction between the college and non-college tracks is not useful by itself; a far more adequate characterization distinguishes between not taking courses, non-college courses, and college prep courses. Therefore, the distinction between not taking and taking a course is preserved.

Before proceeding, however, I investigated whether this collapsed version of the 6×6 table would unduly distort analyses. I tested whether each collapse was a defensible one, using Goodman's (1981) homogeneity criteria. These criteria are appropriate for testing whether one can combine two or more categories.

The results of those tests show that the collapse of the remedial, business and vocational, and lower college categories is defensible in that they are homogenous in their odds-ratios; the collapse of the regular college and elite college preparatory categories also is justified. This collapse still preserves discrepant course locations, which the Chapter 2 analysis suggests one should. Thus, for this analysis I used students' placement in the 3×3 table as the dependent variable.

Two key independent variables in this analysis are math and English achievement. They have been rescaled to have the same range and mean (0), although their variances have been allowed to differ. Rescaling the test scores makes it possible to compare coefficients directly.

The requirements for math and English are also central variables in the analysis. A little less than half of the students have nonmissing data on graduation requirements. However, the data are missing at random because data on course requirements were collected in a random sample of about half of the schools. Thus, the parameter estimates should be unbiased. The other covariates are measured in a straightforward fashion, with relatively small amounts of missing data.

Selection of a Framework

The multinomial logit model is cumbersome to interpret, and there are at least two alternative modeling frameworks one might use. One alternative flows from recent advances that have allowed analysts to add individual-level covariates to log-linear models. Building on the work of Logan (1983), DiPrete (1990) describes a constrained multinomial logit model and Breen

(1994) uses a discrete choice/multinomial (i.e., a mixed conditional) logit model. Both researchers use these models to study social mobility. The advantage of these approaches is that one may combine investigations focused on the meaning of the categories (such as in the levels models in Chapter 2) with investigations focused on the role of individual-level factors on persons' placements. Although being able to maintain both foci simultaneously is an advantage, these approaches are not appropriate here because both require that one (and only one) categorical variable be regarded as a response variable. However, in the present case neither subject is a response variable vis à vis the other. Instead, the response variable is the nexus of the two categorical variables; that is, English placement is not a response to mathematics placement, nor is mathematics placement a response to English placement. Because the multinomial logit model does not require that one of the categorical variables be treated as a response, it is a better way to add covariates to the study of students' placements in two simultaneously differentiated curricula.

A second alternative to the multinomial logit is to estimate RC Model II (Goodman, 1979) and assign scale scores obtained from RC Model II to the categories of math and English placement. Clogg (1982) proposed just this use for RC Model II scale scores. With this transformation, it would be possible to use ordinary least squares regression to analyze students' placement in each subject alone. The major problem with this strategy is that assigning scale scores based on RC Model II requires one to assume that the distances between categories estimated in RC Model II are *absolute* scaling distances. But, as Breen (1984) notes, scaling distances from RC Model II are conditional on the variables in the table. Thus, once individual-level variables are added to the study of association between math and English, the scaling distance may change.

Breen's (1984) example in this context bears repeating. Breen observed that if one fitted RC Model II to two independent, ordered variables, one would obtain a ϕ of zero, indicating no association in the table. The scaling distances would show that no ordering pertained. What the model would tell us was that the *relationship between the variables* did not display an ordering, not that the variables were intrinsically unordered. Thus, the scaling distances from RC Model II are not the absolute distances between the categories, and one should be cautious in using the scaling distances from RC Model II to construct a dependent variable for analysis.

Using the framework of the multinomial logit model, I investigated the association between students' placements in math and English. The standard errors from those analyses were suppressed in the text, but are available from the author.

CHAPTER 4

I used a macro written by Raymond Wong to estimate Goodman's (1979) row and column model II (RC Model II), which is a revision of a macro written by Yu Xie. With RC Model II, a log-multiplicative model, it is possible to obtain order and scaling distances for the categories in a cross-classification table and to obtain a measure of the strength of association. To obtain these, however, requires an oft-unstated assumption. The assumption behind Goodman's model is that the best ordering of the categories would produce an isotropic table (Yule, 1905). This is tantamount to assuming that the most appropriate ordering of categories would produce a bivariate normal distribution. This assumption is much more stringent than the assumptions I made in estimating the levels models.

Although I could have moved directly to RC Model II and estimated models with both complex patterns of association and the attributes of RC Model II, I estimated the levels models first precisely because it was important, given the state of knowledge in this substantive area, to establish findings with a minimum of assumptions. Levels models make fewer assumptions than does RC Model II.

The more stringent assumption purchases ease of comparison. In contrast to levels models, RC Model II can concentrate the differences between two tables into one parameter, increasing our ability to detect differences between them. But, as the assumption is more stringent, one must be willing to reject the model if results are highly counterintuitive, given existing theory (Clogg, 1982). Counterintuitive results (especially strongly counterintuitive orderings) can be viewed as evidence that the stringent assumptions of the model are not met.

I want to also acknowledge that, when faced with counterintuitive orderings, one alternative to outright rejection of the model is validation in other data sets. That is, if data drawn in some other nation, or at some other time, produced the same ordering; if larger sample sizes and smaller sample sizes produced the same ordering; if random samples of the larger sample produced the same ordering—in short, if the counterintuitive result was validated in several different situations—one might begin to question existing theory instead of the model. Because the complex sample design greatly reduces the effective sample size, I have analyzed all of the data I have rather than hold out a cross-validation sample. Thus, such cross-validation must await further work.

Log-Multiplicative Analysis: Model Specification

To estimate Goodman's RC Model II, I use the framework proposed by Xie (1992). To convey that framework, I first consider the following representation of the saturated model for the three-way table (i.e., the model that states that each cell is different):

$$F_{ijk} = \tau \tau_i^R \tau_j^C \tau_k^L \tau_{ij}^{RC} \tau_{ik}^{RL} \tau_{jk}^{CL} \tau_{ijk}^{RCL}$$

where for each dimension the τ parameters multiply to 1. In this equation, τ represents the grand mean, τ_i^R captures the marginal row effects, τ_j^C captures marginal column effects, τ_k^L captures marginal level effects, τ_{ij}^{RC}, τ_{ik}^{RL}, and τ_{jk}^{CL} capture the two-way interactions, and τ_{ijk}^{RCL} captures the three-way interaction. The saturated model always fits the data perfectly, but provides no more information about the association than would a perusal of the table. Thus, what one wants to do is remove terms to make the model more parsimonious than the saturated model, but still useful as a description of the table.

There are several ways one may proceed to develop a more parsimonious model. One may specify Yamaguchi's (1987) uniform layer effect model, identify ways to scale categories *a priori* (Hout, 1984), assume equidistant categories and estimate the uniform association model (Duncan, 1979), adopt a latent class approach to analyzing the table (Clogg, 1981), and more. For the question under consideration, Goodman's RC Model II is an appropriate model to estimate and has the advantages of not requiring an *a priori* order, equidistant categories, or introduction of other variables to scale the categories.

Xie (1992) proposed a log-multiplicative layer effect framework for comparing the level of social mobility in different nations, where "layer" refers to nations. This framework provides a tractable way to extend RC Model II to the m-way case, while allowing analysts to include levels-type terms. In Xie's framework all τs are estimated except the three-factor interaction and τ_{ij}^{RC}; these terms are re-parameterized in a more parsimonious manner than the saturated model, thus making it possible to assess the fit of the model. The re-parameterization is

$$F_{ijk} = \tau \tau_i^R \tau_j^C \tau_k^L \tau_{ik}^{RL} \tau_{jk}^{CL} e^{\phi_k \mu_i \nu_j}$$

such that μ_i and ν_j are scores for the row and column categories *that are estimated from the data*, ϕ_k indicates the strength of association, where $\Sigma\mu_i = \Sigma\nu_j = 0$ and where $\Sigma\mu_i^2 = \Sigma\nu_j^2 = 1$. If $\Sigma\mu_i = \Sigma\nu_j = 0$ is specified alone, then one obtains partially normalized scaling distances, but if one also constrains $\Sigma\mu_i^2 = \Sigma\nu_j^2 = 1$, then one obtains fully normalized scaling distances. It is also possible to constrain μ_i and ν_j scores to be the same across levels (i.e., years) or allow them to vary; I constrained row scores to be equal across academic years, and column scores to be equal across years.

Data Considerations

Again, I had to make some adjustments to analyze the possible role of school environments on the strength of association. Disaggregating the 6×6 table by 12 school environments would lead to very sparse tables. Yule (1905) suggests that sparse frequencies may make the order of categories unstable. Thus, I sought to collapse the table prior to analysis. The same theoretical and empirical reasons that justified collapsing the 6×6 table into the 3×3 table in Chapter 3 apply here.

Thus, for the school environment analysis, I analyzed the six-way cross-tabulation of mathematics by English by academic year by sector by size of place by level of socioeconomic diversity. This $3 \times 3 \times 4 \times 2 \times 3 \times 2$ table can be analyzed using Xie's framework. This approach allows estimation of measures of association for each of 12 types of schools. Measures of association are obtained for each academic year for each school type.

Analysis of Association

I report the ϕ_k, the measures of association. One may obtain standard errors for the ϕ_k by altering the jackknife method proposed by Clogg, Shockey, and Eliason (1990). An alteration is necessary because I have used weighted data. Thus, unlike in the Clogg, Shockey, and Eliason example (1990) in which each case carries equal weight, for my analysis it would be inappropriate to treat each case in cell ij as if it were weighted as $1/f_{ij}$. Instead, to obtain correct standard errors, one would need to drop one case from the unit record data, construct the corresponding cross-classification table of counts, construct the corresponding table of weights, estimate the model, save the estimates, and return the dropped case to the unit record data, and then repeat the process for each case, that is, $n - 1$ more times. This is obviously burdensome and, given the aims of this analysis, not clearly necessary. Standard errors for analogous statistics, such as correlation coefficients, typically are not provided.

To tease out which factors were associated with differences in the strength of association between math and English courses, I regressed the ϕ_k on school factors. I dropped two cases from this analysis because they were extreme outliers. They had undue influence on the regression, with studentized residuals of -5.69 and -4.39 and Cooks' Distance statistics of .42 and .33. In the regression models with them, nothing was statistically significant and virtually none of the variance was explained; when these outliers were dropped from the model, about half of the variance was explained by school factors and academic year.

CHAPTER 5

Chapter 5 uses log-linear models in much the same way as they are used in Chapter 2. Thus, the section on Chapter 2 covers many of the general issues of estimation and analysis that are relevant to the analysis of Chapter 5. This section provides information pertaining to specifics of the Chapter 5 analysis.

Log-Linear Model Specification

In Chapter 5 the basic data are two 3-way, cross-classification tables. Each cross-classification is a $7 \times 7 \times 6$ array (Grade 11 by Grade 12 by Grade 10) because students who drop out before completing tenth grade cannot be observed moving into the eleventh or twelfth grades (2.2% of the cases). Also, each 7×7 subtable contains six structural zeros because students who drop out in Grade 11 are not observed in a school location in Grade 12. But the tenth-grade math or English course of students who drop out in Grades 11 and 12, and the eleventh-grade math or English course of students who drop out in Grade 12, are observed. Thus, the curricular origins of dropouts are known, but their post-dropout behavior is unknown.

In the three-way case there is more than one independence model (see Agresti, 1990, for additional varieties of independence). I estimate the mutual independence (MI) as follows:

$$\log (F_{ijk}) = \alpha + \beta_{1i} + \beta_{2j} + \beta_{3k}$$

where F_{ijk} is the count in cell (i,j,k), α is a parameter for the mean count in each cell, β_{1i} controls for the row marginals, β_{2j} controls for the column marginals, β_{3k} controls for the level marginals, $i = (1, \ldots, 7)$, $j = (1, \ldots, 7)$, and $k = (2, \ldots, 7)$, and $\beta_{11} = \beta_{21} = \beta_{32} = 0$, and where if $i = 1$, $j > 1$, for all k, the cells do not exist. (Because of structural zeros, letting k vary from 2 to 7 means that 2 to 7 signify the same categories for i, j, and k.)

Mutual independence is the appropriate independence model because the central question of this chapter—does tournament mobility describe students' patterns of movement?—implies particular patterns across 3 years of course taking. Tournament mobility theory attempts to explain the association between origin and interim location, interim location and destination, and origin and destination simultaneously. Thus, since they are all the focus of theoreticians' attention, the independence model should fit none of the two-way interactions or the three-way interaction.

The asymmetric mobility model (AM) is estimated as

$$\log (F_{ijk}) = \alpha + \beta_{1i} + \beta_{2j} + \beta_{3k} + \lambda_1 + \lambda_2 + \lambda_3 + \lambda_4 + \lambda_5 + \lambda_6$$

where $\lambda_1 = 0$ if $i \geq j$, $\lambda_2 = 0$ if $i \leq j$, $\lambda_3 = 0$ if $j \geq k$, $\lambda_4 = 0$ if $j \leq k$, $\lambda_5 = 0$ if $i \geq k$, and $\lambda_6 = 0$ if $i \leq k$. This model states that there is an asymmetry, but does not specify the most common direction of movement. Thus, as described in the text, only if this model fits *and* if $\lambda_1 > \lambda_2$, $\lambda_3 > \lambda_4$, and $\lambda_5 > \lambda_6$, can I conclude that there is asymmetric *downward* mobility.

To test varying asymmetry, the heterogenous asymmetric mobility (HAM) model is estimated as

$$\log (F_{ijk}) = \alpha + \beta_{1i} + \beta_{2j} + \beta_{3k} + \lambda_{1ij} + \lambda_{2jk} + \lambda_{3ik}$$

where $\lambda_{1ij} = 0$ if $i = j$, $i = 1$, or $j = 1$; $\lambda_{2jk} = 0$ if $j = k$ or $j = 1$; and $\lambda_{3ik} = 0$ if $i = k$ or $i = 1$.

Quasi-symmetry (QS) is estimated as

$$\log (F_{ijk}) = \alpha + \beta_{1i} + \beta_{2j} + \beta_{3k} + \lambda_{1ij} + \lambda_{2jk} + \lambda_{3ik}$$

where $\lambda_{1ij} = 0$ if $i = j$, $i = 1$, or $j = 1$; $\lambda_{2jk} = 0$ if $j = k$ or $j = 1$; and $\lambda_{3ik} = 0$ if $i = k$ or $i = 1$, and where $\lambda_{1ij} = \lambda_{1ji}$, $\lambda_{2jk} = \lambda_{2kj}$, and $\lambda_{3ik} = \lambda_{3ki}$. This model is diametrically opposed to asymmetric mobility because it says that upward and downward moves are equally likely once marginals are controlled. I also estimate a second variant of QS that conditions the eleventh grade by twelfth-grade parameters on tenth-grade origins.

Commentary

Sociologists have studied mobility in other domains for decades; most prominent among these is the study of social mobility. In-school mobility, therefore, is one example of a generic phenomenon, and findings and methods useful for studying and understanding mobility in other domains may prove useful here. Yet, schools are particular types of institutions, which may distinguish in-school mobility research from other types of mobility research in many ways. Thus, juxtaposing the inquiry into in-school mobility to the comparatively advanced research on social mobility may pay dividends for both.

Two contributions that in-school mobility research may make to social mobility research may be noted. First, the data for this study come from students' yearly registration. Focusing on the last 3 years of high school requires analyzing three-way tables and thus using the rich information on paths through the curriculum that exist. Such detail rarely is exploited in studies of social mobility. Features of occupational attainment make the origin-by-interim-by-destination table difficult to analyze (but see Hope, 1984, for an example). Persons begin their occupational careers at different times, change jobs at varying rates, and have wide variation in the length of time between origin and destination. These features of occupational life mean that conceptual difficulties attend the analysis of more than two-way tables of occupations.

For example, consider the three-way table of parent's occupation, child's first occupation, and child's current occupation. If the time between first job and current job is short (say, by research design), then one may underestimate the rate of mobility and misestimate the pattern of mobility. Moreover, given the increasing age at which formal education is completed and the phenomenon of the returning-to-graduate-school student, one may question to what population the parameters and patterns refer. If, alternatively, the time between first job and destination is long, the value of the interim location for improving our understanding is likely to wane. The sensitivity of social mobility research to the definition of first job is well known (Featherman & Hauser, 1978). If first job becomes an interim location, the sensitivity is not reduced.

All these difficulties follow from the relatively voluntaristic nature of the timing of job change in comparison to the coercion inherent in the institutional mechanism of course registration in school. The latter creates both a forum in which movement from year to year is meaningful to participants and a set of procedures that makes it possible to treat transcripts as the bureaucratic residue of a repeated measures design. To the extent that both in-school mobility and social mobility are general mobility phenomena, results from the analysis of the 3-year sequence of in-school mobility may provide insights that transfer (if only conceptually) to the social mobility case.

The treatment of dropouts provides a second example of how the study of in-school mobility may lend insights to the study of social mobility. Analyses of occupational mobility usually recode unemployed persons to their "usual" occupation or their last occupation. However, this may obfuscate comparisons across time, across race, and across sex. A better approach might be to retain one or two categories to tap a not-in-labor-force status as well as unemployment. Whether this would deepen our understanding of social processes is an empirical question, but whether it is defensible to use such "non-job" codes is a theoretical question that must be answered affirmatively. To the extent that studies of occupational mobility aim to tap *social* mobility, the inclusion of non-job positions would seem necessary. The necessity can only increase as changes in the structure of the economy make many persons economically superfluous (Darity, 1993); the best way to capture such change in studies of social mobility is to retain "non-occupation" positions. Hence, the concept of the dropout, clearly relevant to the study of curricular mobility, can be transferred with suitable revision to the study of social mobility.

CHAPTER 6

The ordered probit model is an appropriate way to study individual-level correlates of placement. If prior location is used as a covariate, the model becomes a model of mobility. The ordered probit model is specified as follows:

$$P(y_i = 0) = \Phi(\mu_1 - \beta'X)$$
$$P(y_i = 1) = \Phi(\mu_2 - \beta'X) - \Phi(\mu_1 - \beta'X)$$
$$P(y_i = 2) = \Phi(\mu_3 - \beta'X) - \Phi(\mu_2 - \beta'X)$$
$$P(y_i = 3) = 1 - \Phi(\mu_3 - \beta'X)$$

where Φ signifies the normal probability density, μs represent thresholds on that density, X represents a matrix of explanatory variables, and β represents a vector of estimated parameters linking variables to the outcome. This approach is straightforward.

The implications of the model are that whatever variable affects one's propensity to reach one destination, also affects one's propensity to reach any of the other potential destinations. Moreover, the coefficient for any given variable is the same across destinations, once the thresholds are scaled appropriately. However, the *same* coefficient will imply *different* effects on the probability of being in different categories, because the implied effect of a given coefficient of a nonlinear model depends on the other variables in the model, that is, it depends on one's location on the curve.

These observations are most important as one considers the dropout destination and all other destinations. The comments above imply that the marginal effect of a variable on whether someone drops out will in general differ from the marginal effect of the same variable on whether that person reaches any other destination, even though the coefficient reported is the same regardless of the destination.

CHAPTER 7

Binary logit models are used to analyze interest in school in Grade 12 and college entry. OLS regression models are used to analyze measured achievement in math and English.

Dropouts

All analyses presented in the text were based on students who did not drop out of school between Grades 10 and 12. However, as Berends (1994) argues, dropping out is itself a sign of interest in school. Thus, removing from the analysis the students who drop out may lower the estimated effect of track location.

Berends (1994) attempts to correct for this problem by estimating a two-equation model, the bivariate probit model with sample selection. One equation predicts whether the student is in school or not, and the second equation predicts the outcome of substantive interest using only the students who are in school. Although Berends's approach is arguably the best way to address sample selection bias, some contend that there are strong assumptions behind these kinds of selection approaches that make them problematic. Manski (1993) questions the value of using these kinds of approaches to adjust for missing data and advocates instead that analysts should attempt to discern bounds to important parameters. Stolzenberg and Relles (1990) report that using the Heckman two-step correction (a similar approach) in small samples may produce *more* biased estimates than simply ignoring missing data. Compared with the bias introduced by dropping the cases with missing data, the bias in the Heckman correction tends to be in the opposite direction. They suggest that analysts should refrain from using these kinds of models when the process they are trying to assess is not well understood. For these reasons, I presented the results from an analysis based only on the students who did not drop out of school.

However, I estimated the models again using a bivariate probit with sample selection and calculated BIC* statistics for each model, that is, using the same technique Berends (1994) uses. Fit statistics from these models are in Table C.1. The qualitative finding did not change; no specification of

Table C.1. Fit Statistics for Bivariate Probit Models of Interest in School in Twelfth Grade (controlling for dropping out) (effective $n = 4,281$)

Model	L^2	df	BIC*
Tracking Ignored	−3391.51	27	−1437.00
Track Placement	−3319.50	51	−1380.34
Consistent Locations	−3334.59	41	−1433.77
Consistent vs. Inconsistent	−3350.94	37	−1434.51
Degree of Discrepancy	−3350.00	44	−1377.87
Track Mobility	−3196.13	114	−1100.27

track location improved the fit of the model. Thus, the findings appear robust against different ways of treating dropouts.

Specifications of Track Location

I used five different specifications of track location. In the track placement model, I used dummy variables indicating the student's joint placement in math and English in Grade 11, and another set of dummy variables indicating the student's joint placement in math and English in Grade 12. In the consistent locations model, I created a dummy variable for whether the student was college prep for both math and English in Grade 11, a dummy variable for whether the student was non-college prep for both math and English in Grade 11, and a dummy variable for whether the student was not taking a course for both math and English in Grade 11. I did the same for Grade 12. This model, then, compares students in each of three concordant locations with students in discrepant locations. It also allows the effects of the concordant locations to differ.

For the consistent vs. inconsistent model, I compared students who were consistent with all other students, but did not allow the college preparatory, non-college preparatory, and not-taking categories to have different effects. A measure of consistent or not was constructed for both Grade 11 and Grade 12. This model investigates whether students who obtain relatively consistent exposures are different from other students.

The degree of discrepancy model uses the original 6 × 6 table of English and math placements to construct dummy variables for degree of discrepancy. Students in the same category for math and English have no discrepancy, students who are in adjacent categories are coded as having only 1 degree of discrepancy, and so on. Finally, the track mobility model specifies track location by referencing the path through the math and the English curriculum the student took. As one can see by the degrees of freedom, the mobility model used many more variables than any of the others. This happened because each of the paths from Grade 10 to Grade 11 to Grade 12 denoted a separate variable.

For interest in school, the track model always fit less well than did a model that ignored track location. Tables C.2 and C.3 contain the coefficients from the baseline models as well as the best-fitting model for each outcome.

Statistical Inference

In the interest in school model, both of the coefficients for consistency are statistically significant at the .05 level. If I were using standard statistical

Table C.2. Coefficients for Baseline Model (without track variables) and Best Tracking Model for Twelfth-Grade Interest in School and Twelfth-Grade English Achievement

Regressors	Grade 12 Interest in School				Grade 12 English Achievement			
	Baseline		Track		Baseline		Track	
	Coeff	S.e.	Coeff	S.e.	Coeff.	S.e.	Coeff.	S.e.
Constant	.140	.098	−.029	.105	.898*	.032	.772*	.037
Math Ach 10	.067	.037	.042	.037	.158*	.016	.140*	.016
Engl Ach 10	.061	.039	.053	.039	.690*	.018	.684*	.017
SES	.090	.071	.060	.071	.166*	.032	.143*	.032
Interest 10	−.255	.191	−.242	.191	—	—	—	—
Male	.311*	.087	−.331	.088	−.153*	.039	−.163*	.039
Black	.816	.172	.788*	.172	−.583*	.065	−.613*	.065
Latina	.338*	.141	.323*	.142	−.600*	.062	−.614*	.062
Other Non-White	.330	.260	.307	.261	−.384*	.118	−.409*	.118
Priv. School	.080	.142	.021	.144	.416	.063	.380*	.063
Consistent 11	—	—	.318*	.095	—	—	.245*	.042
Consistent 12	—	—	.266*	.093	—	—	.115*	.041

Ordinary Least Squares regression is used for the achievement variables; logistic regression is used for interest in school and college entry* = coefficient is statistically significant at $\alpha \le .05$

tests, I would conclude that there is an association between track location and interest in school. However, the BIC* statistic uses a more stringent and, some would argue, more appropriate test.

The BIC* statistic is more stringent in that with a sample size of approximately 3,500, the t-values would have to be on the order of 3.6 in order for one to provisionally accept the model (Raftery, 1995). The t-values for the tracking variables are 3.35 and 2.86. Thus, the BIC and BIC* statistics, the test statistics I have used throughout, provide arguably more stringent tests. Why, then, use the BIC statistic?

I have used the BIC statistic throughout the analysis to use an index that allows the test of nonnested models and also avoids some of the problems of classical statistical tests. The former reasons are detailed above, but the latter reason comes from criticisms of how social science research uses statistical testing. The statistical literature is replete with periodic requests that social scientists stop using the conventional .05 α level in analyses (Carver, 1978; Johnstone, 1988). Several reasons are offered for this request. For example, in the standard case, social scientists estimate many models, report some,

Table C.3 Coefficients for Baseline Model (without track variables) and Best Tracking Model for Twelfth-Grade Math Achievement and Four-Year College Entry

| | Grade 12 Math Achievement | | | | Four-Year College Entry | | | |
| | Baseline | | Track | | Baseline | | Track | |
Regressors	Coeff	s.e.	Coeff	s.e.	Coeff.	s.e.	Coeff.	s.e.
Constant	.338*	.034	1.438*	.060	−1.870*	.076	−2.001*	.037
Math Ach 10	.708*	.018	.596*	.017	.278*	.021	.198*	.022
Engl Ach 10	.187*	.019	.139*	.017	.316*	.023	.269*	.024
SES	.231*	.034	.108*	.032	.933*	.044	.871*	.045
Interest 10	—	—	—	—	−.116	.129	−.077	.134
Male	.246*	.043	.209*	.039	.033	.052	−.036	.054
Black	−.389*	.071	−.554*	.066	.394*	.099	.258*	.102
Latina	−.427*	.068	−.458*	.063	−.248*	.098	−.258*	.102
Other Non-White	−.016	.129	−.138	.119	.083	.144	.007	.150
Priv School	.369*	.069	.141*	.065	.766*	.077	.527	.079
Math11/Eng11								
Coll/Coll			Comparison				.770*	.059
None/None			−.753*	.119			−.344	.195
None/Non-Col			−.840*	.098				
None/Coll			−.761*	.061				
Non-Col/None			−.775*	.162				
Non-Col/Non-Col			−.656*	.094			−.053	.135
Non-Col/Coll			−.565*	.059				
Coll/None			.229	.163				
Coll/NonCol			.056	.101				
Math12/Eng12								
Coll/Coll			Comparison					
None/None			−.840*	.081				
None/Non-Col			−.832*	.085			.727*	.067
None/Coll			−.805*	.065			−.643*	.103
Non-Col/None			−.794*	.106				
Non-Col/Non-Col			−.757*	.098				
Non-Col/Coll			−.706*	.072				
Coll/None			−.070	.156			−.159	.125
Coll/Non-Col			−.142	.102				
Dropout			−1.229*	.108				

Ordinary Least Squares regression is used for the achievement variables; logistic regression is used for interest in school and college entry

* = coefficient is statistically significant at $\alpha \leq .05$

and discuss several coefficients from the models presented. When several coefficients or models are evaluated using a stationary α level, the actual p-value of the test is much larger than the nominal p-value of the independent tests (Miller, 1984). In other words, the more tests conducted, the greater the chance that one will obtain nominally statistically significant results just by chance.

This dilemma has a historical aspect as well. The classical statistical testing approach does not fit a common means of research today. The classical approach calls on the researcher to devise the sample size based on the size of an effect the researcher wants to be able to discern at a specified level of statistical significance, that is, at a specified level of certainty. If researchers design their own studies, including sample size considerations, then this approach is useful. But in many cases analysts use the sample someone else collected for very different purposes. In that case, researchers need to be wary of using arbitrary "cutoffs" to, in effect, denote substantive significance. However, until the culture of referees and editors also changes, it is unlikely that any headway in this battle will be gained. The BIC statistic is one of several useful responses to the sea-change in the organization of statistical research programs and the apparent inertia in the organization of the evaluation of research. (See Atkinson, Furlong, & Wampold, 1982, for an interesting analysis of the use of statistical significance by journal reviewers.) One answer to these problems is provided by BIC for model selection.

For details about how the BIC statistic is a response to this problem, see Raftery (1995, especially p. 142) and for more examples of its effective use, see Hauser (1995). However, for the reasons above as well as others, I have used the BIC and BIC* statistics in model selection throughout. When comparing models, I have given precedence to the BIC statistics over the t-values of the individual coefficients. This is an appropriate use of the BIC statistic. When I do that here, I provisionally conclude that interest in school is not systematically associated with students' track locations.

CONCLUDING COMMENTS

At this point it is important to step back from the decision-by-decision relation of the measurement and statistical operations and detail two or three key foundational assumptions of the analysis. Sociologists of knowledge have taught us that every research effort has embedded within it assumptions about how the world works and without which research could not be conducted (Kuhn, 1962). Assumptions are useful because they allow researchers to focus on some factors and ignore others. This research is no different.

Sociologists of knowledge also have pointed out that every research effort is based on a set of consciously adopted assumptions and a set implicit assumptions, what one might term witting and unwitting assumptions. My blanket acknowledgment that this research is based on assumptions covers both types. This acknowledgment may indeed be useful. But a clear, concise articulation of at least some of the conscious assumptions that guided the research would be far more useful to the scholarly community, for such a statement would enable other scholars to accept, alter, reassess, and eventually reject whatever assumptions I have adopted that stand in the way of future research endeavors. Moreover, a statement of at least some of the consciously adopted foundational commitments will facilitate identification of unwitting and potentially damaging assumptions upon which the research also may be based. Thus, I consider the task of articulating the foundational assumptions of the study to be at least as important as the task of relating the operations of the research, if the aim is to document what was done and why in order to facilitate continued study. Thus, here I want to state directly what I regard to be some of the foundational assumptions upon which the foregoing analysis has been based.

One foundational assumption is that there is a national track system. Even though students are enrolled inside *different* schools, my foundational assumption has been that in principle one can place students into discrete groupings that transcend their individual schools. This foundational assumption does *not* mean that this is the only way to study stratification in school. It does mean that this is *one* way to study stratification in school. I think it is a promising way.

This foundational assumption has an analogy with research into the world of work. It is patently apparent that people work in particular stores, firms, corporations, and other economic entities. Each of these entities has its own organizational chart, division of duties, and so on. Analysts have learned much from investigating one business in-depth or a set of businesses that share some similarities. However, a long line of research has ignored these firm-specific factors, classified laborers into discrete groups (or assigned laborers interval-level scores) that are commensurable at a national and even transnational level, and investigated the adult system of stratification using this as its raw data (Blau & Duncan, 1967; Grusky & Hauser, 1984; Hope, 1982; Treiman, 1977). Most assuredly, close, firm-specific studies are indispensable; however, I also think that analyses of larger entities such as nations has greatly furthered our insights into the structure and process of stratification. The logic of this way of treating people engaged in work can be transferred to students' course taking in schools.

Another foundational assumption of this research is the idea, adumbrated above, that knowledge will increase fastest and be surest if analysts collectively use a healthy diversity of approaches. When only one approach is used, it becomes impossible to discern whether the findings are based on the reality of the social world or, instead, on idiosyncrasies of the method of study. This is an extremely obvious point in research. A classic criticism of much of the 1960s research on social stratification is that it was based on samples of white boys. The criticism had force because, obviously, unless and until researchers studied more varied circumstances, no one could be sure whether the findings generalized or instead were confined to the particular group under study. Researchers subsequently did study more groups and deepened our understanding of how social stratification works.

An analogous claim may be made about the approach researchers adopt to study a phenomenon. Much of the social world can be studied with different methods, and most methods and measures have some advantages and disadvantages. Ideally, researchers will adopt a variety of methods and, through the process of comparing findings across methods and probing a finding obtained with one method by using other approaches, deepen their understanding of the social world that is the focus of study. For this reason I do not see the line of inquiry I have taken as the only line of research worth pursuing. Indeed, the value of the line I have taken depends crucially on existing work in other traditions and continued work in other traditions of educational research.

These few paragraphs have outlined two foundational commitments. It is in the nature of foundational commitments that one often cannot investigate them within the framework for which they serve as the foundation. Thus, I have not exposed these views to empirical analysis in the pages above. Still, I hope that over time they will be exposed to empirical analysis, for although I have good reasons to believe these foundational commitments are appropriate, I also believe that no one gains if the foundation is inappropriate and the ideas are unsound. The only way to discern which is true, however, is through continued theorizing and research. With this short statement of two foundational commitments, coupled with the description of the statistical operations and measurement strategies, I aim to facilitate continued theoretical development, empirical research, and substantive understanding.

References

Agresti, A. (1990). *Categorical data analysis*. New York: Wiley.

Alexander, K. L., & Cook, M. A. (1982). Curricula and coursework: A surprise ending to a familiar story. *American Sociological Review, 47,* 626–640.

Alexander, K. L., Cook, M., & McDill, E. (1978). Curriculum tracking and educational stratification: Some further evidence. *American Sociological Review, 43,* 47–66.

Aronowitz, S., & DiFazio, W. (1994). *The jobless future: Sci-tech and the dogma of work*. Minneapolis: University of Minnesota Press.

Ascher, C. (1992). Successful detracking in middle and senior high schools. *Digest: Clearinghouse on Urban Education, 82.*

Atkinson, D. R., Furlong, M. J., & Wampold, B. E. (1982). Statistical significance, reviewer evaluations, and the scientific process: Is there a (statistically) significant relationship? *Journal of Counseling Psychology, 29,* 189–194.

Bachman, J. G. (1975). *Youth in transition documentation manual*. Ann Arbor, MI: Inter-University Consortium for Political and Social Research.

Barr, R., & Dreeben, R. (1983). *How schools work*. Chicago: University of Chicago Press.

Becker, G. (1964). *Human capital: A theoretical and empirical analysis, with special reference to education*. New York: National Bureau of Economic Research.

Berends, M. (1994). Educational stratification and students' social bonding to school. *British Journal of Sociology of Education, 16,* 327–351.

Bernstein, B. (1977). *Class, codes, and control: Vol. 3. Towards a theory of educational transmissions*. Boston: Routledge & Kegan Paul.

Bishop, Y. M. M., Fienberg, S. E., & Holland, P. W. (1975). *Discrete multivariate analysis: Theory and practice*. Cambridge, MA: MIT Press.

Blau, P. M., & Duncan, O. D. (1967). *The American occupational structure*. New York: Free Press.

Bollen, K. A. (1989). *Structural equation models with latent variables*. New York: Wiley.

Bourdieu, P., & Passeron, J. (1977). *Reproduction in education, society, and culture* (2nd ed.). London: Sage.

Bowles, S., & Gintis, H. (1976). *Schooling in capitalist America*. New York: Basic Books.

Braddock, J. H., II. (1990). Tracking the middle grades: National patterns of grouping for instruction. *Phi Delta Kappan, 71,* 445–449.

Breen, R. (1984). Fitting non-hierarchical and association log-linear models using glim. *Sociological Methods and Research, 13*, 77–107.

Breen, R. (1994). Individual level models for mobility tables and other cross-classifications. *Sociological Methods and Research, 23*, 147–173.

Camarena, M. (1990). Following the right track: A comparison of tracking practices in public and catholic schools. In R. B. Page & L. Valli (Eds.), *Curriculum differentiation: Interpretive studies in U.S. secondary schools* (pp. 159–182). Albany: State University of New York Press.

Campbell, D. T., & Stanley, J. C. (1963). *Experimental and quasi-experimental designs for research.* Boston: Houghton Mifflin.

Campbell, P. B., Orth, M. N., & Seitz, P. (1981). *Patterns of participation in secondary vocational education.* Columbus: National Center for Research in Vocational Education, Ohio State University.

Carey, N., Farris, E., & Carpenter, J. (1994). *Curricular differentiation in public high schools: Fast response survey system e.d. tabs.* Rockville, MD: Westat.

Carver, R. P. (1978). The case against statistical significance testing. *Harvard Educational Review, 48*, 378–399.

Catsambis, S. (1994). The path to math: Gender and racial-ethnic differences in mathematics participation from middle school to high school. *Sociology of Education, 67*, 199–215.

Chubb, J. E., & Moe, T. M. (1988). Politics, markets, and the organization of schools. *American Political Science Review, 82*, 1065–1087.

Cicourel, A. V., & Kitsuse, J. I. (1963). *The educational decision makers.* Indianapolis: Bobbs-Merrill.

Clogg, C. C. (1981). Latent structure models for mobility tables. *American Journal of Sociology, 86*, 836–852.

Clogg, C. C. (1982). Using association models in sociological research: Some examples. *American Journal of Sociology, 88*, 114–134.

Clogg, C. C., & Eliason, S. R. (1987). Some common problems in log-linear analysis. *Sociological Methods and Research, 16*, 8–44.

Clogg, C. C., Shockey, J. W., & Eliason, S. R. (1990). A general statistical framework for the adjustment of rates. *Sociological Methods and Research, 19*, 156–195.

Coleman, J. S., Campbell, E. Q., Hobson, C. J., McPartland, J., Mood, A. M., Weinfeld, F. D., & York, R. L. (1966). *Equality of educational opportunity.* Washington, DC: United States Department of Health, Education, and Welfare.

Coleman, J. S., Hoffer, T., & Kilgore, S. (1982). *High school achievement: Public, catholic, and private schools compared.* New York: Basic Books.

Collins, R. (1979). *The credential society: An historical sociology of education and stratification.* New York: Academic Press.

Darity, W., Jr., with Cotton, J. P., & Hill, H. (1993). Race and inequality in the managerial age. In W. L. Reed (Ed.), *African-Americans: Essential perspectives* (pp. 33–80). Westport, CT: Auburn House.

Dauber, S. L., Alexander, K. L., & Entwistle, D. R. (1996). Tracking and transitions through the middle grades: Channeling educational trajectories. *Sociology of Education, 69*, 290–307.

Davies, S. (1995). Leaps of faith: Shifting currents in critical sociology of education. *American Journal of Sociology, 100,* 1448–1478.

DeLany, B. (1991). Allocation, choice, and stratification within high schools: How the sorting machine copes. *American Journal of Education, 99,* 181–207.

DiPrete, T. A. (1990). Adding covariates to loglinear models for the study of social mobility. *American Sociological Review, 55,* 757–773.

Dougherty, K. J. (1996). Opportunity-to-learn standards: A sociological critique. *Sociology of Education, 69,* E40–E65.

Dreeben, R., & Barr, R. (1988). Classroom composition and the design of instruction. *Sociology of Education, 61,* 129–142.

Duncan, O. D. (1979). How destination depends on origin in the occupational mobility table. *American Journal of Sociology, 84,* 793–803.

Evaluation Technologies Incorporated. (1982). *A classification of secondary school courses.* Washington, DC: National Center for Education Statistics.

Featherman, D. L., & Hauser, R. M. (1978). *Opportunity and change.* New York: Academic Press.

Fennessey, J., Alexander, K. L., Riordan, C., & Salganik, L. H. (1981). Tracking and frustration reconsidered: Appearance or reality. *Sociology of Education, 54,* 302–309.

Finley, M. K. (1984). Teachers and tracking in a comprehensive high school. *Sociology of Education, 57,* 233–243.

Finney, R. L. (1928). *A sociological philosophy of education.* New York: Macmillan.

Fischer, C., Hout, M., Jankowski, M. S., Lucas, S. R., Swidler, A., & Voss, K. (1996). *Inequality by design: Cracking the bell curve myth.* Princeton, NJ: Princeton University Press.

Freedman, F. (1975). The internal structure of the proletariat: A Marxist analysis. *Socialist Revolution, 26,* 41–83.

Gamoran, A. (1987). The stratification of high school learning opportunities. *Sociology of Education, 60,* 135–155.

Gamoran, A. (1989). Rank, performance, and mobility in elementary school grouping. *Sociological Quarterly, 30,* 109–123.

Gamoran, A. (1992a). Access to excellence: Assignment to honors English classes in the transition from middle to high school. *Educational Evaluation and Policy Analysis, 14,* 185–204.

Gamoran, A. (1992b). The variable effects of high school tracking. *American Sociological Review, 57,* 812–828.

Gamoran, A. (1993). Alternative uses of ability grouping in secondary schools: Can we bring high-quality instruction to low-ability classes? *American Journal of Education, 102,* 1–22.

Gamoran, A., & Mare, R. D. (1989). Secondary school tracking and educational equality: Compensation, reinforcement, or neutrality. *American Journal of Sociology, 94,* 1146–1183.

Garet, M. S., & DeLany, B. (1988). Students, courses, and stratification. *Sociology of Education, 61,* 61–77.

Gelb, J. (1979). Beyond the academic, non-academic dichotomy: High school curriculum effects and educational attainment (Report No. 273). Baltimore, MD:

Johns Hopkins University, Center for Social Organization of Schools. (ERIC Document Reproduction Service No. ED 173 504)

Goldberger, A. S., & Cain, G. G. (1982). The causal analysis of cognitive outcomes in the Coleman, Hoffer, and Kilgore report. *Sociology of Education, 55,* 103–122.

Goodlad, J. I. (1984). *A place called school: Prospects for the future.* New York: McGraw-Hill.

Goodman, L. (1979). Simple models for the analysis of association in cross-classifications having ordered categories. *Journal of the American Statistical Association, 74,* 537–552.

Goodman, L. (1981). Criteria for determining whether certain categories in a cross-classification table should be combined, with special reference to occupational categories in an occupational mobility table. *American Journal of Sociology, 87,* 612–650.

Greene, W. H. (1993). *Econometric analysis* (2nd ed.). Englewood Cliffs, NJ: Prentice-Hall.

Grusky, D. B., & Hauser, R. M. (1984). Comparative social mobility revisited: Models of convergence and divergence in 16 countries. *American Sociological Review, 49,* 19–38.

Hallinan, M. T. (1992). The organization of students for instruction in middle school. *Sociology of Education, 65,* 114–127.

Hallinan, M. T. (1994a). Tracking: From theory to practice. *Sociology of Education, 67,* 79–84.

Hallinan, M. T. (1994b). Further thoughts on tracking. *Sociology of Education, 67,* 89–91.

Hallinan, M. T. (1996). Track mobility in secondary school. *Social Forces, 74,* 983–1002.

Hallinan, M. T., & Williams, R. A. (1989). Interracial friendship choices in secondary schools. *American Sociological Review, 54,* 67–78.

Hauser, R. M. (1978). A structural model of the mobility table. *Social Forces, 56,* 919–953.

Hauser, R. M. (1979). Some exploratory methods for modelling mobility tables and other cross-classified data. *Sociological Methodology, 11,* 413–458.

Hauser, R. M. (1995). Better rules for better decisions. *Sociological Methodology, 25,* 175–183.

Hauser, R. M., Sewell, W., & Alwin, D. (1976). High school effects on achievement. In W. Sewell, R. M. Hauser, & D. Featherman (Eds.), *Schooling and achievement in American society* (pp. 309–341). New York: Academic Press.

Hauser, R. M., Tsai, S., & Sewell, W. (1983). A model of stratification with response error in social and psychological variables. *Sociology of Education, 56,* 20–46.

Hayes, F. W., III. (1990). Race, urban politics, and educational policy-making in Washington, DC: A community's struggle for quality education. *Urban Education, 25,* 237–257.

Herrnstein, R. J., & Murray, C. (1994). *The bell curve: Intelligence and class structure in American life.* New York: Free Press.

Heyns, B., & Hilton, T. L. (1982). The cognitive tests for High School and Beyond: An assessment. *Sociology of Education, 55,* 89–102.

Hirsch, D. (1994). Schooling for the middle years: Developments in eight European countries. Washington, DC: Carnegie Council on Adolescent Development. (ERIC Document Reproduction Service No. ED 383 471)

Hollingshead, A. B. (1949). *Elmtown's youth: The impact of social classes on adolescents.* New York: Wiley.

Hope, K. (1981). Vertical mobility in Britain: A structural analysis. *Sociology, 15,* 19–55.

Hope, K. (1982). Vertical and nonvertical class mobility in three countries. *American Sociological Review, 47,* 100–113.

Hope, K. (1984). Intergenerational and career mobility in Britain: An integrated analysis. *Social Science Research, 13,* 20–37.

Hotchkiss, L. (1986). *High school tracking and stratification.* Columbus: National Center for Research in Vocational Education, Ohio State University.

Hotchkiss, L., & Dorsten, L. E. (1987). Curriculum effects on early post-high school outcomes. *Research in the Sociology of Education and Socialization, 7,* 191–219.

Hout, M. (1983). *Mobility tables* (Sage University Paper Series on Quantitative Applications in the Social Sciences, series no. 07-031). Beverly Hills: Sage.

Hout, M. (1984). Status, autonomy, and training in occupational mobility. *American Journal of Sociology, 89,* 1379–1409.

Immigration [An editorial]. (1974). In S. Cohen (Ed.), *Education in the United States: A documentary history* (Vol. 2; pp. 995–997). New York: Random House. (Reprinted from *Massachusetts Teacher,* 1851, 4, 289–291)

Jackman, M. R., & Jackman, R. W. (1983). *Class awareness in the United States.* Berkeley: University of California Press.

Jencks, C. L., & Brown, M. D. (1975). The effects of high schools on their students. *Harvard Educational Review, 45,* 273–324.

Johnstone, D. (1988). Comment on Oakes on the foundations of statistical inference in the social and behavioral sciences: The market for statistical significance. *Psychological Reports, 63,* 319–331.

Jones, C., Knight, S., Butz, M., Crawford, I., & Stephenson, B. (1983). *High School and Beyond transcripts survey (1982): Data file user's manual.* Washington, DC: National Center for Education Statistics.

Jones, J. D., Vanfossen, B. E., & Ensminger, M. E. (1995). Individual and organizational predictors of high school track placement. *Sociology of Education, 68,* 287–300.

Karabel, J. (1972). Community colleges and social stratification: Submerged class conflict in American higher education. *Harvard Educational Review, 42,* 521–562.

Kelley, F. (1903). An effective child labor law. *Annals of the American Academy of Political and Social Science, 21,* 438–445.

Kelly, D. H. (1976). Track position, school misconduct, and youth deviance: A test of the interpretive effect of school commitment. *Urban Education, 10,* 379–388.

Kerckhoff, A. C. (1986). The effects of ability-grouping in British secondary schools. *American Sociological Review, 51*, 842–858.

Kilgore, S. B. (1991). The organizational context of tracking in schools. *American Sociological Review, 56*, 189–203.

Kliebard, H. M. (1995). *The struggle for the American curriculum: 1893–1958* (2nd ed.). New York: Routledge.

Kohn, M. L. (1977). *Class and conformity: A study in values* (2nd ed.). Chicago: University of Chicago Press.

Kohn, M. L., & Schooler, C. (1986). *Work and personality: An inquiry into the impact of social stratification.* Norwood, NJ: Ablex.

Kuhn, T. S. (1962). *The structure of scientific revolutions.* Chicago: University of Chicago Press.

Lareau, A. (1989). *Home advantage: Social class and parental intervention in elementary education.* New York: Falmer Press.

Lenski, G. E. (1954). Status crystallization: A non-vertical dimension of social status. *American Sociological Review, 19*, 405–413.

Levinson, J., Riccobono, J. A., & Moore, R. P. (1975). *National longitudinal study of the high school class of 1972: Base-year and first follow-up users manual: Preliminary with added appendix K.* Washington, DC: National Center for Education Statistics.

Logan, J. A. (1983). A multivariate model for mobility tables. *American Journal of Sociology, 89*, 324–349.

Logan, J. A. (1996). Rules of access and shifts in demand: A comparison of loglinear and two-sided logit models. *Social Science Research, 25*, 174–199.

Long, J. S., & McGinnis, R. (1981). Organizational context and scientific productivity. *American Sociological Review, 46*, 422–442.

Lucas, S. R. (1990). Course-based indicators of curricular track location. Unpublished master's thesis, University of Wisconsin–Madison.

Lucas, S. R. (1992, August). Secondary school track rigidity in the United States: Existence, extension, and equity. Paper presented at the meeting of the American Sociological Association, Pittsburgh.

Lucas, S. R. (1996). Selective attrition in a newly hostile regime: The case of 1980 sophomores. *Social Forces, 75*, 511–533.

Lucas, S. R., & Gamoran, A. (1991, August). Race and track assignment: A reconsideration with course-based indicators of track locations. Paper presented at the meeting of the American Sociological Association, Cincinnati, OH.

Manski, C. F. (1993). Identification problems in the social sciences. *Sociological Methodology, 23*, 1–56.

McClendon, M. J. (1980). Structural and exchange components of occupational mobility: A cross-national analysis. *Sociological Quarterly, 21*, 493–509.

McDonnell, L. M. (1995). Opportunity to learn as a research concept and a policy instrument. *Educational Evaluation and Policy Analysis, 47*, 198–213.

McKelvey, R. D., & Zavoina, W. (1975). A statistical model for the analysis of ordinal level dependent variables. *Journal of Mathematical Sociology, 4*, 103–120.

McNeal, R. B., Jr. (1995). Extracurricular activities and high school dropouts. *Sociology of Education, 68*, 62–81.

Merton, R. K. (1968). The Matthew effect in science. *Science, 159*, 56–63.

Metz, M. H. (1978). *Classrooms and corridors: The crisis of authority in desegregated secondary schools.* Berkeley: University of California Press

Meyer, J. W. (1977). The effects of education as an institution. *American Journal of Sociology, 83*, 55–77.

Meyer, J. W., Ramirez, F., Rubinson, R., & Boli-Bennett, J. (1977). The world educational revolution, 1950–1970. *Sociology of Education, 50*, 242–258.

Meyer, J. W., Ramirez, F., & Soysal, Y. N. (1992). World expansion of mass education, 1870–1980. *Sociology of Education, 65*, 128–149.

Meyer, R. H., & Muraskin, L. (1988). Participation in high school vocational education. In *First interim report from the National Assessment of Vocational Education* (pp. 1–38). Washington, DC: U.S. Department of Education. (ERIC Document Reproduction Service No. ED 290 881)

Miller, A. J. (1984). Selection of subsets of regression variables (with discussion). *Journal of the Royal Statistical Society (Series A), 147*, 389–425.

Moore, D. R., & Davenport, S. (1988). *The new improved sorting machine.* Madison: University of Wisconsin–Madison, School of Education, National Center on Effective Secondary Schools. (ERIC Document Reproduction Service No. ED 316 942)

Muthén, B. (1984). A general structural equation model with dichotomous, ordered categorical, and continuous latent variable indicators. *Psychometrika, 49*, 115–132.

National Center for Education Statistics. (1981). *High School and Beyond, 1980: A longitudinal survey of students in the United States.* Ann Arbor, MI: Inter-University Consortium for Political and Social Research.

National Education Association. (1968). *Ability-grouping: Research summary.* Washington, DC: National Education Association.

Natriello, G., Pallas, A. M., & Alexander, K. (1989). On the right track? Curriculum and academic achievement. *Sociology of Education, 62*, 109–118.

Neter, J., Wasserman, W., & Kuttner, M. H. (1989). *Applied linear regression models* (2nd ed.). Homewood, IL: Irwin.

Oakes, J. (1981). *Tracking policies and practices: School by school summaries: A study of schooling in the United States* (Technical Report Series No. 25). Los Angeles: University of California at Los Angeles Graduate School of Education. (ERIC Document Reproduction Service No. ED 214 893)

Oakes, J. (1985). *Keeping track: How schools structure inequality.* New Haven, CT: Yale University Press.

Oakes, J. (1987). Tracking in secondary schools: A contextual perspective. *Educational Psychologist, 22*, 129–153.

Oakes, J. (1994a). More than misapplied technology: A normative and political response to Hallinan on tracking. *Sociology of Education, 67*, 84–89.

Oakes, J. (1994b). One more thought. *Sociology of Education, 67*, 91.

Page, R. (1989). The lower-track curriculum at a "heavenly" high school: "Cycles of prejudice." *Journal of Curriculum Studies, 21*, 197–221.

Page, R. (1990). Games of chance: The lower-track curriculum in a college-preparatory high school. *Curriculum Inquiry, 20*, 249–281.

Pallas, A. M., Entwistle, D. R, Alexander, K. L., & Stluka, M. F. (1994). Ability-group effects: Instructional, social, or institutional? *Sociology of Education, 67*, 27–46.

Paulsen, R. (1991). Education, social class, and participation in collective action. *Sociology of Education, 64*, 96–110.

Powell, A. G., Farrar, E., & Cohen, D. K. (1985). *The shopping mall high school: Winners and losers in the educational marketplace*. Boston: Houghton Mifflin.

Raftery, A. (1986). Choosing models for cross-classifications. *American Sociological Review, 51*, 145–146.

Raftery, A. (1995). Bayesian model selection in social research. *Sociological Methodology, 25*, 111–163.

Rehberg, R. A., & Rosenthal, E. R. (1978). *Class and merit in the American high school: An assessment of the revisionist and meritocratic arguments*. New York: Longman.

Riehl, C., Natriello, G., & Pallas, A. M. (1992, August). Losing track: The dynamics of student assignment processes in high school. Paper presented at the meeting of the American Sociological Association, Pittsburgh.

Rifkin, J. (1995). *The end of work: The decline of the global labor force and the dawn of the post-market era*. New York: Putnam's.

Rosenbaum, J. E. (1976). *Making inequality*. New York: Wiley.

Rosenbaum, J. E. (1978). The structure of opportunity in school. *Social Forces, 57*, 236–256.

Rosenbaum, J. E. (1980). Track misperceptions and frustrated college plans: An analysis of the effects of tracks and track perceptions in the National Longitudinal Survey. *Sociology of Education, 53*, 74–88.

Rosenbaum, J. E. (1981). Comparing track and track perceptions: Correcting some misperceptions. *Sociology of Education, 54*, 309–311.

Rosenbaum, J. E., Miller, S. R., & Krei, M. S. (1995, August). *Gatekeeping in an era of more open gates: High school counselors' views of their influence on students' college plans*. Paper presented at the meeting of the American Sociological Association, Washington, DC.

Sauthier, R. (1995). *Secondary education in Switzerland*. Strausbourg: Council of Europe.

Schafer, W. E., & Olexa, C. (1971). *Tracking and opportunity*. Scranton, PA: Chandler.

Schwartz, F. (1981). Supporting or subverting learning: Peer group patterns in four tracked schools. *Anthropology and Education Quarterly, 12*, 99–121.

Sobel, M. E. (1983). Structural mobility, circulation mobility, and the analysis of occupational mobility: A conceptual mismatch. *American Sociological Review, 48*, 721–727.

Sobel, M. E., Hout, M., & Duncan, O. D. (1985). Exchange, structure, and symmetry in occupational mobility. *American Journal of Sociology, 91*, 359–372.

Sørenson, A. B. (1970). Organizational differentiation of students and educational opportunity. *Sociology of Education, 43*, 355–376.

Spring, J. H. (1972). *Education and the rise of the corporate state*. Boston: Beacon Press.

Stevens, F. I. (1993). *Opportunity to learn: Issues of equity for poor and minority students*. Washington, DC: U.S. Department of Education.

Stevenson, D. L., Schiller, K. S., & Schneider, B. (1994). Sequences of opportunities for learning. *Sociology of Education, 67*, 184–198.

Stolzenberg, R. M., & Relles, D. A. (1990). Theory testing in a world of constrained research design: The significance of Heckman censored sampling bias correction for nonexperimental research. *Sociological Methods and Research, 18*, 394–415.

Thomas, W. I., & Thomas, D. S. (1928). *The child in America: Behavior problems and programs*. New York: Knopf.

Treiman, D. J. (1977). *Occupational prestige in comparative perspective*. New York: Academic Press.

Turner, R. (1960). Sponsored and contest mobility and the school system. *American Sociological Review, 25*, 855–867.

Upchurch, D. M., & McCarthy, J. (1990). The timing of a first birth and high school completion. *American Sociological Review, 55*, 224–234.

Useem, E. (1992). Middle schools and math groups: Parents' involvement in children's placement. *Sociology of Education, 65*, 263–279.

Valli, L. (1990). A curriculum of effort: Tracking students in a Catholic high school. In R. B. Page & L. Valli (Eds.), *Curriculum differentiation: Interpretive studies in U.S. secondary schools* (pp. 45–65). Albany: State University of New York Press.

Velez, W. (1989). High school attrition among Hispanic and non-Hispanic white youths. *Sociology of Education, 62*, 119–133.

Wells, A. S., & Oakes, J. (1996). Potential pitfalls of systemic reform: Early lessons from detracking research. *Sociology of Education, 69*, E135–E143.

Wells, A. S., & Serna, I. (1996). The politics of culture: Understanding local political resistance to detracking in racially mixed schools. *Harvard Educational Review, 66*, 93–118.

Wheelock, A. (1992). *Crossing the tracks: How "untracking" can save America's schools*. New York: Norton.

Wiatrowski, M. D., Hansell, S., Massey, C. R., & Wilson, D. L. (1982). Curriculum tracking and delinquency. *American Sociological Review, 47*, 151–160.

Willis, P. (1977). *Learning to labour: How working class kids get working class jobs*. New York: Columbia University Press.

Wilson, B. L., & Rossman, G. B. (1993). *Mandating academic excellence: High school responses to state curriculum reform*. New York: Teachers College Press.

Wonnacott, T. H., & Wonnacott, R. J. (1990). *Introductory statistics for business and economics* (4th ed.). New York: Wiley.

Wright, E. O. (1979). *Class, crisis, and the state*. London: New Left Books.

Wright, E. O. (1985). *Classes*. London: New Left Books.

Wrigley, J. (1982). *Class, politics and public schools: Chicago 1900–1950*. New Brunswick, NJ: Rutgers University Press.

Xie, Y. (1992). The log-multiplicative layer effect model for comparing mobility tables. *American Sociological Review*, *57*, 380–395.

Yamaguchi, K. (1987). Models for comparing mobility tables: Toward parsimony and substance. *American Sociological Review*, *52*, 482–494.

Yogev, A. (1981). Determinants of early educational career in Israel: Further evidence for the sponsorship thesis. *Sociology of Education*, *54*, 181–194.

Yule, G. U. (1905). On a property which holds good for all groupings of a normal distribution of frequency for two variables, with applications to the study of contingency-tables for the inheritance of unmeasured qualities. *Proceedings of the Royal Society of London* Series A, *77*, 324–336.

Index

About the Author

Samuel R. Lucas obtained his bachelor's degree from Haverford College in 1986, was awarded a National Science Foundation Minority Graduate Fellowship in 1988, and completed his doctoral degree in Sociology from the University of Wisconsin-Madison in 1994. Lucas has served on the Editorial Board of *Sociology of Education*, and has research and teaching interests in sociology of education, social stratification, methods, and statistics. A co-author of *Inequality by Design: Cracking the Bell Curve Myth*, he is presently undertaking a cross-time comparative analysis of tracking in the United States with his collaborator Mark Berends, and is also completing a book on effects of race and sex discrimination in America. Lucas is currently an Assistant Professor of Sociology at the University of California-Berkeley.